OXFORD HISTORICAL SERIES

Editors

N. GIBBS   R. W. SOUTHERN   J. S. WATSON
R. B. WERNHAM

SECOND SERIES

THE PASSING OF THE
IRISH ACT OF UNION

A STUDY IN
PARLIAMENTARY POLITICS

BY

G. C. BOLTON

OXFORD UNIVERSITY PRESS
1966

Oxford University Press, Ely House, London W.1

GLASGOW NEW YORK TORONTO MELBOURNE WELLINGTON
CAPE TOWN SALISBURY IBADAN NAIROBI LUSAKA ADDIS ABABA
BOMBAY CALCUTTA MADRAS KARACHI LAHORE DACCA
KUALA LUMPUR HONG KONG

PRINTED IN GREAT BRITAIN

ACKNOWLEDGEMENTS

THE thesis on which this book is based was undertaken for the degree of doctor of philosophy at Oxford University, where research was undertaken between 1956 and 1958. A grant from the Beit Trustees facilitated the first year's research; and to Sir Keith Hancock and the Australian National University I owe the privilege of one year's leave in order to complete the first draft of the thesis. My supervisor, Dr. J. B. Owen, became a good friend as well as a good overseer, and I thank him for his interest. I also want to acknowledge the kindness and encouragement of the fellows in history at Balliol College, where I spent four valuable and agreeable years. During my time there my interest in the eighteenth century was fostered by the Master of Balliol and by two fine scholars, now dead: Mr. A. B. Rodger, who first set me thinking about the Anglo-Irish nexus, and Professor Vincent Harlow, whose seminars stimulated so many overseas students.

Most of the manuscript material cited came from public collections, as indicated in the bibliography, and I thank the many archivists and librarians whose help was invoked during my research. For permission to quote from the Wentworth Woodhouse MSS. I thankfully acknowledge the Sheffield City Library and the 10th Earl Fitzwilliam; from the Mount Stewart MSS., the late Marchioness Dowager of Londonderry, D.B.E.; from the Wellington MSS. at Apsley House, the 7th Duke of Wellington; and from the Windsor Castle MSS. Her Majesty the Queen and the Keeper of the Records. In citing contemporary material, I have modernized such forms as 'ye' and 'yt', and I have standardized the use of capitals to conform with current practice. Otherwise no alteration has been made in the spelling or (except where ambiguity would result) in the punctuation of quotations.

In the preparation of this book for publication, I am grateful to Mrs. Jean Thompson, who typed the manuscript. My wife has cheerfully undergone the inconveniences of having

the politics of Ireland around the house, and looking after any task from encouragement to proof-reading; and in the first place I owe all my academic opportunities to the sacrifices of my parents, to whom I dedicate this book.

G. C. BOLTON

Monash University, 1964

CONTENTS

Acknowledgements

ABBREVIATIONS

Add. MSS. = British Museum Additional Manuscripts
C.S.O.   = Chief Secretary's Office papers, Dublin Castle, Dublin, Ireland
H.M.C.   = Historical Manuscripts Commission
H.O.   = Home Office papers (in Public Record Office, London)
H. of C.   = House of Commons (United Kingdom)
Parl. Hist. = William Cobbett (ed.), *Parliamentary History of England . . . 1066 to . . . 1803* (36 vols.) 1806–20
Parl. Reg. = *Parliamentary Register*: a report of the debates in the House of Commons in Ireland on Tuesday and Wednesday 22nd and 23rd Jan. on the subject of an Union . . . (Dublin 1799)
Proc. Royal Irish Acad. = *Proceedings of the Royal Irish Academy*
P.R.O.   = Public Record Office, London
P.R.O.N.I. = Public Record Office of Northern Ireland, Belfast

I

THE ANGLO-IRISH NEXUS

Bind us to you by the only chain that can connect us—the
only chain we will ever consent to wear—the dear ties of
mutual love and mutual freedom.

LORD CHARLEMONT tO LORD ROCKINGHAM, 17 April 1782.[1]

THE Protestant Ascendancy who governed Ireland in
1797 consisted mainly of descendants of English or
Scots families who had migrated in several waves in the
time of the Tudors and Stuarts, imposed their régime on the
original inhabitants, and built up a distinctive outlook and
culture, neither English nor Gaelic. In the closing years of
the eighteenth century they found themselves under challenge from the influences of radical nationalism thrown up by
the American and French Revolutions. A classic revolutionary situation seemed to be brewing with a discontented
peasantry, potential leadership among the urban middle class
and aristocratic rebels, and the backing of a strong outside
power, France. Although the United Irishmen gained their
strongest support from Presbyterian Ulster, the Ascendancy's main fear was that these revolutionary ideas might
provide the Catholic peasantry with doctrine and organization through which to vent their grievances. Even before
1789 French influence had been blamed for the arson, stock-
maiming, and occasional murders committed by peasant
secret societies such as the Whiteboys. In fact these out-
breaks had very little specific political content. The main
source of grievance was a rapid natural increase which multi-
plied the demand for smallholdings for subsistence farming.[2]
But the majority of the Protestant Ascendancy saw the threat
to their régime not merely as a struggle for land, but in terms

[1] Charlemont to Rockingham, 17 April 1782 (H. Grattan, *Life of Henry Grattan*,
5 vols., London, 1839–46, ii, pp. 241–2).
[2] The best work on this subject is K. H. Connell, *The Population of Ireland*,
1750–1845, Oxford, 1950.

of religious and political conflict. The Anglo-Irish were the pattern of a colonial oligarchy; anxious to defend their supremacy against the more numerous native inhabitants, and suspicious of a Home Government on whose protection they depended, but whose interest in their welfare seemed at times lukewarm. During the eighteenth century they had found little community of interest with the metropolitan power. Ireland had been subjected legislatively and commercially to the restraints of colonial status,[1] until the American Revolution provided an example and an opportunity for national self-assertion. The Volunteer Movement, overriding for a time divisions of class, religion, and faction, inspired a strong and well-disciplined pressure which in a few years drove Britain from concession to concession, ending with the abolition of Poynings's Law in 1782, and the Renunciation Act of the following year. Every tie between Great Britain and Ireland was specifically removed, save that of a common sovereign.

Hailed by Irish patriots as a 'final settlement', the constitution of 1782 left many problems of the vexed Anglo-Irish relationship unresolved. The British Parliament considered it 'indispensable' that the connexion between the two nations 'should be established by mutual consent upon a solid and permanent footing'. It seemed essential to successive British Governments—not merely to Pitt, although as his term of office almost coincided with the era of Irish parliamentary independence, the policy is most associated with him—that some formal co-ordination of commerce and defence was necessary between Great Britain and Ireland. This point had occurred to some Irish patriots. Henry Grattan had been willing to concede that all Irish legislation should pass under the Great Seal of England, and in July 1782 his close associate, Robert Day,[2] had urged on Shelburne the desirability of joining the two countries in a 'national compact', a bilateral agreement between the two nations which

---

[1] V. T. Harlow, *The Founding of the Second British Empire, 1763–1793*, i, pp. 501–9.

[2] Robert Day (1745-1841), member of a Kerry family, an intimate friend of Henry Grattan; acted as Grattan's agent in London 1782; M.P. for Tuam 1783–90, Ardfert 1790–7; chairman of quarter sessions at Kilmainham 1789–98; judge of common pleas 1798–1818.

would stand independently of the Crown, and would commit Ireland to be '*ipso facto* at war with the enemies and at peace with the friends of Great Britain'.[1] But Grattan could not appear too eager about offering the Home Government terms, confronted as he already was with the rivalry of Henry Flood for a more radical leadership of the national movement; and the situation was not formally clarified. Although Ireland was unlikely to go its own way in foreign affairs, it was probable that commercial competition would lead George III's two kingdoms into divergent policies. Yet constitutionally there could be no check on such divergencies except the royal veto. This point was understood and accepted by the Home Government under Portland: 'The plan here is to leave the government of Ireland to its Parliament, exercising the king's negative only in extraordinary cases, but then with decision.'[2] But was common sovereignty an adequate symbol of imperial unity? It had not sufficed for the American colonies, and at this very time politics at Westminster tended to divide precisely on the question of defining George III's authority in the choice and control of ministers and their policies.

These ambiguities presented peculiar difficulties for the King's representative in Ireland, the Lord Lieutenant. Like his sovereign, the Lord Lieutenant had to work through ministers who, if not accountable to the Irish House of Commons, should at least be capable of its management. Before Lord Townshend (Lord Lieutenant, 1767–72) most Viceroys were often absent from Ireland, leaving patronage management and the control of government business largely in the hands of the Undertakers, a small clique of officials and nobles. Conforming with George III's policy in England, Townshend had endeavoured to restore full control of government business to the Crown. The leading Undertakers, the duke of Leinster, Lord Shannon,[3] and the

---

[1] Day to Shelburne, — July 1782 (E. B. Day, *Mr. Justice Day of Kerry*, Exeter, 1938, pp. 126–7).

[2] Knox to Pery, 12 Sept. 1783 (*H.M.C. Emly MSS.*, p. 178).

[3] Born 1727: married a daughter of John Ponsonby; succeeded his father as 2nd earl 1764; a patron of from 10 to 13 members in county Cork; in opposition 1768–75, 1780–1, 1789–93, otherwise supported various governments; K.P. 1783; died 1807.

Speaker, John Ponsonby,[1] had seized the earliest pretext for
going into opposition, reinforcing the unconnected country
gentlemen and a few city 'radicals' who had hitherto provided
its nucleus; and in consequence they had been stripped of
their offices. Ponsonby's post as Chief Commissioner of
Revenue, a position considered to give the holder wide
patronage powers, went eventually to John Beresford,
Lord Waterford's brother,[2] so stimulating rivalry between
two of Ireland's most extensive parliamentary families. The
management of government business passed to a Chief
Secretary appointed from England. Successive Lords Lieutenant found patronage only a doubtful aid in securing a
parliamentary majority, especially in the face of any determined expression of articulate public opinion. Lord Harcourt
created eighteen peerages for the elections of 1776, but
could count on no more than ninety-two supporters in a
House of Commons of 300; and during the life of this Parliament his successors were harassed by a 'patriot' opposition
critical of British-imposed commercial and constitutional
restraints.

The possibility arose that an Irish Opposition, attacking
ministers and policies approved by the British Cabinet,
would make common cause with the British Opposition,
particularly since, under the inspiration of the Rockingham
whigs, a systematic concept of party was slowly taking shape
at Westminster. Writing with the hindsight of 1795, Edward
Cooke compared the Undertakers to the 'domination of the
old Whig families against the king',[3] and Fox's language in

---

[1] Born 1713, brother of the 2nd earl of Bessborough; married a sister of the 4th
duke of Devonshire; Speaker 1756–71; died 1789. Of his sons, William Ponsonby
was born 1744; M.P. for Cork city 1764–76, Bandon Bridge 1776–83, co. Kilkenny
1783–1806; joint Postmaster-General 1784–9; Baron Ponsonby 1806; died 1806;
and George Ponsonby was born 1755; M.P. for Inistioge 1783–97, Galway town
1797–1800, co. Wicklow 1801–6 and 1816–17, Tavistock (U.K.), 1807–12, and
Peterborough (U.K.) 1812–16; counsel to commissioners of revenue 1782–9; proposed for attorney-general by Fitzwilliam 1795; Lord Chancellor of Ireland 1806–7;
leader of the opposition 1807–17.

[2] Born 1738, second son of 1st earl of Tyrone; M.P. co. Waterford 1761–1805;
P.C. (Ireland) 1767, (Great Britain) 1786; Commissioner of Revenue 1770–80;
Chief Commissioner 1780–1802; Commissioner of Treasury Board 1793–1805;
also Taster of Wines, Joint Storekeeper of Dublin, and Commissioner for Wide
Streets; died 1805.

[3] Cooke to Nepean (confidential), 27 Jan. 1795 (P.R.O. 30/8/326).

later years certainly suggested that there had been some
rapport between English and Irish oppositions before 1782.[1]
Portland, as Lord Lieutenant in 1782, dismissed some of the
appointees of the preceding administration, and as leader of
the Fox–North coalition in 1783 looked forward to creating
'the nest egg of a real whig party' in Ireland, centred on his
Ponsonby kinsmen. But such an alignment of interests was
possible only while the English whigs were strange to office.
Fox as Home Secretary soon took as tough a line as his
political opponents in resisting Irish 'patriot' pretensions.
Lord Northington and Thomas Pelham,[2] respectively Lord
Lieutenant and Chief Secretary under the coalition, found it
desirable to court support from many Irish members who
were anything but whigs. As the Irish 'patriots' split under
the pressure of Flood's reform movement, it became possible
to dissociate Irish politics from British party alignments.
This emerged clearly on the downfall of the Fox–North
coalition, when the Irish House of Commons was nearly
unanimous in quashing a new member's move for delivering
an address to the King in support of Pitt's new ministry.
There was a common dislike of 'entering into the politics of
the other country'.[3] Pitt's Viceroys continued the policy of
dissociation. Irish offices formerly held by English appointees, such as Lord Chancellor and Chancellor of the Exchequer, passed between 1784 and 1789 to members of the
Irish Parliament; only the Chief Secretary was appointed
from London. At the same time parliamentary support was
drawn not only from the families of Dublin Castle office-
holders and place-hunters, but also from former oppositionists such as the Ponsonby cousinhood, Thomas Connolly,[4]

---

[1] In a speech in Dec. 1798 he stated: 'Mr. Grattan was during the American War
at the head of the Opposition in Ireland, acting on the same principles as the
Opposition with which I am connected here.' But he may have been over-simpli-
fying, in the light of the evolution of both Oppositions between 1782 and 1798.

[2] Born 1756; Chief Secretary for Ireland 1783–4, 1795–8 (and intended by Fox
in 1789); Secretary of State 1795–1801; Home Secretary (U.K.) 1801–3; succeeded
his father as 2nd earl of Chichester 1805; died 1826.

[3] Tighe to Buckinghamshire, 26 Jan. 1784 (*H.M.C. Lothian MSS.*, p. 427).

[4] Born 1738; brother-in-law of 3rd duke of Richmond, 2nd earl of Buckinghamshire, 1st earl of Rosse, 1st earl Howe, and John Staples (q.v., p. 29); uncle of 2nd
duke of Leinster and Lady Castlereagh; M.P. Malmesbury 1759–68 and Chichester
1768–80 in British House of Commons; M.P. co. Londonderry 1761–1800; P.C.

and the Agars of Kilkenny, whose ties of kinship and connexion were all with the Foxites of England. If, as one Lord
Lieutenant feared, Fox aimed to 'make his harvest in Ireland',[1] he seemed doomed to disappointment.

Yet the inadequacies of the Anglo-Irish nexus were soon
apparent. In 1785 Pitt proposed free trade between Great
Britain and Ireland in return for a permanent Irish defence
contribution and specific legislation binding the Irish to
enforce all trade and navigation laws passed in Great Britain.
The scheme fell foul of the well-organized lobbying of business pressure-groups in England, as well as the reluctance
of the Irish to surrender their power of regulating trade to
a possibly hostile British House of Commons. At the height
of the crisis the Irish Government's usual majority of around
seventy dropped to nineteen, only to return to normal as soon
as the commercial propositions were abandoned. So ended
one of the most promising plans for securing Anglo-Irish
co-ordination within the framework of the 1782 constitution.
Union, at this stage, was hardly thought of. At the very
beginning of the eighteenth century the Irish Parliament,
fortified by the writings of Molyneux, had requested a
legislative union with England as the best means of over-
coming Ireland's colonial disabilities; but the suggestion was
spurned. During the reign of George III, as Irish demands
for autonomy became louder, plans of Union had been
sketched by Chatham and by the Ulster magnate Lord
Hillsborough, then a British Cabinet minister; and in 1779
and 1780 North's ministry had gone so far as to probe Irish
official opinion, only to be discouraged. 'The idea of an union
at present would excite a rebellion,' wrote a former Chief
Secretary, Sir George Macartney, 'and yet without an union,
how loose and feeble is the connexion of Ireland with England.'[2] After the heady achievements of 1782 Irish opinion
was even less favourable, and although the dispute over the
1785 commercial propositions found the General Chamber
of British Manufacturers advocating 'a real Union with

1772; owner of Ballyshannon and Newtown Limavady boroughs, which he sold in
1795; died 1803.

[1] Rutland to Pitt, 16 June 1784 (*Pitt–Rutland Correspondence*, p. 47).
[2] Macartney to North, 8 Jan. 1780 (D.O.D. 8/572: P.R.O.N.I.).

Ireland, under one legislature', the Lord Lieutenant warned Pitt that anyone suggesting Union in Dublin would be tarred and feathered for his pains.[1]

Until 1788 the potential strains in Anglo-Irish relations remained hidden. By that year the Government seemed strongly placed in the Irish Parliament. The last major opposition faction, under the duke of Leinster,[2] had been reconciled to the administration, and the Lord Lieutenant, the marquess of Buckingham, had even made a start on cleaning up official malpractices. But with the onset of the Regency crisis party divisions sharpened once more. In England George III's insanity produced a reversal of traditional attitudes, with Pitt maintaining Parliament's right to impose limitations on the Regent's powers, and Fox arguing for the transmission of unlimited sovereignty to the Prince of Wales. Since the person of the sovereign was the sole constitutional link between Great Britain and Ireland, it would be a grave embarrassment to Pitt if the Irish Kingdom endorsed the Foxite view. Grattan and the Irish 'patriots', however, disliked the suggestion that their regency arrangements must of necessity follow the British Government's lead, and saw this issue as a means of wresting policy control from Dublin Castle. It was their hope that, if an Irish Parliament granted the Prince of Wales the regency without limitations, the incoming whig Lord Lieutenant would select his advisers as recommended by the Irish 'patriots' and introduce an agreed programme of reforms.[3] The old ministers were to be turned out, and the incoming Chief Secretary presented with the names of those who would constitute his Irish Cabinet. This would have represented a degree of practical autonomy never before acceded to Irish politicians; unfortunately it also had the effect of firmly linking Irish party politics to British alignments, and even of confirming the Ponsonby versus Beresford feud as one of the shibboleths of party. Thomas Burgh, a veteran civil servant and one of Leinster's following, wrote to Thomas Pelham, who was expected to

[1] *Parl. Hist.* xxxiv, p. 736.
[2] Born 1749; M.P. for Dublin city 1768–73; succeeded his father as 2nd duke 1773; in opposition except 1768–71, 1780–4, 1788–9, and 1795–6; K.P. 1783; Master of the Rolls 1788–9; Clerk of the Hanaper 1795–8; died 1804.
[3] Grattan to Forbes, n.d. [early in January 1789] (Forbes MSS.).

return as Chief Secretary under the whigs: 'Let me recommend you to come as soon as possible. If party is not stopp'd
in time, we shall get into such a strange state that the country
will not be worth coming to. Heretofore Court and Country
party have been our political distinction, except a small
interruption which you happily put an end to.'[1]

It was too late. Many office-holders had deserted Dublin
Castle to invite the Prince to assume the Irish regency, and
to vote censure on Buckingham for refusing to transmit the
address. On 2 March 1789 news of the King's recovery to
health reached Dublin. Those who had voted censure on
Buckingham issued a manifesto stating their determination
never to accept office under the Crown if any one of them
was victimized for his conduct. This combination commanded the votes of one-third of the House of Commons;
but its solidarity melted when Buckingham offered amnesty
to those who would quit opposition immediately, and dismissal to the others. By the end of April the Government's
majority was secure; and after the 1790 elections their
majority was forty on a division over the Speaker's re-election
which tested the feeling of the House. The Regency crisis
had permanently aligned the British and Irish Oppositions,
symbolized in 1790 when Leinster, Charlemont, and the
Ponsonbys joined in the formation of an Irish Whig Club
designedly modelled on the English Opposition. The irre-
sponsibility of Irish officials to the Irish House of Commons,
and their reliance on the British-appointed Lord Lieutenant,
had produced a situation where those urging a change of
administration had perforce to oppose the English ministry.

This situation arose partly because the cabinet system was
less maturely developed in Ireland than in England. In practice the Irish Cabinet consisted of those members of the
Privy Council whom the Lord Lieutenant saw fit to consult,
irrespective of office, although it would have been a drastic
step to exclude either the Lord Chancellor or the Chief
Secretary. The influence of the Irish Cabinet varied with the
Lord Lieutenant, but by 1790 events were tending to increase their power; as old hands whose experience of Irish
politics and administration grew with the years, they seemed

[1] Burgh to Pelham, 25 Jan. 1789 (Add. MSS. 33100).

increasingly valuable to a series of Lords Lieutenant and Chief Secretaries. The Lord Lieutenancy demanded a taste for the minutiae of patronage, enough wealth and conviviality for lavish entertaining, and willingness to forgo the pleasures of London society for several years. Such qualities were usually to be found in a young nobleman 'caught wild at Brooks's', whose second-rate abilities and limited experience made him expendable at home. Westmoreland, the Lord Lieutenant appointed in 1789, was a spineless creature who was soon completely in the hands of his Dublin Castle advisers. The Chief Secretary, too, was usually a man at the outset of his political career, without claims to a more important or congenial office, but fortified by the knowledge that his post was becoming a recognized jumping-off ground for entry into British politics. Between 1789 and 1793 the Chief Secretary was Robert Hobart, a sociable, cynical young man who never went against the tide.

Outstanding among Westmoreland and Hobart's advisers was the Lord Chancellor, John, Lord Fitzgibbon.[1] Somewhat of a lone wolf, Fitzgibbon was an able, reforming, hardworking law officer, mordantly forthright, an unscrupulous political intriguer, and bitterly anti-Catholic as only the grandson of a Catholic peasant could be. He was connected by marriage with the Beresford family, that powerful clan whom contemporaries believed to control one-quarter of the offices in Ireland and 'undoubtedly govern the kingdom'.[2] This picture was an exaggeration. John Beresford, chief commissioner of revenue, was a shrewd old stager with widespread patronage; but his main concern was providing for his numerous family rather than exercising any voice in the creation of policy. As a commercial adviser, he was perhaps overshadowed by the proud and intelligent John Foster,[3] a man noted equally for his hostility to the Catholics and his

---

[1] Born 1749; M.P. for Dublin university 1777–83 and Kilmallock 1783–9; at first in Opposition, but soon a Government spokesman; Attorney-General 1784–9; Lord Chancellor 1789–1802; baron 1789; viscount 1793; earl of Clare 1795; died 1802.

[2] [T. Knox], 'The State of the Irish House of Commons, 1791' (ed. Dr. E. M. Johnston), *Proc. Royal Irish Acad.*, Mar. 1957, p. 48.

[3] Born 1740; M.P. Dunleer 1761–8, co. Louth 1768–1821; Customer of Dublin Port 1780; Chairman of Committees 1780; Chancellor of the Irish Exchequer 1784–5, 1804–6, and 1807–11; Chairman of the Linen Board 1784–1811; Speaker 1785–1800; Baron Oriel 1821; died 1828.

careful protection and encouragement of Irish industries. The first Irish-born Chancellor of the Exchequer, Foster since 1785 had been Speaker, a post which far more than its English equivalent still retained a traditional prestige as spokesman of the House of Commons in its dealings with the executive. His successor at the Exchequer was a close friend, Sir John Parnell,[1] whom Jonah Barrington described (for once, not unfairly) as 'a sloven and a gentleman';[2] he was a popular and fairly able figure, but lazy, easy-going, and always anxious to avoid trouble. Foster and Parnell were understood to be closely in touch with Irish mercantile and manufacturing interests, and their ideas did not always chime with Beresford's. The Attorney-General, the Solicitor-General, and the Prime Serjeant were law officers whose duties traditionally included the defence of government measures in the House of Commons. Others consulted at Dublin Castle usually included one of the more politically minded prelates of the Church of Ireland—in the 'nineties it was the ambitious Archbishop Agar of Cashel—and a few of the Government's more prominent supporters in the House of Lords. From these sources the Lord Lieutenant received a narrow view of the Protestant Ascendancy's interests, marked by a strong resistance to change and reform.

But change and reform were in the air. Encouraged by the apparent liberation of France from its *ancien régime*, some of the elements in Ireland who considered themselves under-privileged began to raise their claims. In 1791 the United Irishmen revived the issue of parliamentary reform among the middle class and artisans of Ulster and Dublin. But Dublin Castle's chief concern was with the Roman Catholic community, which commanded at least the nominal allegiance of about three-quarters of the population, as well as the sympathy of such public men as Edmund Burke, Henry Grattan, and the Ponsonbys. In the autumn of 1791 a deputation representing Irish Catholics went to London to demand abrogation of the remaining penal laws, and admission to full

---

[1] Born 1746; M.P. Bangor 1767-8, Inistioge 1777-83, Queen's County 1783-1801; 2nd baronet 1780; Commissioner of Excise 1780; Chancellor of Exchequer 1785-99; P.C. 1786; Vice-Treasurer of Ireland 1793-9; died 1801.

[2] J. Barrington, *Historical Anecdotes and Secret Memoirs of the Legislative Union between Great Britain and Ireland*, London, 1809, p. 19.

rights of citizenship. It was not an unpropitious moment. In Britain Catholics had just been admitted to the practice of law, and in Canada a new constitution had secured the rights of French-speaking Catholics. Admission of Catholic free-holders to the vote and Catholic gentry to parliament might allay religious discontents in Ireland, and perhaps insure against increased agrarian unrest by divorcing sectarian and economic grievances.

Pitt was notoriously uninterested in Irish affairs,[1] and at Whitehall the responsible minister was the Home Secretary, Henry Dundas, whose non-English, non-Anglican back-ground suggested that he would not be unsympathetic. Having sounded Westmoreland and found him opposed to concessions, the hard-bitten Dundas warned him that, if violence resulted from ignoring the reasonable demands of the Catholics, the British taxpayer could not be expected to subsidize the cost of the forces required to pacify Ireland.[2] Completely identifying himself with the conservative wing of the Ascendancy, Westmoreland in reply posed a dilemma.[3] If the British ministry insisted on removing all religious dis-abilities, they would lose control of the Irish Parliament to a 'Protestant' coalition, which would reject the measures and defy England: and if, without reform, Ireland underwent civil commotions tempting other nations to intervene, it would be impossible for Great Britain to stand aside and witness the Ascendancy's overthrow. The British ministry dropped for the time all but a few minor schemes of relief, but Pitt was by now stimulated to reopen the whole question of Anglo-Irish relations, for 'they must look to a permanent system which they could stand upon'.[4] During 1792 the situation in Europe deteriorated, and the Catholic agitation

[1] 'I believe as you candidly acknowledged to me before I came hither,' wrote Camden as late as 1796, 'that Ireland occupys little of your thoughts': and his complaint was echoed by other Viceroys, especially Westmoreland (Westmoreland to Pitt, 12 Oct. 1790 (P.R.O. 30/8/331); Camden to Pitt, 6 May 1796 (P.R.O. 30/8/326)).

[2] Dundas to Westmoreland, 26 Dec. 1791 (secret and confidential; Fane MSS., P.R.O., Dublin).

[3] Westmoreland to Dundas, 2 Jan. 1792 (private and confidential; 11 Jan. 1792 (official); 14 Jan. 1792; (Fane MSS.). Westmoreland to Pitt, 1 Jan. 1792 (secret; P.R.O. 30/8/331).

[4] Hobart to Westmoreland, 25 June 1792 (Fane MSS.).

continued. Pitt and Dundas resumed their pressure on West-moreland to ascertain precisely the depth of resistance to Roman Catholic concessions. In November 1792 Pitt con-fidentially threw at Westmoreland the notion of combining Catholic emancipation with a union of the two legislatures. 'The idea . . .', he wrote, 'has long been in my mind. . . . The admission of Catholics to a share of the suffrage could not then be dangerous—the Protestant interest in point of power, property and Church establishment would be secure because the decided majority of the supreme legislature would neccessarily be Protestant. . . .'[1] Westmoreland's reply was discouraging. Whatever his defects as an administrator, he had a certain cunning in patronage matters which enabled him to assess pretty accurately many of the difficulties which would confront Union. The great magnates who feared the ruin of the Ascendancy and Church Establishment might acquiesce, and the Catholics 'would probably not be averse . . . but the city of Dublin would be outrageous and that description of politician who can cabal and job here, but would either not reach, or be lost in the magnitude of the court of London . . .'.[2] However, he had previously noted that 'The Pro-testants frequently declare they will have an union rather than give the franchise to the Catholics, and the Catholics that they will have an Union rather than submit to their present state of degradation. It is worth turning in your mind how the violence of both parties might be turned on this occasion to the advantage of England.'[3]

Nevertheless, when in January 1793 the Home Govern-ment compelled Westmoreland to sponsor a proposal for enfranchising Catholic forty-shilling freeholders, at once the Lord Lieutenant concluded that Pitt was using the Catho-lics to coerce the Ascendancy: 'Do you mean by the fer-mentation to force the Protestants to a Union?'[4] This suspicion was fairly widespread—the whig Charlemont[5] had

---

[1] Pitt to Westmoreland, 18 Nov. 1792 (Fane MSS.).
[2] Westmoreland to Pitt, 28 Nov. 1792 (Fane MSS.).
[3] Same to same, 24 Nov. 1792 (Fane MSS.).
[4] Same to same, 18 Jan. 1793 (ibid.).
[5] Born 1728; 4th viscount Charlemont 1748; created earl 1763; patron of many of the young patriots; general of the Volunteer Movement 1782; K.P. 1783; died 1799.

voiced it over a year earlier[1]—and Fitzgibbon, the Lord Chancellor, became from this time convinced that nothing but Union could save Ireland from 'a Popish democracy'.[2] But a more common viewpoint was probably that of a whiggish young county member who argued that Union would be needed only if the British Government failed to carry through a policy of reform.[3] His name was Robert Stewart, soon to be better known as Lord Castlereagh.[4]

During 1793 and 1794 Pitt endeavoured to secure Anglo-Irish co-operation, within the framework of the existing system, by a judicious programme of administrative reforms, some of which had been urged by the Irish Opposition. The climate of opinion was favourable; on the outbreak of war with France in 1793 Grattan and his associates pledged their support to the war effort, although in no way coalescing with the Government. The veteran office-holders of Dublin Castle also had their reasons for supporting reform: 'We are all afraid of the Guillotine' wrote one during this period.[5] The Catholic forty-shilling freeholders were enfranchised, although a motion to admit Catholics to Parliament was defeated by 163 votes to 69. Other measures paralleled the British economic reforms of 1782 and assimilated Irish administrative usage to that of Great Britain. The Irish Treasury Board, with its seven commissioners appointed to exercise a much-needed supervision over the departmental management of Irish finances, was designedly modelled on that of England.[6] Electoral reforms included a reduction in the number of pensions, and the disqualification of certain placemen from sitting in the Commons, including the holders of all offices created after 1793. Those appointed to other

---

[1] Charlemont to Halliday, 15 Dec. 1791 (*H.M.C. Charlemont MSS.* ii, p. 183).

[2] Clare to Auckland, [8 June 1798] (Add. MSS. 29475).

[3] Stewart to Camden, 26 Jan. 1793 (Mt. Stewart MSS.).

[4] Born 1769; eldest son of 1st earl and marquess of Londonderry; grandson of 1st marquess of Hertford; step-nephew of 2nd Earl Camden; married a sister of Lord Hobart and niece of Thomas Connolly; M.P. for co. Down 1790–1805, 1812–21, and for various English boroughs 1806–12, 1821–2; Keeper of the Signet 1796; Chief Secretary of Ireland 1798–1801 (acting rank Mar.–Nov. 1798); President of the Board of Control 1802–6; Secretary for War and Colonies 1805–6, 1807–9; Foreign Secretary 1812–22; 2nd marquess of Londonderry 1821; died 1822.

[5] Lees to Auckland, 24 Mar. 1794 (Add. MSS. 34452).

[6] Douglas to Pitt, 16 Oct. 1794 (P.R.O. 30/8/327).

offices of profit were obliged to seek re-election, and an equivalent of the Chiltern Hundreds was provided in the Escheatorships of Munster, Leinster, and Ulster. Revenue officials were disqualified from voting. And the reconstruction of a new House of Commons was authorized, to replace the building destroyed by fire in 1792; an expenditure which certainly suggested that Union was not yet regarded as inevitable.

All these reforms were potentially capable of causing a shift in the balance of Irish political power. The enfranchisement of the Catholics eventually led, under the inspiration of Daniel O'Connell in 1826–9, to their emergence as a pressure-group which no landlord could control; but in 1793 it was assumed that Catholic tenantry would obey their landlords, and there does not seem to have been any comment even on the added weight which their enfranchisement might give to the Catholic provinces of Munster and Connaught. The provision of escheatorships, on the other hand, made for more flexible management of the House of Commons. Hitherto it had been impossible for a member to vacate his seat during the lifetime of a Parliament. Now, as well as retiring because of ill health, residence abroad, or desire to transfer to another constituency, a member could vacate his seat whenever it facilitated official arrangements or suited the wishes of his patron. But for this provision it is doubtful if the Union could have been carried. Among other reforms, the limitations on placemen and revenue officers were aimed at curbing the worst forms of local jobbery, and in particular gave a check to John Beresford's influence in government appointments. Early in 1794 the movement for clean government looked like taking a personal turn when Foster, Lord Ely,[1] and others normally found on the Government's side were pressing hard for an inquiry into Beresford's conduct with respect to the sale of certain government property in Dublin.

Grattan and the Ponsonbys, however, were after more

---

[1] Born 1738; son of Sir John Tottenham, Bart.; M.P. for Clonmines 1761–76, Fethard 1776–83, co. Wexford 1783–5; Collecter of Drogheda; succeeded to the estates of his uncle, the earl of Ely, 1783; baron 1785, viscount 1789, earl 1794, marquess of Ely 1800; Lord Loftus (U.K.) 1801; died 1806.

substantial concessions. Following the relaxation of the Navigation Acts in 1793, to admit Ireland to the East India trade, they went on to press for complete free trade. As William Ponsonby put it: '. . . if Ireland gave its hearty support to England in the war as an equal independent nation connected with the other in a mere federal union, it had a right to demand a total relinquishment of the colonial government, and to be put on a footing of complete equality with respect to its trade.'[1] Their other objectives could be summarized in the terse phrases of Thomas Connolly: 'Destroy all the new and useless places, you want your money for the war. Trust to the good sense of the real landed and monied aristocracy of the kingdom. Give the Catholic gentlemen of property the right to sit in Parliament. Pay the Catholic clergy from the publick treasury, as you do the Dissenters, and above all take care that neither your militia nor your standing army be made a job of.'[2] Nevertheless, the reforms of 1793–4 had revived confidence in the goodwill of the British Government, and had laid a promising foundation for Westmoreland's successor, especially after the admission of the Portland whigs into coalition with Pitt at the end of June 1794 gave rise to hopes of a like broadening of the Irish ministry.

An important aim of the Portland whigs in taking office was that 'Ireland may be saved and made a peacefull and usefull member of the British Empire',[3] and it had been agreed that Portland himself should have the Home Office, with surveillance of Irish affairs, while his old associate Lord Fitzwilliam, absentee landlord of large estates in county Wicklow, was persuaded after initial reluctance to accept the Lord Lieutenancy. The choice was disastrous; Fitzwilliam's high principles were clouded by invincible self-righteousness and a complete lack of political finesse.

Even before Dublin Castle had received word of his coming Fitzwilliam was in touch with the Irish whigs, promising a 'purified administration' and the implementation of their

[1] Douglas to Pitt, 23 Jan. 1794 (P.R.O. 30/8/326).
[2] Connolly to Fitzwilliam, 30 Aug. 1794. Cf. Charlemont to Fitzwilliam, 1 Sept. 1794; Leinster to Fitzwilliam, 4 Sept. 1794 (Wentworth Woodhouse MSS., F. 29).
[3] Portland to Fitzwilliam, 14 June 1794 (Wentworth Woodhouse MSS., F. 31 [b]).

policies. As well as admitting the Ponsonbys and their supporters to office, Fitzwilliam saw himself as a new broom
ousting such unpopular elements as Fitzgibbon and the
Beresfords. This could have been due to the crass refusal of
the Castle junta to accept the moderate reforms needed to
keep Ireland quiet; unfortunately, in view of the known
resentment of the Irish Opposition at the outcome of the
Regency crisis, it could equally be construed as 'the old and
sleepy game of patronage'.[1] The Pitt–Portland coalition
nearly split over this in October 1794. Lord Grenville
roundly condemned 'the system of introducing English party
into Ireland, the principle of connecting changes in Government here with the removal of persons high in office there',[2]
and Pitt nearly provoked Fitzwilliam's resignation by insisting that '. . . all idea of a new system of measures, or of new
principles of government in Ireland, as well as of any separate and exclusive right to conduct the department of Ireland
separately from any other in the King's service is disclaimed
and relinquished'.[3] But, after lengthy discussions between
the ministers and visiting Irish politicians, a programme was
devised on the basis of which Fitzwilliam consented to take
office. Fitzgibbon was to remain Lord Chancellor, provided
he continued to support the Government, and the Ponsonbys
and their followers should be brought in at the earliest
opportunity through a gradual reshuffle of offices. The reduction of unnecessary offices, as urged by Grattan and William
Ponsonby, could be taken into consideration in Ireland.
Anglo-Irish commercial intercourse would be regulated on
the principle of equalization of duties. The Convention Act
of 1793 restricting public meetings was to be repealed or
modified. And Catholic Emancipation was not to be proposed by the Government, but left open for study and
exploration.[4] Pitt's ministry had not closed the door on

---

[1] Stanhope, *Life of Pitt* [1879 ed.], ii, p. 85, quoting Lord Auckland.

[2] Lord Grenville to Thomas Grenville, 15 Oct. 1794 [Buckingham: *Courts and Cabinets of George III*, ii, p. 315].

[3] Stanhope, op. cit. ii, pp. 84–85. Similar expressions occur in Pitt to Westmore-land, 19 Oct. 1794 (P.R.O. 30/8/325).

[4] *H.M.C. Dropmore MSS.* iii, pp. 35–38: memorandum drawn up for Portland by Grenville in Mar. 1795, recapitulating the course of events leading to Fitz-william's recall. There is a memorandum in the Fitzwilliam papers, entitled 'Heads

further reform, but insisted on the need for an accurate first-hand assessment of Irish problems before new legislation was proposed.

Once on the spot in January 1795 Fitzwilliam, urged by friends who had been too long out of office and whose advice on Irish affairs he had trusted for years, moved precipitately. Two days after arrival he dismissed John Beresford because of the unproven allegations against his probity, and followed this by removing two of the under-secretaries, Sackville Hamilton[1] and Edward Cooke,[2] who were alleged to exercise more power than their situations warranted. He also set about securing the retirement of Wolfe and Toler, the Attorney-General and the Solicitor-General, to make room for members of the Ponsonby faction, and studiously avoided consulting Fitzgibbon. Fitzwilliam's conduct was capable of two interpretations. One was that he was the pliant instrument of the Irish whigs, and was throwing himself too much into the hands of the Ponsonbys and Grattan. But his own interpretation was that he was restoring the Lord Lieutenant's powers as the direct representative of the Crown, choosing ministers and policies irrespective of Irish or English party politics. In 1795, however, the representative of the Crown was the representative of George III; and Fitzwilliam came to grief over his schemes for Catholic relief. For, although counselled to caution by some of the Irish moderates, Fitzwilliam within a month of his arrival had concluded that Catholics should be admissible to Parliament forthwith, in order to allay popular discontent and facilitate the raising of largely Catholic yeomanry divisions for defence purposes. A widespread outburst of petitioning stimulated Grattan to foreshadow the introduction of an Emancipation Bill in the Irish House of Commons. This proposal, coming as

of conversation, 15 Oct. 1794', which substantially confirms this account. (Wentworth Woodhouse MSS., F. 29/2.)

[1] Born 1732; secretary to the Revenue Board 1771–80; M.P. St. Johnstown 1780–3, Rathcormuck 1783–90, Clogher 1790–7; under-secretary in Civil Department 1780–96; a commissioner to assess compensation to the owners of boroughs abolished at the Union 1800–3; died 1818.

[2] Born 1755; came in Lord Buckingham's entourage; Collector of Kinsale and Customer of Baltimore 1789; M.P. Old Leighlin 1790–1800; Under-Secretary Military Department 1789–95, 1795–6, Civil Department 1796–1801, War and Colonies (U.K.) 1804–6, 1807–12, and Foreign Office (U.K.) 1812–17; died 1820.

it did with Fitzwilliam's encouragement, caught George III unprepared, and at once aroused his antagonism. When they met on 7 February Pitt's Cabinet had before them Fitzwilliam's demands for immediate support, and the King's obdurate insistence that 'the subject is beyond the decision of any Cabinet of Ministers . . .'.[1]

By now Fitzwilliam had succeeded in raising, simultaneously and in baffling complexity, almost every contentious aspect of the relationship between Great Britain and Ireland. First, there was the question of the Lord Lieutenant's powers. The British Government viewed the Lord Lieutenant as the ultimate source and origin of Irish legislation, even although this in practice gave the Crown in Ireland a greater initiative than it had been in the habit of exercising in recent years in England. But how far was he entitled to override previous agreements or instructions emanating from his cabinet colleagues in Britain, and how far could he press proposals for the King's service without first securing the acquiescence of the King? And on what grounds might the Lord Lieutenant introduce widespread ministerial changes in Ireland? Were Irish party alignments partly or totally independent of English? If the Lord Lieutenant exalted the Ponsonbys at the expense of the Beresfords, was he compromising his independence, and could he resist the pressure of the Irish whigs towards complete ministerial accountability to the Irish House of Commons, thus materially diminishing the British Government's power to control events in Ireland? Alternatively—and, to judge from the private correspondence of the Beresfords and Lord Downshire, the possibility was not far-fetched[2]—might not the proposal for Catholic Emancipation provoke many of the Protestant Ascendancy magnates to go into opposition, perhaps wresting control of the House of Commons from the Lord Lieutenant, and stimulating dissensions throughout Ireland? Finally, the implications of

---

[1] Memorandum to Pitt, quoted Stanhope, op. cit. ii, pp. 433–6.

[2] Lord Downshire had certainly instructed his members to vote against Catholic emancipation, and one of his satellites told Westmoreland that a committee including Lords Downshire, Shannon, and Enniskillen, controlling between 120 and 140 M.P.s, and observing perfect discipline, had agreed to resist Grattan's Bill. Downshire to Reilly,—Jan., 5 Feb., and 20 Mar. 1795 (Downshire MSS.); for Lord Waterford's attitude, Waterford to Westmoreland, 27 Feb. 1795 (Fane MSS.).

Catholic emancipation raised many disturbing thoughts for the British ministry. The welfare of the Established Church was a very real consideration for such ministers as Portland. How controllable were the Catholic pressure-groups, who could bring forward such concerted petitioning immediately after Fitzwilliam's arrival? Could they safely be admitted to the yeomanry and militia? How could the measure be reconciled to the views of George III, whose dislike of the idea, and insistence that the decision lay ultimately with himself alone, were already plain? (He had not yet taken his final stand on the Coronation Oath, although the doctrine was to be communicated to him some time during February 1795, originating indirectly with Lord Chancellor Fitzgibbon.)

On 21 February the British Cabinet decided on Fitzwilliam's withdrawal from Ireland. He was recalled to his old post as Lord President of the Council, and Portland even volunteered to retire from the ministry if that would facilitate Fitzwilliam's reinclusion. From Portland's letter it was quite clear that the cabinet intended no loss of face to Fitzwilliam, and, without passing judgement on any single action of his, was mainly fearful that the Lord Lieutenant was losing control of the management of Irish politics to an Irish faction based on 'popularity'.[1] Hurt by his colleagues' lack of confidence, however, Fitzwilliam chose to regard himself as recalled in disgrace, and published two open letters implying that Pitt's Government had allowed him to hold out hopes of Catholic emancipation and other relief measures, only to break faith immediately the Dublin Parliament had voted generous taxation for the war. Not altogether surprisingly, he attributed the frustration of his reforms to Pitt's tenderness for the corrupt Fitzgibbon–Beresford clique. Such a view, although unsupported by any of his colleagues—least of all the other Portland whigs—found ready acceptance in Ireland. The prospect of Catholic emancipation and new men in Dublin Castle had raised popular expectations to such a pitch that Fitzwilliam's recall could not be viewed dispassionately. Many Irishmen lost confidence in the good faith of the British ministry and in the Dublin legislature's capacity

[1] Portland to Fitzwilliam, 21 Feb. 1795; same to same, 23 Feb. 1795 (Wentworth Woodhouse MSS., F. 5).

for reforming itself. As the imprisoned United Irishmen after the 1798 rebellion asserted: 'Whatever progress the united system had made among the Presbyterians of the North, it had, as we apprehend, made but little way among the Catholics throughout the kingdom until after the recall of earl Fitzwilliam.'[1]

During the controversy over Fitzwilliam's recall, there was considerable speculation in Ireland about the likelihood of a legislative union. From an oblique phrase in one of Portland's dispatches, Fitzwilliam had inferred that the British Cabinet had this objective in mind, unpopular though it still was in Ireland. The assumption was unwarranted. The most that could be said was that at this stage Union became a little more firmly established as one of a number of practical possibilities. Even Fitzgibbon (now to be promoted earl of Clare), who since 1793 had lost no seasonable opportunity of privately urging the measure on British politicians, saw no prospect of action before the end of the war. The incoming Lord Lieutenant and Chief Secretary thought it wise to disclaim any such intentions, and the Lord Chancellor somewhat disingenuously drafted a declaration promising 'to support the constitution as established in 1782 and still further assimilated to Great Britain by acts that have since passed'.[2] This phrasing at once repudiated Union and Catholic emancipation, and sufficiently expressed the intention of Fitzwilliam's successors to attempt no changes. But the pressures for change grew stronger as the threat of French invasion reinforced the spread of agrarian outrages and the mounting influence of the United Irishmen. Whether middle class and peasant unrest were to be met by concessions or coercion, Dublin Castle's policies could be enforced only with the backing of British arms and British money. Increasingly, despite the reluctance of the Protestant Ascendancy, essential decisions affecting the future of Ireland would be made in London; and increasingly, to an administratively logical mind like Pitt's, Union would appear a feasible answer to the Irish problem.

The qualifications of the new Lord Lieutenant and Chief

---

[1] Memoir of the State Prisoners, 1798 (*Castlereagh Correspondence*, i, p. 356).
[2] Pelham to Portland, 30 Mar. 1795 (Add. MSS. 33113).

Secretary gave little promise of a new direction to Dublin Castle policy. Lord Camden,[1] the Viceroy, combined pleasing manners with admirable intentions of forming independent judgements about Irish conditions and personalities; but after a few months of this exercise he lapsed into a steady dependence on the views of the old Dublin Castle Cabinet. Foster and Parnell may have been consulted somewhat more, Clare and Beresford a little less, but essentially it was the mixture as before; narrow, acquisitive, and unpopular. The Chief Secretary was Thomas Pelham, the honest and sympathetic Portland whig who had held the office for a few months in 1783, and who now took up the post as if it were a task to be discharged conscientiously until the earliest opportunity of returning to a pleasanter berth in England. The main aim to which Camden and Pelham addressed themselves was the conciliation of as many as possible of the Ascendancy gentry. Most country gentlemen, busy with militia and the pacification of their neighbourhood, were content to support in general the policies of Dublin Castle. Pelham began with hopes of retaining the Irish whigs who had come over under Fitzwilliam, and won a few converts such as John Forbes and Lodge Morres;[2] but his generosity fell short of attempting to win over Grattan, and the Ponsonbys 'put themselves out of the reach of all communication'.[3] Isolated in a 'Foxite' Opposition, voicing unpopular criticisms of the Government's defence measures, the Irish whigs were now irrevocably linked with the British opposition, and resolutely deaf to further overtures from Pitt. The propertied members of the Irish Parliament, threatened by rebellion and invasion, had little patience with pleas for Catholic relief, or even for reviving the question of

---

[1] Born 1759, son of 1st earl Camden; M.P. Bath 1780–94; 2nd earl 1794; Lord Lieutenant of Ireland 1795–8; Secretary at war 1804–5; Lord President of the Council 1805–6, 1807–12; marquess Camden 1812; died 1840.

[2] Portland to Pelham, 20 Apr. 1795 (Add. MSS. 33101); Camden to Pitt, 8 Aug. 1795 (P.R.O. 30/8/326). Forbes was appointed to a judicial post in the Bahamas. Morres became a commissioner of the Treasury and was promised a peerage. (Morres to Pelham, 11 and 14 July 1797 (Add. MSS. 33105).) As William Ponsonby observed: 'I suppose one end of him ach'd strongly for a coronet, and the other for a seat at the long table in the Council Chamber' (Ponsonby to Fitzwilliam, 5 June 1796 (Wentworth Woodhouse MSS., F. 30a)).

[3] Camden to Pitt, 21 May 1795 (P.R.O. 30/8/326).

Anglo-Irish free trade. In the divisions of 1796 and 1797 the opposition minority was often under twenty, and after the ignominious failure of one last motion for parliamentary reform Grattan and the Ponsonbys, following the example set by Fox in England, announced their intention of withdrawing from the sittings of Parliament. This left only a few diehards among the county members, such as Flood's former disciple, Sir Lawrence Parsons.[1] Several former Opposition stalwarts were selling their boroughs to proprietors more likely to support the Government, possibly because of financial embarrassments.[2]

For continuing unrest weakened confidence in the financial system just when the Irish Government wanted to make increased provision for military purposes. The moneyed interest declined advances to the Government except on steep terms. Placemen and pensioners created in palmier days complained if their allowances were not paid with punctilious regularity.[3] Landlords refused bank-notes and insisted on cash for their rents, thus decreasing an already low public confidence in the currency.[4] Parnell did what he could, but he was scarcely an adequate Chancellor of the Exchequer. In April 1796 he was obliged to seek a delay of several months in the repayment of advances drawn on the English Paymaster-General by the Irish board of treasury. By November 1796 the Government's credit was so strained by attempting to raise 30,000 yeomanry that the Bank of Ireland refused to advance £150,000 required for maintaining the public service. Shortly afterwards the long expected French invasion fleet set out for Ireland, but met such bad

---

[1] Born 1758; M.P. Dublin university 1782–90, King's County 1791–1807; succeeded his father as 5th baronet 1791, and his uncle as 2nd earl of Rosse 1807; Commissioner of Treasury 1805; P.C. 1806; Postmaster-General of Ireland 1809–17; died 1841.

[2] The duke of Leinster, who sold Harristown to the banker John Latouche for £14,000, was certainly reputed to be in financial difficulties; but I have no such evidence about William Burton, the Ponsonbys' cousin, who sold Carlow borough to a young peerage-hunter in 1795, nor about Thomas Connolly, who was still reckoned the richest of Ireland's country gentlemen when in 1795, despite advice to await better prices after the war, he sold Ballyshannon to the earl of Belmore, and New-town Limavady to Lord Londonderry (Lady Louisa Connolly to Thomas Connolly, 15 June 1795 (Bunbury MSS.)).

[3] Cooke to Pelham, 28 Jan. 1797 (Add. MSS. 33103).

[4] Camden to Portland, 10 July 1797 (H.O. 100/69).

weather at the mouth of Bantry Bay during the last week of
1796 that it withdrew without landing. The invasion scare
created a run on specie, and killed the Government's last
hopes of raising a loan in Dublin. Camden appealed for the
immediate advance of 200,000 guineas in cash and for British
assistance in raising a loan of £300,000. Pitt demurred at the
size of this request, but consented to obtain the sanction of
the British House of Commons for a loan of £150,000 for
the use of the Irish Government.[1] There was little difficulty
in securing the assent of the British Parliament, even though
this measure meant that their credit was raising revenue over
whose disposal not they, but the Lord Lieutenant and Commons of Ireland would have control.

The implications of this step did not escape one experienced Irish whig. More clearly than any of his associates
Lord Charlemont perceived the interrelation between the
assumption of financial responsibility for Ireland by the
British Parliament and a consequent enlargement of their
interest in Irish affairs; as he wrote to Camden in May 1797:

Does the nation or parliament of Great Britain mean to give an
unconditional support, by supplies of money, to any measures whatso-
ever to which the ministers of Ireland may think proper to apply it?
Is it unknown to the nation or parliament of Great Britain that a state
of civil war is actually declared to exist in a great part of Ireland. . . .
Surely, before they involve themselves, even in a dubious adoption of
the war, they should address the king to inquire into the state of Irish
grievances, and to lay them before parliament together with the topics
of redress requested by the Irish nation; that the parliament, together
with their supply, may combine their advice for the application of
it. . . .[2]

Although it was rather too much to hope that any intervention by the British Parliament would be on the side of
liberalism, it was indicative of whig feeling that still less
could be expected from the existing régime in Dublin. But
in times of stress the British Government would introduce
no new measures, lest it should seem to act under duress;
and in more tranquil periods they declined to disturb the

---

[1] Camden to Pitt, 26 and 31 Jan. 1797 (P.R.O. 30/8/326); Pitt to Camden,
10 Feb. and 23 Mar. 1797 (P.R.O. 30/8/325).
[2] Charlemont to Camden, 8 May 1797 (H.M.C. Charlemont MSS. ii, p. 297).

calm by introducing controversial legislation which might upset the ultra-Protestants.

'The independent constitution' of 1782 had been granted in consequence of the stresses imposed on Great Britain by one war. It had been an emergency measure, and had proved inadequate to last through the next war. Procrastination and lack of understanding on the part of the British Government, party pettiness and sectarian rancour on the part of too many of the Irish ruling class, each had tended to make it unworkable. Two possibilities remained. Either rebellion would be followed by alliance with republican France: or a closer connexion with Great Britain would entail the sacrifice of some of the privileges of 1782, which the Irish legislature had been unwilling or powerless to use. Considerations of defence and finance, and the increasing interrelation of British and Irish political groupings alike called for greater intervention and more constant supervision of Irish affairs by the Westminster Government. However unpalatable and imperfect Union might have been, an independent Irish legislature seemed unable to cope with the problems arising since the onset of the French war. The party in power offered nothing more than sterile repression, the Opposition groups were divided, exclusive, and had no clear programme. But the deepest causes of Irish discontent were insoluble under the existing condition of governmental machinery. A fast-growing population pressed on agricultural resources misused by an uneconomic and disheartening land system, whose maintenance was becoming an issue inseparable from religious and political grievances. Insufficient capital or raw materials were available for the large-scale industrialization which might have alleviated Ireland's situation. Instead, Ireland was to be left at a permanent economic disadvantage compared with Great Britain, for reasons scarcely realized by the legislators of the Act of Union.

II

THE ELECTIONS OF 1797

My answer to their offer was that my ambition as a
gentleman and a soldier has always been to keep respectable company and to serve my King and Country, and
that as I was unable to discover how a seat in the Irish
parliament would conduce to either of these purposes, I
hoped they would excuse my non-compliance with their
obliging proposal.

COLONEL GEORGE NAPIER to VISCOUNT CASTLEREAGH,
6 January 1799.[1]

THE abortive French invasion of December 1796 and the
Ulster risings of the following few months stimulated
much hard thinking in official quarters. At the beginning of May 1797, with the fortunes of war at their nadir,
the Navy disaffected, and no prospect of successful peace
negotiations with the French, the British Cabinet decided
that Camden's appeals for a Commander-in-Chief in Ireland
more capable than the bigoted, unpopular earl of Carhampton[2] could no longer be ignored. Whitehall suggested the
Master-General of the Ordnance, the marquess Cornwallis.[3]
Tough-minded, patient, with a wry sense of humour expecting little of human nature, Cornwallis at nearly 60 years of
age had already served more than his fair share of difficult
assignments, and was not particularly eager to go to Ireland;
but his sense of duty obliged him to consider the proposal,
although he firmly resisted Camden's offer to yield up the

[1] Napier to Castlereagh, 6 Jan. 1799 (Mt. Stewart MSS.).
[2] Simon Luttrell, born 1743; M.P. for Bosinney 1768–9, Middlesex 1769–74
(which he contested against John Wilkes); succeeded his father as 2nd earl of Carhampton 1787; Irish Commander-in-chief 1795–7, and then Master of the Irish
Ordnance; died 1821.
[3] Charles Cornwallis, born 1738; succeeded as 5th earl 1762, and was made 1st
marquess Cornwallis 1793; second-in-command in North America 1776–81,
surrendered at Yorktown; K.G. 1786; Governor-General of India 1786–93, 1797,
and 1805; Master-General of the Ordnance 1795–1801; Lord Lieutenant and Commander-in-Chief in Ireland 1798–1801; commissioner at Treaty of Amiens 1802;
died 1805.

Lord Lieutenancy to him.[1] Meanwhile, Pitt tried once more to conciliate the Irish Opposition. A go-between asked Fitzwilliam whether they would support the administration if Catholics were admitted to Parliament. Fitzwilliam replied that this would be throwing away the last chance of winning over the Irish public unless at the same time Clare and his more odious colleagues were dismissed and replaced by Grattan and the Ponsonbys. These were stiff terms; as Fitzwilliam wrote to William Ponsonby, 'I think, as Pitt thinks, that from that moment you become the arbiters of this Government as well as of that. I know not how an administration can exist here, to which you refuse your confidence.'[2] But Ponsonby thought the offer too vague, and unhesitatingly refused: 'No—there is but one person from whom such a proposal could come to us and be complied with, and even then it must be through you and the result of your *own* direct and personal communication.'[3] To such an extent had Irish and British party politics become mingled that neither the Castle clique nor their chief opponents would consider an alignment of Irish parties independent of the arrangements prevailing in England. It must be confessed that the leading Irish whigs had no very realistic notions about the cure for Irish disorder. In June 1797 they dispatched an agent to England beseeching the Prince of Wales to come over as Lord Lieutenant; 'no agent under Heaven', they wrote, 'could be found so fitted to perform the miracle of rescuing this unhappy nation from her present deplorable circumstances . . .'.[4] Were they still hankering after the prospects which had opened before them momentarily during the Regency crisis? The Prince, as it happened, was sufficiently well advised to decline the invitation.

Meanwhile, Camden got wind of the British Cabinet's interest in Catholic emancipation, and on 1 June wrote to Pitt stressing the need to crush all rebellion before there was any thought of concessions; 'if more concessions are to be

---

[1] Camden to Cornwallis, 23 May 1797 (*Cornwallis Correspondence*, ii, p. 327).
[2] Fitzwilliam to Ponsonby, 20 May 1797 (Grey of Howick MSS.).
[3] Ponsonby to Fitzwilliam, 29 May 1797 (ibid.; also Wentworth Woodhouse MSS. F. 30f).
[4] A draft of this letter is enclosed with Conolly to William Ponsonby, 17 June 1797. Cf. same to same, 13 June 1797 (Grey of Howick MSS.).

made,' he urged, 'persuade the King to employ others to . . . be the instruments of these measures, which you can never adopt with credit at present . . .'.[1] If emancipation were conceded, the Catholics would not be satisfied until parliamentary reform followed,

> . . . and if both these points are conceded, do you not lose the best, the only chance of adopting that measure which can alone render this country and England so united, as that it should be an advantage to it, instead of its being a point dreadfully vulnerable in all future wars?— I mean an Union. I do not feel I can be the instrument to carry this measure into effect. It should be entrusted to a deeper statesman or to a general of the highest ability and reputation, and during the alarm which exists amongst the leading persons in the country, I conceive it might be attempted successfully. If that measure is too bold, do not suffer the Catholic emancipation to be concluded in a hurry, or as an expedient to procure a temporary relief.[2]

Others close to Dublin Castle were thinking about Union in these difficult months; a fortnight later John Beresford, usually alert to shifts in government policy, was pumping Lord Auckland very guardedly about the same subject.[3] Whitehall, however, showed no sign of interest. The negotiations with Cornwallis fell through after it emerged that he would accept the post of Commander-in-Chief only if a system of concessions to Roman Catholics was adopted, or in the event of an emergency so threatening that he could not decently refuse.[4] The proposal was allowed to lapse the more readily because the Ulster rising had been suppressed, and quiet was returning.

Before June was out Camden sought and received permission of the Home Government for a dissolution of Parliament. Its term was due to expire within a year, and the weakness of the Opposition, the patriotic mood of the country gentlemen, and the tightness of the money market (which discouraged expensive electioneering) meant that the usual

[1] Camden to Pitt, 1 June 1797 (P.R.O. 30/8/326).
[2] Ibid.
[3] Beresford to Auckland, 19 June 1797 (Add. MSS. 34454).
[4] Portland warned Camden that the King knew nothing of the overtures to Cornwallis—a remarkable illustration of the independence of Pitt's ministry. Camden to Portland, 3 June 1797; Portland to Camden, 10 and 29 June 1797 (H.O. 100/69).

excitements of contested elections might largely be avoided.[1] The alternative—prolonging the life of the current Parliament—was not considered; Camden thought that a new Parliament could deal with such topics as Catholic emancipation more fitly than the old one which had thrice rejected the measure.[2] Besides, the decision took the Irish gentry by surprise. Scarcely three weeks elapsed between the first intimation of a general election and the return of most of the writs, so that there was not a great deal of time for the usual logrolling in the counties.[3] The gravity of the times induced many of the country gentlemen to suspend old rivalries and adhere to the existing balance of representation. County Down was fiercely contested between Lords Downshire[4] and Londonderry[5] in 1783 and 1790, and would be again in 1805 and 1812. But in 1797 Camden thought it worth while to write seeking Downshire's support for Castlereagh, stressing the necessity for calm.[6] Downshire was financially in no position to stand another marathon contest, and wrote to John Reilly, his man of electoral affairs: 'I agree with you that for peace sake the old members are best. I pray most sincerely there may be no contest.'[7] Nor was there, although Castlereagh was not universally popular with the other gentry of Down, and Colonel John Meade, another prospective candidate, made it clear that he withdrew not from want of confidence, but simply to avoid a contest.[8] And in the neighbouring county of Armagh, William Richardson, M.P. since 1783, declined for similar reasons to vie with the sons of Lords Charlemont and Gosford: 'In times like the present nothing short of the moral certainty of success could warrant any man in involving his county in a tedious contest: how ill

[1] Camden to Pitt, 22 June 1797 (H.O. 100/69).

[2] Same to same, 3 June 1797 (H.O. 100/69).

[3] Letters were sent to Lords Downshire, Hertford, and other borough-owning notables on 10 and 11 July, informing them of the election (H.O. 100/70). Most returns had come in by the first week of August.

[4] Arthur Hill, born 1746; M.P. for co. Down 1773–93; succeeded his father as 2nd marquess 1793; removed from Privy Council 1800; died 1801.

[5] Alexander Stewart, born 1739; M.P. for co. Down 1771–83; baron Londonderry 1789; viscount 1795; earl 1796; marquess 1816; died 1821.

[6] Camden to Downshire, 15 July 1797 (Downshire MSS.).

[7] Downshire to Reilly, 20 July 1797 (Downshire MSS.).

[8] *Belfast Newsletter*, 7 Aug. 1797; also Lane to Downshire, 3 Aug. 1797 (Downshire MSS.).

then should I have requited the many favours I have received from mine, had I continued to disturb the peace of it by a perseverance in a poll, the event of which was at best doubtful.'[1]

By Irish standards the elections were remarkably quiet, with few contests. Even in the North, where Camden had feared the return of two or three radicals, the only county poll was in Antrim where one sitting member, E. J. Agnew, was defeated by his colleague John Staples (brother-in-law of Thomas Connolly) and Edward McNaghten, backed by the marquesses of Hertford and Donegall. The poll was as large as usual, despite the recent unrest, final voting figures being Staples, 1,568, McNaghten, 1,195, Agnew 777.[2] Skirmishes also occurred in one or two midland counties; in Meath and Cavan the sitting members were challenged, but won without difficulty. Camden expected contests in Cork and Wicklow, but nothing eventuated. There were several contests in boroughs, of which possibly the most significant was at Carrickfergus, where the entrenched interests were challenged by a candidate of 'democratic' leanings, James Craig. But the poll ended with 611 votes for Lord Spencer Chichester (son of the marquess of Donegall), 523 for a sitting member, Ezekiel Wilson, and 363 for Craig. At the declaration of the poll, Craig observed: 'Contested elections at this time are generally disapproved of—for two reasons—the danger of dividing the harmony and unanimity of the people —and the inability and inefficacy of sending delegates to Parliament under the present system of representation.'[3] No doubt he spoke with justification, but where borough contests occurred, they tended to centre exclusively around the same local and parochial issues as made up the stuff of politics in less stirring times. At Limerick the twelve-year-long attempt of a sitting member, John Prendergast Smyth, to monopolize both seats for his family, came to an end with his retirement. One seat went to his colleague and nephew, Charles Vereker, the other to Henry Deane Grady, junior counsel for the petitioners who had maintained a series of lawsuits against Smyth, impugning the voting rights of absentee freemen. This was the result of a deal by which

[1] Ibid.   [2] *Belfast Newsletter*, 4 Aug. 1797.   [3] Ibid.

Grady gave the support of his 'independent' following to Vereker, receiving in return the second votes of absentees from Clare, Galway, and Tipperary. As a result another independent candidate, one of the Monsell family who had been prominent on the corporation for many years, was shut out.[1] The contest at Drogheda resulted, as usual, in the return of two independent members who usually sat in Opposition, keeping out a third candidate whose return, it was thought, would make the Speaker, John Foster, 'the tyrant of Drogheda'.[2] At Downpatrick Edward and South-well Trotter tried to wrest control from Lord de Clifford's kinsmen, the Rowleys; but, as the Trotters put it, 'lordly influence shackled you with its ignominious fetters', and the voters rejected them by 114 votes to 15.[3]

The anti-unionists were subsequently to complain that the 1797 elections were got over at a time when the usual amount of canvassing was impossible; but the turnover of new members was much the same as at past elections. There were 123 new members in the 1797 Parliament, of whom eighteen sat for counties. This may be compared with an intake of 116 newcomers (nineteen of them county members) in 1790. But the Ascendancy had never rallied to the Government so zealously as they did in 1797, threatened by the French and the unknown number of French sympathizers in Ireland. Of 300 M.P.s returned in 1797, no more than fifty at most could be counted as regular members of the Opposition. The Ponsonby family and their friends numbered twenty-two; about the same number represented counties or 'open' boroughs; and a few young lawyers, with the nominees of two or three noblemen of Foxite inclinations, completed the tally. It was later to be argued by Castlereagh that the cheapness of borough seats encouraged the entry into Parliament of young barristers of small fortune and Opposition sympathies.[4] In fact, of the twenty-four unconnected members

---

[1] H. of C. Reports of Committees, vol. ii (1820), 'Report of the committee appointed to inquire into the conduct of the election at Limerick city . . .'.

[2] R. B. McDowell, Irish Public Opinion, 1750–1800, London, 1944, citing a broadsheet in the Massereene and Ferrard MSS. The Foster family achieved dominance in Drogheda in 1807.

[3] Belfast Newsletter, 11 Aug. 1797.

[4] Castlereagh to Pitt, 30 Jan. 1799 (P.R.O. 30/8/326).

ERRATA

Page 31, footnote 1. *Delete existing note and substitute* [1] Many were inexperienced, and sat only in this parliament.

Page 239, line 3, l.h. column. *For* Armeigh *read* Armagh.

who purchased borough seats in the 1797 Parliament, at least twelve were supporters of the administration, and only seven (not all of them in opposition) were lawyers. Altogether 200 of the members elected in 1797 could reasonably be expected to vote with the Government, if they attended. Of the fifty members unaccounted, many were independents or new-comers who were not necessarily ill disposed towards Dublin Castle.[1] The radicals had vanished: Lord Edward Fitzgerald sat no more for county Kildare, and Arthur O'Connor, having broken with his uncle who returned him for Philipstown, was prevented from standing for county Antrim by his arrest in February 1797 on a charge of seditious libel.[2] Even in Dublin city the government candidates, John Wolfe[3] and John Claudius Beresford,[4] were returned unopposed to the plaudits of a street crowd.

Despite the apparent success of this 'khaki election', there were factors implicit in it which would act against the success of the Union proposals of 1799. Of the 200 members who usually supported, only ten sat directly for government boroughs.[5] Four others were law officers who purchased their seats: seven were independent county members: four sat for their own boroughs: and twelve had purchased borough seats. All the remaining 163 members were attached to parliamentary connexions, and in the event of a crisis, it was questionable whether they would remain attached to the Government and its patronage, or join the head of their faction in opposition. The oldest-established connexions tended to be the biggest. The Beresfords had eleven members, Lords Shannon and Ely each ten, Lord Downshire had eight. But new families were coming to the fore. Two brothers-in-law,

---

[1] See Appendix I for an analysis of the 1797 Parliament.

[2] *Belfast Newsletter*, 6 Feb. 1797.

[3] Born 1740; Solicitor-General 1784-9; Attorney-General 1789-98; Lord Chief Justice 1798-1803; murdered during Emmet's rebellion, 1803; had associations with the Beresford faction; a humane but conformist lawyer.

[4] Born 1766, 3rd son of John Beresford, nephew of 1st marquess of Waterford; M.P. for Swords 1790-7; Dublin city 1797-1804; co. Waterford 1806-12; Lord Mayor of Dublin 1814-15; Inspector-General of Exports and Imports; Registrar General of Tobacco (resigned both offices, Jan. 1799); General Secretary of Orange Lodges 1799-1800; head of bank which failed in 1820 crisis; died 1840.

[5] Two each for the 'bishop's boroughs', Armagh, Clogher, St. Canice, and Old Leighlin, and two by gift or purchase.

the earls of Belmore[1] and Enniskillen,[2] had between them in 1797 a following of nine members; eight years earlier Belmore had none and Enniskillen but one.[3] The marquess of Abercorn[4] in the same period increased his following from two to seven.[5] The earl of Kingston[6] had two relatives in the Commons in 1796 and six in 1797.[7] The banking house of Latouche had bought two boroughs since 1780, now had five members in the House, and was supplanting the duke of Leinster as the biggest interest in Kildare. Another rising magnate, John Bagwell, finding little scope in his native Cork, had built up influence in Tipperary. In 1797 he was member for the county, had one son in Parliament, would shortly bring in another, and was assuming control of Cashel borough from the Pennefathers; while his brother-in-law and nephew, William and Richard Hare, sat for purchased seats at Athy. While all these groups supported the Government at a time of crisis, with a compliant Lord Lieutenant who followed the tenets of the Protestant Ascendancy pretty closely, they were an unpredictable element in the business of normal parliamentary management; especially at a time when the Chief Secretary, burdened with the responsibilities

[1] Armar Lowry-Corry, born 1740; M.P. for co. Tyrone 1768–81; High Sheriff of Tyrone 1769 and Fermanagh 1779; baron 1781, viscount 1789, and earl of Belmore 1797; died 1802.

[2] William Willoughby Cole, born c. 1730; M.P. for co. Fermanagh 1761–76; succeeded his father as 2nd baron Mountflorence 1776; earl of Enniskillen 1789; very prominent supporter of Orange Lodges; died 1803.

[3] Lord Belmore returned two members for Belturbet (purchased from Lord Lanesborough before 1789) and Ballyshannon (purchased from Thomas Connolly); Lord Enniskillen had two members for Enniskillen (where he had sold the seats, 1776–90) and was father-in-law to Owen Wynne, M.P. for Sligo borough. Their sons, Lords Corry and Cole, sat for counties Tyrone and Fermanagh.

[4] John James Hamilton, born 1756; succeeded his uncle as 7th earl of Abercorn 1789; created marquess 1790; died 1818.

[5] Having inherited Strabane borough in 1789, he purchased Augher and formed an alliance with the Knox family, proprietors of Dungannon. This gave him six members, and the Hon. Henry George Knox, M.P. for Dublin University, 1797–1807, was the seventh.

[6] Edward King, born 1724; succeeded to the family estates 1755; baron, viscount, and earl of Kingston 1771; died 1797. The 2nd earl, Robert (1754–99), and 3rd earl, George (1771–1839), each bore the title of viscount Kingsborough before succeeding to the earldom.

[7] They were: Lord Kingsborough, M.P. for co. Cork (2nd earl of Kingston, Nov. 1797); Edward King, M.P. for co. Roscommon (3rd earl, Apr. 1799); Henry and Robert King, M.P.s for the family borough of Boyle; and Gilbert and James King, co-proprietors and members for Jamestown.

of defence and finance, had neither time nor resources for the details of patronage. Moreover, the low price at which borough seats sold in 1797 militated against a legislative union. In John Beresford's words: 'As to the boroughs, many of the proprietors are very poor, and have lived by the sale of them. Upon the late general election, boroughs did not sell readily, and several of the proprietors were obliged to come in themselves. They cannot be expected to give up their interest for nothing: and those who have bought their seats cannot be expected to give up their term for nothing.'[1] Since the overthrow of the Undertakers in 1767, the normal price for a seat in one Parliament had been pretty constant at £2,000. In May 1796 John Toler[2] paid Stephen Ram £2,300 for the tenure of a seat at Gorey, the money to be refunded to his heirs if Toler died before the next elections.[3] But between 1796 and 1798 tight money and fear of rebellion and invasion combined to depress the value of boroughs by one-third or more; early in 1798 Richard Herbert, successfully seeking a seat as a government supporter, put up £1,200 as a fair offer, 'as several were sold for this price during this session'.[4] This recession hardly affected the big borough proprietors, such as Ely, Shannon, or the Ponsonbys, for they never sold, but were often in the market to buy a seat for some additional kinsman or follower. It was as a rule a sign of need to sell seats; and it was not to be wondered at if the small borough-owners, who treated their constituencies as an investment, opposed the passing of an Act of Union which might abolish their holdings before they had better opportunities of making another few thousand pounds on them. The speed and facility with which the 1797 elections were

---

[1] Beresford to Auckland, 6 Feb. 1799 (*Beresford Correspondence*, ii, p. 210).

[2] Born 1745; M.P. Tralee 1776–83, Philipstown 1783–90, Gorey alias Newborough 1790–1800; Chairman of Kilmainham Quarter Sessions 1780; Solicitor-General 1787; Attorney-General 1798; Chief Justice of Common Pleas 1800–27; his wife a baroness 1797; himself baron 1800 and earl of Norbury 1827; died 1831.

[3] Receipt dated 20 May 1796, made out by Stephen Ram (C.S.O. 509/22/5).

[4] Herbert to Castlereagh, 29 Apr. 1798 (C.S.O. 511/49/6). In computing the amount required for compensation if Union passed, Castlereagh in his memorandum of 1 Feb. 1799 noted: 'The purchasers into the present parliament are very numerous supposing only fifty, at £1500 each, seats being peculiarly cheap, gives £75,000' (H.O. 100/85).

arranged disguised the emergence of new factors in Irish politics. Since few counties were contested, the potential influence of the Roman Catholic freeholders was hardly guessed. It has been suggested that after Catholic enfranchisement in 1793 landlords started to subdivide their estates into minute freeholdings, in order to increase their electoral influence;[1] but I have found no evidence of it before the Union. More attention was paid to the rise of the Orange Lodges as an influential pressure-group, especially in the North. Within the boroughs, added control was given to patrons by the operation of escheatorships. Even in the House of Commons the withdrawal of the Ponsonbys (who, however, had taken steps to secure their re-election to the Parliament in which they disdained to sit) did not imply an end to all opposition. Perhaps because the Government's majority seemed assured, less attention was paid to cajoling the back-bencher. It was not to be expected that the management required for so controversial a measure as a legislative union would be altogether plain sailing.

Corruption had been of little importance in securing the Government's majority. The act of 1793 had curbed some of the Government's influence through place-giving and the Revenue Board. By deliberate policy, the creation and promotion of peers was limited to a smaller extent than attended the 1776 and 1790 elections, both of which resulted in the return of much larger Oppositions.[2] Threatened by the French and by an unknown number of French sympathizers within Ireland, many of the Ascendancy rallied to the Irish Government more zealously than in quieter times. This was reflected in the Dublin legislature. For the Parliament on College Green was not just a 'noisy sideshow'[3] irrelevant to the mainstream of Irish history. As accurately as any other eighteenth-century legislature, it reflected the interests and preoccupations of the governing class: in this case the Anglo-Irish colonial oligarchy. Although in Ireland the system of land tenure was complicated by acerbities unknown in England,

---

[1] For instance, by E. Strauss, *Irish Nationalism and British Democracy*, London 1951, p. 13.
[2] Pelham to Portland, 8 July 1797 (B.M. Add. MSS. 33105).
[3] M. Corkery, *The Hidden Ireland*, 3rd ed. 1941, p. x.

yet in Ireland as in England, land was the touchstone of political power. From ownership of land respectability and independence were assumed; during the Union controversy both Government and Opposition took pains to demonstrate that the majority of property, rather than the sheer weight of numbers, was on their side.[1] More than any other factor, political loyalty apart, landed estates governed admission to the House of Lords. No man with a rent-roll of under £5,000 a year could hope for a peerage, and most grantees had a considerably higher income.[2] For most of the Ascendancy gentry, their rents were their main source of revenue. Ireland's economy was less diversified than England's, and the younger sons of gentlemen were in any case unwilling to stoop to trade. Some families benefited from urban property; thus the rise of Belfast brought the marquess of Donegall[3] the largest annual income in Ireland. But the Ascendancy's standard of living was expensive. It was an age of great building, and hospitality was by tradition lavish. The minor gentry aped these customs, and the son of a Queen's County squireen wrote of his kind: 'Their habits were in general unadapted to public business, and many of them though possessed of extensive demesnes, had inadequate fortunes. The hospitable disposition and convivial habits of the Irish gentry of the day, by creating an expenditure far beyond the limits of their income, had a sensible effect on the independence of their situations.'[4] For many public office seemed the

---

[1] The Opposition-produced division list of Jan. 1799 marked out those members with a rent-roll of over £4,000 a year. For the Government, Edward Cooke assessed the attitude of such divided counties as Galway and Roscommon by computing the rent-rolls of local gentlemen on either side (Mt. Stewart MSS.; also Castlereagh to John King, 2 Apr. 1800 (P.R.O. 30/8/326)).

[2] *Sketches of Irish Political Character* (1799) indicates that all the landed proprietors worth £15,000 a year were in the House of Lords, except Thomas Conolly, M.P. for co. Londonderry, who prided himself on his status as a leading independent country gentleman. Cf. Drogheda to Buckingham, 16 Aug. 1789 (Buckingham MSS.) or Mullins to Castlereagh, 31 May 1799 (Mt. Stewart MSS.), where aspirants to promotion in the peerage set forth their landed income as a qualification.

[3] Born 1739; succeeded as 5th earl of Donegall 1757; a British peer 1790; marquess of Donegall and earl of Belfast 1791; died 1799.

[4] Sir Jonah Barrington, *Historical Anecdotes and Secret Memoirs of the Legislative Union between Great Britain and Ireland* (1809–13 ed.), p. 33. A not untypical figure was George Ogle, M.P. for co. Wexford 1768–97, of whom it was observed, '. . . by excess, riot, and a dissolute life, pompous apparel banquetting and prodigal spending has consumed a monstrous estate, however there is a good one remaining'.

only respectable way of supplementing their livelihood, and the quest for patronage became their main object in politics.

Patronage, to politically minded landowners, was not necessarily only a means of aggrandizing themselves or providing for their families. It was through the personal goodwill earned by patronage that standing was built up within a county. The debt owed by a county member to the support of a great landowner was thus described by Lord Downshire to the mother of an aspiring candidate:

> It never was my intention to have given up without certain conditions to any one the fruit of all my labours and expenses, but madam, give leave to assure you that I could not propose any conditions that were illiberal or unbecoming any gentleman. If I do a man a material piece of service, is not a return natural and becoming. I offer my friendship's interest and support to a man who wishes to represent a county. He obtains his wishes without trouble, expense, is it not right, proper, and necessary that that friend should always act with and co-operate in such measures as are necessary to keep up that interest in every or any shape. Whilst that friendship last, surely no friend by concurrence can be deemed dishonorable or improper.[1]

The development of a county interest by a great landowner required constant attention to the minor details of local patronage, for his standing with Dublin Castle was measured by his ability to deliver the goods. Thus the earl of Altamont[2] wrote to Under-Secretary Cooke in 1798, pushing the claims of a candidate for the Surveyorship of Newport, worth £35 yearly: 'I am sure both you and Lord Castlereagh must be aware that if we cannot put into *such* offices, in a town which is my own property, and which must be managed from the persons who are principles in it, the O'Donels doing everything hostile both to us and the Government, that we can be of little use to them or to ourselves there.'[3] While at a moment of crisis during the Union controversy, Lord Downshire found occasion to grumble to one of his members:

(Fr. M. Bodkin (ed.), 'Notes on the Irish Parliament in 1773', *Proc. Royal Irish Acad.*, 1942.)

[1] Downshire to Lady Clanwilliam, — October 1793 (Downshire MSS., D.O.D. 607/484).

[2] Born 1756; succeeded his father as 3rd earl of Altamont 1780; marquess of Sligo 1800; died 1809.

[3] Altamont to Cooke, no date, endorsed 1798 (C.S.O. 511/47/35).

'I shall long to hear from you by the next post, remember I have nobody that writes to me on these subjects in the county, and I depend upon you . . .; if a boatman or tide-waiter's place is vacant, I get letters plenty, and four sides full, and put in a white blank sheet, but if any plan or measure is to be adopted or thought of, then I am not thought of. . . .'[1]

Nor was the magnate expected to confine his benevolence to personal dependents. Lord Ely in 1800 presented the town of Wexford with a supply of drinking water, after their political support had just sustained him over the Union controversy. Lord Waterford[2] interrupted his demands for personal patronage with a plea for an improved service of mail coaches between Cork, Waterford, and Dublin. Colonel John Meade was returned for county Down in 1805; among the arguments advanced in his favour was the benevolence of his grandfather, who many years previously had given his tenantry annual leaseholds in perpetuity at 2s. 6d. an acre.[3] Some families, not necessarily the most affluent or powerful, won so respected a local reputation that their members were returned for their county long after the reforms of 1829–32. Such were the O'Neills of Antrim, the Archdalls of Fermanagh, the Brownlows of Armagh; although parallel cases are harder to find in the South after Catholic Emancipation.[4]

Thus the gentry of the Protestant Ascendancy exercised a powerful influence in county elections. The franchise was vested in occupants of lands valued at forty shillings, the bulk of whom were tenants at will. Many landlords secured control of their tenantry's politics through the custom of

1 Downshire to Reilly, 13 Oct. 1799 (Downshire MSS.).

2 Born 1735; succeeded his father as 2nd earl of Tyrone 1763; a British peer 1786; marquess of Waterford 1789; died 1800.

3 *County of Down Election*, 1805.

4 Harder, but not impossible. The Fitzwilliam interest prevailed in Wicklow until 1880. Even the Beresfords, whose defeat in 1826 had been the first striking success of the organized Catholic vote, were not entirely ousted from Waterford: Lord Charles Beresford sat for the county as late as 1874–80. In the North, members of the O'Neill family have sat in the House of Commons for co. Antrim or for mid-Antrim 1783–93, 1802–37, 1863–80, and 1885–1959, as well as providing members and two cabinet ministers in the Parliament of Northern Ireland since 1922. Earlier members of the family represented the borough of Randalstown for considerable intervals in the eighteenth century. They claim descent from Niall, High King of Ireland in the early part of the fifth century.

'hanging gale', which by allowing them to accumulate arrears of rent rendered them liable for eviction unless they voted obediently. Even the liberal-minded earl of Charlemont, who more than most of his class disliked coercion, felt entitled to guide his county Armagh tenantry. 'Is it arrogance . . .', he wrote, 'to think that the recommendation of a man who has lived but to serve them, and who has never had an interest separate from theirs, ought to have some weight?'[1] There are a few—a very few—examples of a landlord forbearing to direct his tenantry. Lord Fitzwilliam, who controlled both seats for county Wicklow, returned one member and allowed his tenantry free choice in voting for the second. Few who wished to cut a figure in politics could afford such magnanimity.[2] When a landlord was uninterested or an absentee, the right to canvass his tenantry was eagerly solicited. Sometimes Government influence was invoked; for instance, both in the 1790 and 1797 elections the Lord Lieutenant of the time wrote to Pitt suggesting how absentee landlords could best use their influence in county Wexford. In 1807 competition in this county became so keen that the retiring member, John Colclough, was shot dead in a duel by his successor, William Alcock, for trespass in canvassing the freeholders of an elderly widow.

Because of the expense of a lengthy poll, contested elections were sometimes avoided by prior negotiations. This was understandable, when a candidate for a county could expect to pay at least £250 in fees to the sheriff and other officials, and often more; the sheriff of Mayo made 2,750 guineas out of the by-election of 1813–14. The unofficial expenses in securing the tenantry of supporters must have been higher, particularly since drunkenness, riot, and intimidation were not unusual. Sir Lucius O'Brien claimed to have spent £2,000 on the county Clare election of 1768. By 1802 his son was prepared to give a rival candidate £4,000 to withdraw from the contest and purchase a borough; this was cheaper than competitive bidding for the tenantry of the local

---

[1] Charlemont to Halliday, 29 Apr. 1790 (*H.M.C. Charlemont MSS.* ii, p. 125).

[2] Fitzwilliam to George Ponsonby, 6 Oct. 1795 (Wentworth Woodhouse MSS., F. 30a). Cf. *Belfast Newsletter*, 7 Aug. 1797, where the tenantry of Noah Dalway, later M.P. for Carrickfergus, insert an advertisement thanking him for allowing the free disposal of their votes at the Antrim county elections.

squireens.[1] Perhaps the record was the £60,000 reputedly spent on the great contest for Down in 1790 between the candidates of Lord Downshire and Lord Londonderry.[2]

The cost of elections helped to ensure that political power stayed in the hands of local landowners, and towards the end of the century the large borough-owning families were extending their grip over a number of county seats. Of sixty-four county members elected to the 1797 Parliament, sixteen were the heirs to peerages. It was a recognized ambition of every parliamentary family to put up the eldest son for a county seat, and some families had no aversion to seeming to press hereditary claims.[3] In Wexford, after a contested return, a seat was won by Lord Ely's eldest son in 1791; the family had never before represented the county. The earl of Enniskillen commanded one seat for Fermanagh after 1783, while the Beresfords, who already returned a member for Waterford, contrived to have the 18-year-old earl of Tyrone brought in for Londonderry in 1790. Other families had older traditions. Lord Shannon could always command one county seat in Cork, and sometimes both; the marquess of Downshire held similar sway over Down. Until after 1790 the duke of Leinster completely controlled Kildare and three of its four boroughs. Lords Altamont and Tyrawley divided Mayo, and between 1761 and 1800 there was always a Rochfort sitting for Westmeath, a Ponsonby for Kilkenny, and a Foster and a Fortescue for the two seats in Louth. Even in more open counties, representation was often shared or contested among a handful of families. The members for Roscommon were all named Crofton, French, or Mahon. The Coopers, O'Haras, and Wynnes rang the

---

[1] O'Brien to Charlemont, 2 June 1775 (*H.M.C. Charlemont MSS.* i, p. 330); Robert Day, Diary, 2 Aug. 1802, quoted in E. B. Day, *Mr. Justice Day of Kerry*, p. 273.

[2] *Castlereagh Correspondence.* Introduction by the 3rd marquess of Londonderry, i, p. 7. H. M. Hyde (*The Rise of Castlereagh*, p. 67) could only find evidence for expenditure of £6,000 by Lord Londonderry's family. Lord Downshire's campaign cost £30,000 (Downshire to Clanwilliam, 24 Oct. 1793 (Downshire MSS.)).

[3] The editor of *An Historical Account of the Late Election . . . for the co. of Down,* etc. (1784) writes of Lord Hillsborough's family: 'And indeed, from their weight and consequence, we think ourselves at liberty to say that soliciting *one seat only*, and that too for the *heir of the family* (exclusive of his personal recommendations) was a strong proof not only of their moderation, but of their respect for the peace and harmony of the country.'

changes in Sligo. Family influence was perhaps weakest in the presbyterian northern counties, where Ulster tenant right gave the forty-shilling voters greater security from eviction, and in the metropolitan area around Dublin; but it was nowhere negligible. Yet, as in England, it was thought an honourable ambition to represent one's county in the House of Commons. Sharing the same dislike of taxation and centralized government as the country gentlemen of England, the Irish county members were a necessary ingredient of any effective opposition to Dublin Castle. At no time between 1776 and 1793 could the Government reckon on the support of a majority of county members. War and rebellion had their effect, and after the 1797 election the Government could normally count on the votes of at least forty of the sixty-four county members.

It was through the boroughs that Governments usually hoped to make up their majorities, for it was here that the Irish parliamentary system came closest to caricaturing the British. Of the 118 boroughs, sixty-six had a closed corporation, comprising a returning officer and about a dozen self-perpetuating members, not necessarily resident. Designed by the early Stuart viceroys to secure the return of a loyal majority to the Dublin Parliament, these corporations had all fallen by the Hanoverian era into the control of local landowners, who either packed them with their relations and dependents, or else permitted them to become extinct. Provision had been made for the creation of freemen in these boroughs, but the custom was sedulously neglected. In thirty boroughs, however, freemen were created; of these twenty-four had less than a hundred freemen, incapable of affecting the patron's control, but six had 200 or more. These last were all boroughs in which rival interests had fought for control, in the process endowing many of their respective tenantry with the freedom of the borough. The future duke of Wellington, at a time when the Wellesleys were struggling to retain their borough of Trim, succinctly described the three classes of people entitled to become freemen: 'Those who were made to repel a party striving to turn the old family interest out of the borough; the man who had been attorney in the cause, had been of use to the corporation, and might be more so in the case of a general election; and the inhabitants of the town who were to be the possessors of lots of commons.'[1] By 1790 Trim, owned by an absentee land-lord and within range of unsettling influences from Dublin, was the only borough of this type in which contests were still likely. In the others competition had ended either through the elimination of all but one party, or through a compromise by which the two most prominent families shared the seats.

Few of the twenty-two 'open' boroughs were really inde-pendent. Eight were potwalloping, in thirteen the franchise lay in the forty-shilling freeholders and freemen (not neces-sarily resident), and the electorate of Dublin University comprised the provost, fellows, and about seventy scholars of Trinity College. Except at Swords, where one seat was usually purchased by a member of the Beresford connexion and the other went to the highest bidder on the open market, no potwalloping borough in normal circumstances[2] was en-tirely free from aristocratic influence, although it was difficult to impose on such a constituency a complete stranger without local interest. In the smaller potwalloping boroughs, such as Baltimore and Randalstown, resident proprietors held undis-puted patronage, but in larger communities the dominant family often met opposition, both from local rivals and from the influence of revenue officials. Control became somewhat easier after the reforms of 1793 disenfranchised revenue officials, and an act of 1795 limited the potwalloping franchise to £5 householders; but absentee and negligent landlords still risked losing control from want of personal attention.[3]

Of the urban boroughs, the city of Dublin was noted for its independence, although even there attempts were some-times made to push the nominees of the oligarchical Court of Aldermen, and, on the other hand, the duke of Lein-ster's family enjoyed considerable popular strength.[4] Smaller

[1] Wellesley to Mornington, 8 May 1790 (Wellington MSS.).

[2] Lisburn, normally the absentee Lord Hertford's preserve, returned two indepen-dent reforming Volunteers in 1783.

[3] Baltimore between 1768 and 1783 and Downpatrick in 1802 were lost by the previously dominant families, owing to neglect or absenteeism, but merely passed into the influence of another magnate.

[4] The 2nd duke, when marquess of Kildare, was M.P. for the city 1767–73, and his brother, Lord Henry Fitzgerald, sat as Grattan's colleague 1790–7. Subsequently

boroughs with an independent tradition were Waterford and Drogheda. Each usually returned unconnected members inclined to oppose Dublin Castle, and each was at some pains to fend off the intervention of a nearby landowning family— the Beresfords at Waterford and the Fosters at Drogheda. At Carrickfergus, the marquess of Donegall controlled one seat, provided that he did not interfere with the choice of the second member, representing the townspeople.[1] In general, boroughs with even so limited an independence were exceptional, and the number was lessening. Since 1759 Cork city had fallen under the influence of the Hely-Hutchinson and Longfield families, and Londonderry after 1768 was dominated by the 'nabob' Lord Caledon and the Hill family, allies of the Beresfords. In Limerick and Galway, the dominant families depended on the votes of absentee freemen. Galway was controlled by two branches of the Daly family who, although differing violently in politics, had combined in 1771 to fight legal proceedings to disenfranchise the absentee freemen. After a struggle, during which there were for some years two rival mayors and corporations in Galway, the mayoralty had been held since 1777 exclusively by members of the Daly family.[2] Limerick was similarly controlled by the Pery and Vereker families, but since the retirement of Speaker Pery in 1785 the Verekers had held both seats, thus arousing considerable antagonism.[3] But once an Irish borough had thrown in its lot with a parliamentary clan of any consequence, it was exceedingly difficult to reduce the patrons' influence.[4]

the banking family of Latouche, which supplanted them in Kildare, also replaced the Leinster family in representing Dublin city.

[1] However, the marquess of Downshire had some interest in the town, and his tenantry were called in when it was necessary to defeat a candidate of 'democratic' leanings (Camden to Downshire, 8 Jan. 1798 (Downshire MSS.)).

[2] A list is given in J. Hardiman, *The History of the Town and County of Galway* . . . (Dublin, 1820), appendix iii, showing that this state of affairs prevailed at least until 1820. The family included Charles Daly, M.P. for the county 1761–8; his brother James, M.P. for Galway town 1768–9; his sons, Denis, M.P. for the county 1768–90, and the town 1765–8 and 1790–1; Anthony, Peter, and St. George, respectively M.P. for the town 1770–90, 1792–7, and 1797–1801. Denis Bowes Daly, 'runner' or whip for the Ponsonby group, and M.P. for the town 1776–90, was a cousin.   [3] See pp. 29–30, *supra*.

[4] This tendency continued some years after the Union. After a reverse in 1807, the marquess of Donegall clinched his hold on Carrickfergus, where previously his

Thus the Irish House of Commons at the end of the eighteenth century readily merited the criticisms of parliamentary reformers. In Ireland, as in England, parliamentary influence was derived from property; but the structure of politics in eighteenth-century Ireland, although employing similar techniques of connexion and patronage to contemporary England, could not make the same claim of 'virtually representing' all interest, because of conflicting views over land and religion. Many Ascendancy landlords resisted the admission of Catholics to Parliament, because they believed this would strip all justification from the 'close borough' system on which their political influence rested. 'The very moment they get into Parliament', wrote John Beresford of the Catholics, 'they would endeavour to inforce Reform, because while boroughs stand as they do, they could not get the power of Parliament into their hands, which if they had they would separate the two countries in one session.'[1] Others feared a Catholic challenge to the supremacy of the Established Church, perhaps to the very title by which (after ousting the native possessors on religious and political grounds) the Protestant Ascendancy landlords held their acres.

Yet despite its manifest imperfections, the Irish Parliament could not be written off as a nest of place-hungry oligarchs. Its members did not legislate in a vacuum, and could not be unresponsive to contemporary public opinion, limited though this public opinion was by the absence of a sufficiently numerous and articulate middle class, and by the economic and religious barriers which checked the growth of popular radicalism. Even Henry Grattan, after many frustrating years in opposition to the Dublin Castle reactionaries, could argue:

How came the Irish parliament, with all its borough members in 1779 to demand a free trade—in 1782 to demand a free constitution? Because it sat in Ireland—because they sate in their own country—because, however influenced, as many of its members were, by places—

interest was limited, in 1812: and the Needhams recovered Newry in 1818. Later, however, several decisions of the House of Commons, adverse to the voting rights of absentee freemen, weakened family interests in Galway (1818), Limerick (1820), and Wexford (1830).

[1] Beresford to Auckland (private), 19 June 1797 (Add. MSS. 34454).

however uninfluenced, as many of its members were, by popular representation, yet were they influenced by Irish sympathy and an Irish law [*sic*] opinion; they did not like to meet every hour faces that looked shame upon them—they did not like to stand in the sphere of their own infamy.[1]

These considerations applied equally to the Parliament which carried the Union. Although the Volunteer Movement, and later the United Irishmen, had endeavoured to arouse a spirit of nationalism, Irish politics, especially at election times, were still fought very much on local and personal considerations. The pre-eminence of an Altamont in Mayo or an Ely in Wexford depended not merely on the amount of government patronage he could attract to himself, but on his standing with the neighbouring gentry, and the effectiveness with which he and his members served as go-between from their county to the Administration. Whether members supported or opposed, Dublin Castle was always prepared to ensure their better behaviour by listening to their demands. Although this system had its abuses, for which, then as later, Ireland enjoyed some notoriety, even the most venal Irish Parliament was not entirely unrepresentative of articulate public opinion, as expressed by the propertied classes. It is not really enough to explain the passing of the Act simply as the result of 'an orgy of corruption',[2] or, more magisterially, 'that it was conceived in treachery, and carried out in corruption, and that it was constitutionally illegal'.[3] The fact is that the Irish Government, which at no time in 1799 or 1800 diverged in its bestowal of places and honours from the code of practice already in Irish parliamentary usage, found that patronage was helpful in counties where government and anti-unionists were evenly matched, but it could retain its usefulness only if it was not employed indiscriminately. The pattern of voting over the Union was intelligible in terms of regional, economic, social, and religious interests, whose influence may be discerned in the recasting of several of the Union's provisions before its eventual passage, and to whose activities the processes of corruption were largely

[1] *Debates*, 15–16 Jan. 1800, p. 127.
[2] G. O. Trevelyan, *History of England* (1956 ed.), p. 591.
[3] P. S. Hegarty, *A History of Ireland under the Union*, London 1952, p. 16.

irrelevant. Nor could it be otherwise with a question which so intimately concerned the future nature of the links between Great Britain and Ireland. For the Anglo-Irish nexus, and its effect on the domestic politics of Ireland, had been for a generation the fundamental preoccupation of Irish politicians, and the catalyst through which parties had formed and regrouped.

III

PREPARATIONS FOR UNION
1797–1798

I am very happy that Mr. Pitt is thinking on the subject
of Ireland, the great misfortune of which country has
been that for many years Ministers have never thought
of her, except when she became extremely troublesome
to them, when by some temporary expedient they have
patched up a temporary quiet and left things to chance
until another crisis called upon them to think again.

JOHN BERESFORD to LORD AUCKLAND, 9 August 1798.[1]

D
EFENCE and finance were the chief problems con-
fronting the newly elected Irish Parliament. 'We are
getting on in a very *handsome* manner,' wrote John
Beresford in reviewing the year 1797, 'our expenses now
exceeding our income by 2,700,000£ (in round numbers).'[2]
It was sometimes argued by the Irish Opposition that the
country's financial troubles arose from the number of places
and sinecures on the public pay-roll required to keep an
unpopular government in power.[3] In fact the deficits of
1797–8 developed almost entirely from the military expenses
incurred in repressing an agrarian and radical discontent
levelled impartially against the whole ruling class. Beresford
estimated the Government's receipts in 1797 at £1,940,000,
of which £650,000 came from customs and excise (the
hereditary revenue) and £1,290,000 from taxes voted by
Parliament. Expenditure included £264,075 for the civil
list; £350,000 for permanent grants to such official agencies
as the linen and canal boards, whose activities fostered Irish
commerce; £698,829 interest on the national debt, which
now totalled £9,500,000; and no less than £3,324,410 for
the military establishment, whose needs had quadrupled
within the last five years. Although Customs revenue had

[1] Beresford to Auckland, 9 Aug. 1798 (Add. MSS. 34454).
[2] Same to same, 19 July 1798 (*Beresford Correspondence*, ii, p. 16).
[3] e.g. Grattan to Fitzwilliam, 10 Dec. 1796 (Wentworth Woodhouse MSS., F. 30a).

decreased slightly since the outbreak of war in 1793, Excise had risen considerably; but most of the increased expenditure had been financed by new taxes and loans, and by October 1797 Beresford was gloomily observing: 'We are in a sad way for want of money. The taxes of last year were nonsense, and I believe they know not what to tax this year.'[1] The Irish loan market was unpredictable and unreliable, and in 1797 Ireland's finances had only been saved by a loan raised for their service in the British House of Commons. Pitt had expressed the hope that Ireland would soon become self-supporting once again, but by November 1797 it had become apparent that the Irish Government's credit would enable it to raise by loan no more than £400,000, and that another £200,000 would be needed from other sources.[2] In 1798 the British House of Commons were induced to raise a credit for that amount, to be applied as the Irish legislature should direct.[3]

Meanwhile, the newly elected Dublin Parliament was exploring other methods. Many of the country gentlemen who had financed and officered the yeomanry and the militia were critical of their absentee neighbours, whose neglect of their tenantry was held to lead to disaffection. The scheme of a land tax on absentees, who spent all their Irish revenues abroad, had been brought forward with official sanction in 1773, and again mooted by the remains of the Opposition in 1797. It was now espoused by one of the most respected independent members of the Commons, the banker David Latouche. Citing the 1773 precedent as grounds for expecting the British Government's approval, several members expressed their support when Latouche gave notice of motion introducing this measure in January 1798.[4] Immediate protest ensued from the absentee interests in England, who had been warned by Portland that the move would command considerable backing.[5] The absentees—who included noblemen

---

[1] Beresford to Auckland, 24 Oct. 1797 (*Beresford Correspondence*, ii, p. 149).
[2] Camden to Pitt, no date, but forwarded to Pitt on 22 Nov. 1797 (P.R.O. 30/8/326).   [3] Pitt to Camden, 8 Feb. 1798 (P.R.O. 30/8/325).
[4] But Camden expected opposition from the resident landed proprietors: cf. Camden to Pitt, 12 Feb. 1798 (P.R.O. 30/8/326).
[5] Portland to Upper Ossory, 29 Jan. 1798 (Wentworth Woodhouse MSS., F. 30g); cf. Portland to Camden, 29 Jan. 1798 (H.O. 100/75).

of such diverse political opinions as Fitzwilliam, Bessborough, Lansdowne, Hertford, Clermont, and Upper Ossory[1]—were not sanguine about resisting the proposal. Lord Egremont hoped its application might be limited as a war tax,[2] while the marquess of Hertford grumbled:

> We certainly stand a worse chance of success now than in former years, 1st because the pressure of finance is much greater, 2d. because some great men, as they are called, in Ireland will endeavour to throw a load upon us from selfish motives in order to avoid a general land tax, and 3d. because the open Irish loan of last winter, to which it was expected the absentee proprietors should subscribe, failed completely, and that failure is imputed to us.[3]

Pitt, however, came down firmly against the proposal. Having just secured an advance of £200,000 for the Irish Government, he wrote to Camden in strong terms:

> It really seems to me in principle to be no inconsiderable step towards cutting off the little that now remains of union between the two countries, which ought on the contrary to be drawn closer on every practicable occasion. I wish it also to be seriously considered in Ireland whether they can suppose it possible that I should propose to raise a loan here on our credit, and with the effect of draining us of our money, on no other ground but the common interest of the two countries, when the Parliament of Ireland will at the same moment be creating and making a separation of interests by the most invidious measure they can adopt. It seems to me that, if the idea is persisted in, the option must be put fairly to them between an Absentee Tax and an English loan. I hope however that a tax on absentees will be relinquished, and a general land tax, to which I cannot imagine a real objection, substituted in its room.[4]

Camden, although he found Irish members reluctant to oppose the absentee tax, succeeded in persuading Latouche to withdraw his sponsorship of the motion, which was taken

---

[1] All these noblemen wrote to Fitzwilliam between 29 Jan. and 9 Feb. 1798 (Wentworth Woodhouse MSS., F. 30g). Bessborough and Fitzwilliam, cousins of the Ponsonbys, were in opposition, where they were frequently joined by Lansdowne (formerly earl of Shelburne). Hertford and Clermont, on the other hand, were both courtiers.

[2] Egremont to Fitzwilliam, 1 Feb. 1798 (Wentworth Woodhouse MSS., F. 30g).

[3] Hertford to Fitzwilliam, 29 Jan. 1798 (ibid.).

[4] Pitt to Camden, 8 Feb. 1798 (P.R.O. 30/8/325).

up by Crofton Vandeleur. On 22 February, the proposal was defeated by 104 votes to 40. The division affords no clue about members' sentiments towards a legislative union. The supporters of the tax included future unionists such as Vandeleur, Martin, and Sir John Blaquiere, of whom the latter at least was not normally in opposition: its opponents were evenly divided between those who would favour and those who would denounce the plan for Union. Characteristically, the earl of Ely's pack abstained.[1]

The increasing financial dependence of Ireland upon Great Britain was not easily compatible with the theoretical independence of the Dublin legislature. Pitt was acutely conscious that there was no constitutional redress if the Irish Parliament failed to make the necessary provision for defraying the interest and charges on loans raised for the Irish service by the British House of Commons.[2] The Ascendancy of Ireland were likewise under conflicting pressures. They needed strong military support to shore up their régime against the threat of rebellion, yet they could afford this protection only by submitting to the financial domination of Great Britain. Far from welcoming British intervention unreservedly, the Ascendancy magnates tended to complain that the English authorities were too scrupulous in their handling of the crisis, and they particularly resented any restraint or criticism of their own cavalier methods. And the Ascendancy showed its teeth to some effect in the affair of Sir Ralph Abercromby. Appointed Commander-in-Chief in Ireland in September 1797, this experienced professional found himself coping with a motley militia whose fighting calibre had hitherto been tested mainly by such exploits as wrecking seditious newspaper offices and the roughshod performance of elementary police duties. On 20 February 1798

---

[1] Opponents of the absentee tax included the Chancellor of the Exchequer, Sir John Parnell, J. M. O'Donel, Charles O'Hara, and William Tighe, all subsequently strong anti-unionists: but also St. George Daly, Edmond Stanley, and Henry Kemmis, lawyers who became prominent supporters of the Union. For comments on this motion see Camden to Portland, 15, 22, and 24 Feb. 1798 (H.O. 100/75).

[2] Pitt to Cornwallis, 13 July 1798 (P.R.O. 30/8/325). This is a review of the whole policy of English loans to Ireland. The question had arisen whether the Irish Parliament should provide for a contribution to the British Sinking Fund in proportion to the amount of the loans raised for Ireland in 1797 and 1798.

he issued a general order calling for a tightening of discipline, and described the Irish forces as being 'in such a state of licentiousness as to render them formidable to every one but the enemy'. This was unpalatable language to the aristocracy of Ireland, many of whose regiments were raised from among their own friends and tenantry. A storm of criticism and protest assailed Abercromby, who thereupon handed in his resignation.[1] Camden, although disapproving strongly of such forthright language, made a few languid attempts to persuade him to remain, but Abercromby insisted on leaving, and Camden renewed his plea for the appointment of some military man, preferably Cornwallis, as Lord Lieutenant.[2] As Thomas Pelham had fallen dangerously ill in March 1798, a new Chief Secretary was also needed. Camden's kinsman, Castlereagh, was proving perfectly satisfactory *locum tenens*, but Camden suggested the appointment either of Sylvester Douglas or the experienced Treasury official, Thomas Steele.[3]

The disturbances in Ireland were now looking serious. On 30 March the military were authorized to disperse tumultuous assemblies and to take all necessary measures for preserving the peace, without awaiting the authority of the civil magistrates. During April and May the triangles and cat-of-nine-tails were used unsparingly, and in the eyes of men like Beresford and Cooke, successfully. Quantities of home-made arms were confiscated, many arrests made, and suspects interrogated by methods which rankled for generations in long Irish memories. Nationalist historians have not hesitated to assert that these excesses were directly instigated by Pitt and Camden, in order to provoke the Irish to open rebellion, and thus reduce the country to helplessness so that the Union could be passed. Swift MacNeill, writing in 1917—well after Lecky—quoted sympathetically verses which he attributed to an Irish judge:

---

[1] 'You know how the Chancellor, Speaker, etc., work when they have a point to carry,' wrote Wellesley Pole to Mornington on 9 June 1798, 'and from all I can learn, I don't believe they ever labour'd more about any thing than they did in the affair of Sr. Ralph Abercrombie.' (Add. MSS. 37308.)

[2] Camden to Portland, 15 and 26 Mar. 1798 (H.O. 100/75); Camden to Pitt, 26 Mar. 1798 (P.R.O. 30/8/325).

[3] Camden to Pitt, 15 Dec. 1797 and 26 Mar. 1798 (P.R.O. 30/8/326).

How did they pass the Union?
  By perjury and fraud;
By slaves who sold their land for gold
  As Judas sold his God.
By all the savage acts that yet
  Have followed England's track,
The pitch-cap and the bayonet.
  The gibbet and the rack;
And thus was passed the Union
  By Pitt and Castlereagh;
Could Satan send for such an end
  More worthy tools than they?[1]

As early as October 1798 Fitzwilliam, perhaps hardly an objective critic, was commenting about the Union:

. . . it is a comical remedy for the disease, and whatever might have been my confidence in it as a specifick, I would never have stimulated the disease for the pleasure of applying the remedy. For myself I am of too timid and diffident a nature to have plung'd, with my eyes open, into all the risks and dangers of a rebellion for the purpose of bringing to bear the doubtful policy of an Union. *Le jeu ne vaut pas la chandelle*.[2]

This was just irresponsible gossip. It was, of course, perfectly true that before any notion of the Union was known in Ireland, some of the more hot-headed Protestants had been clamouring for open conflict with the United Irishmen and Catholics, so that disaffection could be brought to a head and annihilated.[3] More responsible reactionaries, such as John Beresford, were inclined to deplore such talk:

You say that some people imagine we are too eager to drive the people to a crisis, and that we wish to govern and to punish by martial law. Can any man in England imagine that the landed property of Ireland, the Parliament, the Privy Council, and the Cabinet Council

---

[1] Quoted by J. Swift MacNeill, *The Constitutional and Parliamentary History of Ireland till the Union*, London, 1917, p. 382.

[2] Fitzwilliam to the bishop of Ossory, 21 Oct. 1798 (Wentworth Woodhouse MSS., f. 30e).

[3] Thus the Revd. William Elliot of Trim, writing to Arthur Wellesley on 9 Mar. 1798, stated: 'It is my firm and deliberate opinion that the re-establishment of good order among us is only to be obtained or hoped for thro' the violent means of previous open rupture and great national convulsion: every hour confirms me still more in this idea, that it is impossible by gentle degrees ever to settle again into a state of subordination to the laws and good wishes to the British government.' (Wellington MSS.)

should wish for martial law, or that the law of the land should in any degree be suspended, if they did not clearly see that there was an absolute necessity for very strong measures. . . . How could we wish to provoke the people to crimes that would be our ruin?[1]

The only piece of near-contemporary evidence to assert that the rebellion was forced in order to pave the way for the Union may be found in Grattan's *Life*. Here the younger Henry Grattan relates an anecdote which he claims to have had from a relative by marriage, Dean Scott, nephew of the earl of Clonmel:

> Shortly before his death he sent for his nephew, Dean Scott, got him to examine his papers, and destroy those that were useless. There were many relating to politics, that disclosed the conduct of the Irish Government at the period of the disturbances in 1798. There was one letter in particular, which fully showed their duplicity, and that they might have crushed the rebellion; but that they let it go on, on purpose to carry the Union, and that this was their design. When Lord Clonmel was dying, he stated this to Dean Scott, and made him destroy the letter; he further added that he had gone to the Lord Lieutenant, and told him that as they knew of the proceedings of the disaffected, it was wrong to permit them to go on—that the Government, having the power, should crush them at once, and prevent the insurrection. He was coldly received, and found that his advice was not relished. That of Lord Clare, Mr. Foster, and Bishop Agar had predominated, and, in consequence, he was not summoned to attend the Privy Council on business of state.[2]

Like many Irish politicians a generation after the Union, the younger Grattan was much inclined to seek sinister motives in British policy towards Ireland, and his story should be taken with a grain of salt. It can be corroborated from other sources that Clonmel was at loggerheads with Clare and other Irish officials, and that there was a difference of opinion at the Castle over timing the arrest of suspects.[3] That this

---

[1] Beresford to Auckland, 10 Apr. 1798 (Add. MSS. 34454).

[2] Grattan, *Life*, iv, p. 349. John Scott (1739–98), earl of Clonmel, was Lord Chief Justice of Ireland 1784–98.

[3] At a Privy Council in Feb. 1798 it was Foster, the Speaker, who urged the arrest of known revolutionary leaders, and who was discouraged by Camden and the British Cabinet (Camden to Portland, 8 Feb. 1798; Portland to Camden, 15 Feb. 1798 (H.O. 100/75)).

had anything to do with the project of a legislative union is less certain.[1] It is a major flaw in the story that Clonmel died on 24 May 1798, the very day on which the rebellion broke out. It would be difficult for a man on his deathbed to predict the extent, duration, and consequences of this rebellion, especially since only a day or two earlier the officials of Dublin Castle had been congratulating themselves on having averted trouble by firm measures: on 21 May that well-informed man Edward Cooke wrote to Lord Auckland, 'A rising is not given up: but I think it will not take place.'[2] It is highly unlikely that Foster and Agar, whose initial reaction to the Union proposals was strenuous opposition, would have joined with Clare in conniving at a dangerous insurrection designed to ease the passage of the Union. If there is the slightest scrap of documentary evidence now in existence to prove that Dublin Castle knew of the adoption of Union as the policy of the British Government before the outbreak of the rebellion in May 1798, it has yet to come the way of the present writer.

Nevertheless, it is likely that in April or May 1798, Pitt and a few intimates began to give serious consideration to an Anglo-Irish union. 'From the time of General Abercrombie's return', wrote Lord Chancellor Loughborough in June, 'I have thought it would become necessary',[3] and it seems fair to presume that his sentiments were shared by other members of the British Cabinet. It may be that the Abercromby episode was the last straw which convinced Pitt and his ministers that the defence, finance, and administration of Ireland in war-time could not safely be left to a domineering minority. There is no evidence to suggest that any definite decision was made about timing the measure until the end of May, when the Irish situation deteriorated rapidly.

---

[1] It should be noted that the United Irishmen's organization was often referred to as 'the Union' in 1797–8, and this may have led to some confusion in the transmission of the story from Scott to Grattan.

[2] Cooke to Auckland, 21 May 1798 (Add. MSS. 34454). John Lees wrote to Auckland on 10 May, 'Treason and rebellion have certainly been check'd' (ibid.). 'From the favourable turn which affairs have taken within a few days,' wrote Camden to Portland on 21 May, 'I trust there is every reason to expect that by a perseverance in the same system we may be enabled to restore the kingdom to quiet' (H.O. 100/75).

[3] Loughborough to Pitt, 13 June 1798 (P.R.O. 30/8/329).

Insurrection was reported from Kildare, Wicklow, and Wexford: in the latter county, where the conflict was sharpened by religious animosities, the rebels seized control of a considerable area and were joined, perhaps reluctantly, by several of the gentry. A smaller outbreak was reported from among the republicans of Down and Antrim. Just after news of these risings reached London, reports came of an expedition under Bonaparte which had left Toulon on 19 May, in fact for Egypt, but it was feared for Ireland.

Desperate with fear, Camden appealed to Pitt for the immediate dispatch of 10,000 British troops. On 2 June Pitt sent 5,000, with an injunction that in employing them the Lord Lieutenant should 'resist with as much firmness the intemperance of your friends, as you do the desperate efforts of the enemy'.[1] It was probably on the same day that he conferred with Grenville and took the decision to effect a legislative union as soon as possible.[2] Auckland, one of the Government's regular advisers on Irish affairs, was informed two days later, and wrote immediately sounding the views of the Irish Lord Chancellor Clare.[3] An opportunity of putting the policy into effect arose—perhaps fortuitously—with the receipt on 10 June of a letter written four days earlier by Camden, in which he appealed for more troops, dilated upon the inadequacies of General Lake (temporarily in charge of

---

[1] Pitt to Camden, 2 June 1798 (P.R.O. 30/8/325).

[2] The evidence that Union was discussed is indirect but suggestive. On 1 or 2 June, Pitt wrote to Grenville announcing the Toulon expedition: 'In the mean time', he added, 'we must redouble diligence to make use of the few weeks left before his reaching Ireland (if he ever comes). There are one or two leading points on which I should like much to have an hour's conversation with you, if you could conveniently call here any time this evening.' (*H.M.C. Dropmore MSS.* iv, p. 229.) On 3 June, having heard from his brother Grenville about the measures proposed to counter the Toulon fleet, the marquess of Buckingham wrote from Colchester: 'I am content. But I shall not be so unless you urge, upon the spur of this occasion, the question of a Union, which never can be if it be not now.' (Ibid. iv, p. 227.)

[3] On 4 June, Pitt wrote to Auckland advising him that he and Grenville had 'had a great deal of discussion lately on the subject of following the termination of the present crisis in Ireland by immediate steps for a Union'. (*Auckland Correspondence,* iv, p. 2; the original, and a memorandum drawn up by Grenville at the same time do not now appear to be among the *Auckland* papers in the British Museum.) Auckland's letter to Clare has been lost, but from internal evidence, Clare's reply can be dated 8 June 1798 (Clare to Auckland, 'three days after the battle of New Ross', Add. MSS. 29475). From the tenor of this letter, it is possible that Auckland may merely have sounded Clare on the issue without informing him of the Government's decision.

the Irish forces) and recommended that Cornwallis should be Lord Lieutenant and Commander-in-Chief. 'His inclination to the Catholic cause ought not to weigh against him', Camden urged, adding that, if necessary, front-line defence might be undertaken by the Commander-in-Chief of the British Army, the duke of York himself.[1] Twice before Camden had vainly proffered this suggestion: but this time, not a moment was lost in acting on it. On the very day the letter arrived the King's consent was obtained for the appointment of Cornwallis to the combined offices.[2] By 20 June the new Lord Lieutenant was in Dublin to succeed Camden—who, now that his request for a competent military successor had been granted, was rather aggrieved at the alacrity with which he had been supplanted.[3]

In endorsing this new appointment the King, with habitual bluntness, referred to the motives which inspired the change of personnel in Ireland: 'I cannot think any forces sent there can be of real avail unless a military Lord Lieutenant, and that the Marquiss of Cornwallis with Mr. Pelham as his Secretary, be instantly sent there. The present Lord Lieutenant is too much agitated at the present hour and totally under the control of the Irish Privy Councillors, whose hurry have been the real cause of the two failures, which, if repeated, will by degrees teach the Irish rebels to fight.'[4] So far from being compliant to the Irish 'junta' and their methods, the King and ministers were convinced of the bankruptcy of their ideas and of their inability to pacify Ireland. No other body of Irish politicians could be found in their stead, who were not limited in their usefulness by local prejudices or compromised by association with Fox and the British Opposition. The intervention on a permanent basis of the Westminster Government, which already had so often provided guidance during the last few years, appeared to be the only solution. Nor can it be wondered that the British Government were misinformed of the strength of the main argument against this solution, the power of Irish nationalism. The King, Pitt,

[1] Camden to Pitt, 6 June 1798 (P.R.O. 30/8/326).
[2] George III to Pitt, 10 June 1798, 6.30 p.m. (P.R.O. 30/8/104).
[3] Camden to Pitt, 16 June 1798 (P.R.O. 30/8/326).
[4] George III to Pitt, 10 June 1798, 6.30 p.m. (P.R.O. 30/8/104).

and Dundas had never visited Ireland; Portland and Grenville had only stayed there a few months in the abnormal
circumstances of 1782–3; and their expert advisers, retired
Viceroys such as Buckingham and Westmoreland and the
officials into whose hands the timorous Camden had fallen,
were not the men to convey an adequate notion of a spirit
with which they lacked all sympathy.

Yet no clear plan of Union had been devised. In acknow-
ledging the desirability of the scheme—which seems to have
been broached to him a day or two after the appointment of
Cornwallis was approved—the King observed with unmis-
takable emphasis:

> . . . the new Lord Lieutenant . . . must not lose the present moment
> of terror for frightening the supporters of the Castle into an Union
> with this country, and no farther indulgences must be granted to the
> Roman Catholics, as no country can be governed where there is more
> than one established religion, the others may be tollerated but that
> cannot extend further to leave to perform their religious duties accord-
> ing to the tenets of their Church, for which indulgence they cannot
> have any share in the government of the State.[1]

Thus, at the very outset of the Union negotiations, a point
of the greatest difficulty was touched upon. For Cornwallis
was already known to be in favour of some form of concession to the Catholics, and Pitt himself was inclined to take
the matter into consideration.

Finding Pelham unable to return to Ireland with him, and
Thomas Grenville reluctant to accept a situation 'very much
below his calibre and time of life'[2] Cornwallis decided to
continue Castlereagh as acting Chief Secretary.[3] In some
respects, however, Castlereagh was not the ideal man for the
post at that time. Able, loyal, hard-working, he was, at the

---

[1] Same to same, 13 June 1798, 7.36 a.m. (ibid.).
[2] Buckingham to Grenville, 12 June 1798 (*H.M.C. Dropmore MSS.* iv, p. 235).
Thomas Grenville thought that Camden and Cornwallis should have been appointed
joint Lords Deputy, because military duties would prevent Cornwallis from attending to the civil arrangements and patronage business of the Lord Lieutenancy, and
too much influence would be thrown into the hands of the Irish Cabinet. (Ibid.,
p. 236.)
[3] Cornwallis to Portland, 8 July 1798 (H.O. 100/77); his good opinion of Castlereagh appears in Cornwallis to Ross, 9 July 1798 (*Cornwallis Correspondence*, ii,
p. 363).

age of 29, one of the most capable members of the Irish legislature: but many of his contemporaries were antagonized by his shy, cold manner and lack of that eloquence which was regarded as the hall-mark of an Irish statesman. Jealousy had been kindled by his rapid rise to office, helped by his relationship to Camden, and his deft abandonment of a youthful flirtation with the whig radicalism of Belfast. To place the management of the House of Commons and the patronage of the Chief Secretary's office in the hands of a comparative novice viewed dubiously by his contemporaries was not the surest way of securing a tractable legislature. Attention to this point was especially necessary with a Lord Lieutenant such as Cornwallis, who was disinclined to flatter or cajole the old gang that held power under Westmoreland and Camden, and whose notions of toleration and clemency were unpalatable to many of the Ascendancy.

For the insurrection had thrown many of the gentry into a kind of panic rage, in which they were prepared to condone any excesses committed against the rebels. John Beresford, who believed that floggings of up to 300 lashes were at once more humane and more effective in restoring order than summary executions, could write with perfect sincerity and accuracy: 'I see every man I meet full of passion and resentment, they actually want to hang every person taken, some even without trial, while Government certainly move very slow and show the greatest reluctance in punishing any man.'[1] Colonel Robert Ross, M.P. for Newry, was more outspoken: 'I hope in God our Govt. will have orders to try Jackson, Bond, &c. &c. by martial law. I fear much for courts, big wiggs, and jurys . . . such proceeding is fighting pikes and firelocks with full bottoms. For God's sake let the innocents be hanged, and then when the rebellion is extinguished, a bill of indemnity cures all; any other proceeding is rank insanity, and common sense tells you if the hydra head is not taken off it will produce shortly a second rebellion.'[2] Some ministerialists were not slow to point out that the most prominent victims of the rebellion, Lords Mountjoy and O'Neill, had been among the advocates of Catholic

---

[1] Beresford to Auckland, 30 May 1798 (Add. MSS. 34454).
[2] Ross to Downshire, 16 June 1798 (Downshire MSS.).

concessions, and argued from that the impolicy of liberality.[1]
As Cornwallis soon found:

> The principal persons of this country, and the Members of both
> Houses of Parliament are, in general, averse to all acts of clemency,
> and . . . would pursue measures that could only terminate in the ex-
> tirpation of the greater number of the inhabitants, and in the utter
> destruction of the country. The words Papists and Priests are for ever
> in their mouths, and by their un-accountable policy they would drive
> four-fifths of the community into irreconcilable rebellion; and in their
> warmth they lose sight of the real cause of the present mischief, of that
> deep-laid conspiracy to revolutionize Ireland on the principles of
> France, which was originally formed, and by wonderful assiduity
> brought nearly to maturity, by men who had no thought of religion but
> to destroy it. . . .[2]

The news of Cornwallis's appointment was not received
with enthusiasm by the Irish governing classes. John Beresford wrote: 'I hope and trust that Lord Cornwallis's eyes are
now opened as to the R: Catholicks, should he come here
with the sentiments he some time since entertained of them,
I cannot say what might be the consequence.'[3] While
Mr. Under-Secretary Cooke grumbled: 'I don't like this
manœuvre of a change at all; nor can I possibly see what
good can result from it except loss of reputation to my Lord
Lieutenant.'[4] There was a real possibility that the ultra-
Protestant wing of the Irish Cabinet, emboldened by their
success in ousting Fitzwilliam, dominating Camden, and
precipitating the resignation of Abercromby, were considering the withdrawal of their support from the new Lord
Lieutenant; especially when it emerged that he was not to
be mastered by his advisers. Dean Warburton may only have
been retailing political gossip when he wrote to Fitzwilliam
in July: 'Lord Cornwallis is open to information from any
man, but consults no man: he sees the ruinous effect of the
late administration, and does not favor the opinions of the
old Cabinet—a cabal is forming against him—I believe he

---

[1] Henry Alexander to Pelham, 10 June 1798 (Add. MSS. 33105).
[2] Cornwallis to Portland, 8 July 1798. Cf. Buckingham to Grenville, 6 July 1798
(Buckingham, *Courts and Cabinets of George III*, ii, p. 404).
[3] Beresford to Auckland, 15 June 1798 (Add. MSS. 34454).
[4] Cooke to Pelham, 16 June 1798 (Add. MSS. 33105).

is aware of it, and seems determined to withstand it.'[1] A more circumstantial story is given by Lord Sheffield, who was usually well informed on Irish affairs, in a letter to his old crony Auckland:

on the arrival of Lord Cornwallis, matters were very critical, for a very few days in respect to the old Cabinet, when suddenly the Chancellor entered into support in the warmest manner: one found the ground hollow, another refused to go on, but sulked and retired. The Speaker, I understand, took up the battle, and with others, held a very dissatisfied language, which at length came to the Lord Lieutenant; and the Secretary and the Knight of Kerry in the House of Commons noticed in strong terms the clamour excited by men of high consideration; the discontented appeared to be disconcerted, and did not say one word, and the Speaker is since gone out of town. I rejoice extremely that the Chancellor has arranged himself thus, for if he and the Speaker could have agreed, and had continued disgusted with measures, the consequence would have been worse than the existing rebellion. . . .[2]

Apart from Clare and Castlereagh, no Irish official of consequence could be found to back Cornwallis whole-heartedly in his policy of clemency, and this rift between the Lord Lieutenant and his senior advisers was hardly propitious for the success of a scheme, such as the Union, requiring dexterous parliamentary management. The backing of Clare was useful—he certainly could not be accused of softness towards the Catholics, but, whatever his defects, he was too courageous to share the demand, born of panic, for an extra-legal White Terror. And Cornwallis was unperturbed by the reactionaries: 'I am on good terms with the Speaker, but do not see much of him. I have totally set aside the Irish Cabinet which Lord Castlereagh told me was very inconvenient and embarrassing to Lord Camden.'[3] But even though his proposals for an amnesty commended themselves to the old Opposition, this was hardly likely to conciliate the staunch

---

[1] Warburton to Fitzwilliam, 31 July 1798 (Wentworth Woodhouse MSS., F. 30e).
[2] Sheffield to Auckland, 12 Aug. 1798 (Add. MSS. 34454).
[3] Cornwallis to Ross, 16 Aug. 1798 (*Cornwallis Correspondence*, ii, p. 387). Cf. Ross to Downshire, 11 July 1798: 'I understand from every body that none of the old Cabinet are consulted. That body is now composed of English or Scotch generals, who can know little indeed of the country or the dispositions of the inhabitants. I hear of nothing but general discontents, and all wishing Lord Camden back. . . .'

backwoodsmen in the Government ranks, who expressed
their fear that 'in the end he'll find himself in wrong hands,
as will Ireland'.[1]

With this want of confidence between the Lord Lieutenant and the official class, it was not surprising that Cornwallis
showed the utmost caution in talking about the proposed
Union. Clare was in the know: so before long, was Castlereagh.[2] Those who have seen in Clare the most persistent and
urgent advocate of the scheme must have overlooked the fact
that almost his first reaction was to urge caution, and to
advise against the introduction of the measure until the conclusion of the war with France. His letter to Auckland,
intelligently anticipating many of the difficulties, but biased
by his religious prejudices, went into some detail:

The main difficulty which it strikes me you will have to encounter
at the outset of this very important business to which your last letter
alludes is our strong national love of jobbing, which must receive a
fatal blow in the ultimate success of the measure—this creditable feeling
altho' by no means extinguished, has been very much counteracted by
an apprehension, not ill founded, for the safety of our persons and
estates, and I shd. hope will ultimately yield to it. I think the general
feeling of the landed interest is in favour of the measure, and when the
advantages of it in a commercial point of view are understood, I suppose
the commercial interest of the country would then be generally and
strongly for it. The Catholicks will, I make no doubt, oppose it with
violence as will the Northern republicans, and therefore before the
measure is avowed, it will be essentially necessary to have a strong British
military force here, nor in my opinion will it be prudent to avow it, until
Great Britain is at peace with her foreign enemies. The Speaker will,
I believe, be against the measure, and I know the Archbishop of Cashel
will oppose it vehemently. Lord Shannon, I think, sees the necessity
which presses for it, and I am pretty confident that the general feeling
of the House of Lords is in favour of it. Our proprietors of boroughs
which would not be represented will demand compensation. If this
should be practicable, I make no doubt a great many of them will
acquiesce.[3]

---

[1] Ross to Downshire, 1 Aug. 1798 (Downshire MSS.). For a favourable view of
Cornwallis from a leading member of the Opposition cf. Parsons to Charlemont,
27 July 1798 (*H.M.C. Charlemont MSS.* ii, p. 330).

[2] 'It seems perfectly clear', wrote Clare to Castlereagh on 13 Aug., 'that the old
system, if not worn out, is certainly so shaken that scarce a hope remains of our
being able to reinstate it.' (Mt. Stewart MSS.)

[3] Clare to Auckland, 3 July 1798 (Add. MSS. 34454).

These arguments weighed with Cornwallis, who wrote on 20 July:

> If the rebellion should now be completely subdued, there remains much to be done to put this country into a tolerable state of security, and how or when to bring forward or even to broach the great point of alternate settlement is a matter in which I cannot see the most distant encouragement. The two or three people whom I have ventured in the most cautious manner to sound, say that it must not be mentioned now, that this is a time of too much danger to agitate such a question, but if a period of safety should come when boroughs will be considered as a sure property, and all good jobs again appear within our grasp, that moment will not, I am afraid, be found propitious for expecting those sacrifices which must be required.[1]

This does not sound like the language of a Viceroy preparing for 'an orgy of parliamentary corruption' to push through an unpopular measure.

Although Cornwallis, aloof from the backstairs politics of Dublin Castle, may have imagined that the prospect of Union was a secret only to be confided to a few trusted advisers, there exists a considerable body of evidence to indicate that the idea was already leaking out. In part this was very probably due to the presence in Dublin of the marquess of Buckingham, who had come over at the end of June with his militia regiment, and who, as a former Lord Lieutenant, had been put in the know by his brother, Grenville.[2] The presence of this touchy grandee was later to be a source of embarrassment to Cornwallis, but at the moment he was 'all goodness and friendship',[3] and plumed himself on being the only man in Dublin, apart from Cornwallis, Clare, and Lord Hobart, to be in the secret.[4] However, it was not in his nature to refrain from gossiping, and he passed on the information not only to his brother-in-law, the earl of Carysfort but also to a rather less intimate acquaintance, William Wellesley Pole.[5] Possibly there were others: the knowledge was not

---

[1] Cornwallis to Pitt, 20 July 1798 (P.R.O. 30/8/326).

[2] This emerges from his letter to Grenville, 23 July 1798 (*H.M.C. Dropmore MSS.* iv, pp. 264–7).

[3] Cornwallis to Ross, 1 July 1798 (*Cornwallis Correspondence*, ii, p. 357).

[4] Buckingham to Grenville, 26 Sept. 1798 (*H.M.C. Dropmore MSS.* iv, p. 315).

[5] Pole wrote to his brother, Mornington, on 24 Aug. 1798: 'Bucky lives up 7 pr of stairs in the dirtiest hole you ever saw in Dublin barrack—he has not taken his

confined to friends of the Government. Dean Warburton, whose opinions were so liberal that they permanently exiled him from the bench of bishops, wrote at the end of July: 'A Union has been so much talk'd of, that many people begin to think it done—and very many gentlemen, who formerly flew out at the bare mention of Union are now earnestly wishing for it. The late events have revived and establish'd religious animosity so much that moderate men are of opinion it will be necessary to remove from this Kingdom the object of political contention, and they think if we have no parliament, we may have peace and security.'[1] The question was already sufficiently in agitation for sides to be taken. At a by-election for the independent borough of Drogheda, Edward Hardman pledged his constituents to resist the measure of Union, if it was brought forward.[2] On the other hand, a body of Catholic merchants, fearing that resentment against Papist outrages in Wexford would incur 'such jealousies as cannot otherwise be got over without further bloodshed' contemplated applying to Cornwallis to bring about a Union, under which they might feel more secure. An approach was made to consult with Richard Annesley, a ministerialist M.P. whose active role on the Board of Revenue brought him into contact with commercial opinion, but nothing ensued.[3] This growth of public speculation was paralleled in England[4] and Pitt was beginning to display impatience.[5] Throughout July and August he had been discussing details of the scheme with Dundas and Grenville, yet in that time Cornwallis had taken no further steps except to arrange for Clare to go over to England in the autumn, ostensibly for reasons of health,

seat as an Irish Peer . . . and he patters much about a Union. He affects to attend to nothing but his Regt.' (Add. MSS. 37308).

[1] Dean Warburton to Fitzwilliam, 31 July 1798 (Wentworth Woodhouse MSS., F. 30e).

[2] Hardman to Castlereagh, 15 Jan. 1799 (Mt. Stewart MSS.).

[3] Richard Annesley to Downshire, 22 Aug. 1798 (Downshire MSS.).

[4] The scheme was becoming well known in English political circles. As early as 4 July, Hatsell, the Clerk of the House of Commons, had written to Auckland expatiating on its difficulties. Sheffield's letter of 12 Aug. expressed surprise that none of his Irish correspondents had adverted to the subject, and by 30 Aug. the earl of Carlisle (Lord Lieutenant 1780-2) knew about it (Auckland MSS., Add. MSS. 34454).

[5] Pitt to Grenville, 5 and 6 Aug. 1798 (*H.M.C. Dropmore MSS.* iv, pp. 273 and 275). Cf. Dundas to Grenville, 10 and 19 Aug. 1798 (ibid., pp. 278 and 284).

but actually to confer with the British ministers about the Union.[1]

It was at this juncture that on 22 August the French general Humbert made a surprise landing at Killala in Mayo, with a force of just over 1,000 men. Striking swiftly inland, the invaders met with one or two initial successes against ill-equipped militia units, until compelled to retreat by the approach of a much larger force, of which Cornwallis himself had insisted on taking personal control, although seriously ill.[2] Pursued through Leitrim and Sligo, and finding less support from the local peasantry than expected, Humbert surrendered at Ballinamuck on 8 September. Greatly alarmed by the invasion, the Ascendancy increased their attacks on the policy of clemency. Several leading United Irishmen, in custody in Dublin, had been spared a trial and promised no other punishment than exile, in return for information about the nature of their society. This information—which contained no details which might incriminate any individual—was incorporated in the report of a secret committee appointed by the House of Commons. Alleged extracts from the reports of the prisoners' evidence found their way to the newspapers, and it was held to be an aggravation of their offence when, on 27 August, three of the prisoners published an advertisement in the Dublin press to deny the authenticity of some of the reports. This act was deemed by many to repudiate the whole agreement over the confessions, and Members of Parliament were not lacking to demand the blood of the prisoners—unsuccessfully—and to deplore the impolicy of the 'treaty of Newgate'.[3]

'Every one loud against Lord Cornwallis,' wrote Buckingham,[4] 'some with reason but most without any.' By now many of the Irish gentry were only too ready to take offence at Cornwallis's every action, and a pretext for more outcry was discovered in the phrasing of part of the General Orders,

---

[1] Cornwallis to Ross, 12 Aug. 1798 (*Cornwallis Correspondence*, ii, p. 386).

[2] The campaign is described in the *Cornwallis Correspondence*, ii, pp. 390–404; *Castlereagh Correspondence*, i, pp. 320–4, 339; and Fremantle to Buckingham, 29 Aug. 1798 (*H.M.C. Dropmore MSS.* iv, p. 297).

[3] Johnson to Downshire, 3 Sept. 1798 (Downshire MSS.); Castlereagh to Wickham, 27 Aug. and 5 Sept. 1798 (H.O. 100/77 and 100/78).

[4] Buckingham to Grenville, 16 Oct. 1798 (*H.M.C. Dropmore MSS.* iv, p. 321).

in which Cornwallis congratulated his forces on the surrender of the French: '. . . The Corps of Yeomanry in the whole country through which the army has passed, have rendered the greatest services, and are peculiarly entitled to the acknowledgement of the Lord Lieutenant, from their not having tarnished that courage and loyalty, which they displayed in the cause of their King and country, by any acts of wanton cruelty towards their deluded fellow-subjects.'[1] It was held that by implying that 'acts of wanton cruelty' could conceivably have been attributed to them at other times, the Yeomanry were made the subject of a gross calumny.[2] As Abercromby had found before, an English general who was less than flattering in his references to the local militia, invited the abuse of the gentry who officered them. The legend grew, to reach full maturity during the Union debates, that only the exertions of the yeomanry had saved Dublin from the French, that the local men and their leaders had been fully adequate to suppress insurrection, and that the regulars under Cornwallis had been inept and outgeneralled.[3] This view, although widespread, showed singular forgetfulness of the panic of early June.[4]

The resultant unpopularity of Cornwallis was enhanced by the Whollaghan affair. On 13 October, Hugh Whollaghan, a corporal of the Mount Kennedy corps of yeomanry was acquitted by a court martial of the murder of an unarmed peasant, of whose death the facts clearly showed he had been guilty without provocation. The president of this court martial was the earl of Enniskillen, a Fermanagh magistrate of pronounced Orange tendencies.[5] Cornwallis, indignant at the attitude displayed in this case, ordered the immediate

---

[1] *Cornwallis Correspondence*, ii, pp. 403–4.

[2] Johnson to Downshire, 13 Sept. 1798 (Downshire MSS.).

[3] See, for instance, the remarks of Frederick Falkiner, M.P. for co. Dublin, and Jonah Barrington, M.P. for Clogher, in *Parliamentary Register*: a report of the debates in the House of Commons in Ireland on Tuesday and Wednesday 22nd and 23rd of Jan. on the subject of an Union . . . , Dublin, 1799 (hereafter listed as *Parl. Reg.*).

[4] Camden to Pitt, 30 May 1798 (P.R.O. 30/8/326); Castlereagh to Wickham, 12 June 1798 (Mt. Stewart MSS.).

[5] Robert Day (E. B. Day, op. cit., p. 263) describes in his diary (28 July 1801) a procession of 4,500 Protestants through Enniskillen, led by his son, Lord Cole, 'the Prince of Orange of county Fermanagh'.

dismissal of Whollaghan from the yeomanry, and directed that Enniskillen and the other officers involved should not in future sit on any court martial.[1] The immediate effect of this was to antagonize from the Castle Enniskillen, his brother-in-law Belmore, and their considerable parliamentary following. From this time, too, observers noted that the disgruntled yeomanry and the Orange Lodges were drawing closely together.[2] Every criticism of Cornwallis was sedulously retailed to the British ministry by the marquess of Buckingham. Cornwallis had affronted him by refusing him leave to command a detachment of his regiment against the French, and by politely ignoring his suggestions that he, or another, should be appointed Lord Deputy to take up the Government of Ireland with a Council of State, in the event of Cornwallis's death in action.[3] Buckingham's constant carping certainly had its effect on Grenville, who had also begun to complain of the infrequency with which Cornwallis communicated with the Home Government.[4] He indeed showed less taste for paper work than had his verbose predecessors Westmoreland and Camden, but this was hardly a sign of idleness.[5]

Towards the end of September, Cornwallis dispatched to England Robert Marshall, an official in the Chief Secretary's Department, to act as a liaison officer between the British

---

[1] Taylor to Craig, 18 Oct. 1798 (*Cornwallis Correspondence*, ii, p. 421).

[2] 'There is reason to dread', wrote Cooke to Auckland on 2 Nov. 1798, 'that whatever measure be brought forward by Ld. Cornwallis, it may be opposed by the yeomanry and by the Orange Party because it is *his* measure. . . . This may be momentary; but I fear the system of not consulting and of having no Irish cabinet will continue, and that I consider as fatal.' (Add. MSS. 34455.) 'The great question of Union will be hurt by this measure, as however *unjustly*, it will indispose, I fear, a very important party to whatever seems to be a favourite measure of the Government', wrote Camden to Castlereagh on 4 Nov. 1798 (Mt. Stewart MSS.). For comments on the effects of Enniskillen's disgrace on public opinion cf. Richard Annesley to Downshire, 24 Oct. 1798; Ross to Downshire, 27 Oct. 1798 (Downshire MSS.).

[3] Buckingham to Grenville, 26, 28, and 31 Aug., 5, 8, and 10 Sept. 1798; Cornwallis to Buckingham, 31 Aug. 1798 (*H.M.C. Dropmore MSS.* iv, pp. 286-9, 291-2, 300-4.

[4] 'I protest', wrote Grenville to Buckingham early in Sept. 1798, 'that I am not more a stranger to Buonoparte's government of Egypt than to that of Ireland' (Buckingham, *Courts and Cabinets of the Reign of King George III*, ii, pp. 404-7).

[5] Portland later voiced the same complaint until overruled by Pitt; cf. the draft of a dispatch from Portland to Cornwallis (not sent) of 4 Nov. 1798 (H.O. 100/79); also Elliot to Castlereagh, 4 Nov. 1798 (Mt. Stewart MSS.).

Cabinet, the absent Chief Secretary Pelham (still recuperating from his illness at home in Sussex), and Dublin Castle. He found the outlines of an Act of Union taking shape in Whitehall.[1] It was suggested that Ireland should send to the Westminster Parliament thirty-two representative peers, six of them to be bishops, and 100 commoners. The method of selecting the latter was to cause much argument and experiment, but the mode then favoured was that there should be one member from each of the thirty-two counties and eighteen most considerable towns, and that the other fifty members should be chosen from the 100 smaller boroughs[2] 'two places choosing members either jointly or alternately'. No principle of compensation had yet been devised. The Protestant establishment would be secured in the same form as the articles of union with Scotland: Roman Catholics would be eligible for all offices, taking the oath of 1793, but it had yet to be decided whether they would be allowed to sit in Parliament. The tithe question, which Cornwallis had held up as a major cause of religious and agrarian discontent, if not dealt with under the articles of union, should be settled soon afterwards. A State provision should be made for the Catholic clergy, on the same lines as the *regium donum* which had been granted to the Presbyterian clergy of Ulster since the time of Charles II. The existing civil taxes of each country would remain applicable to its own internal welfare, but new land and income taxes might be generally applied. Interest charges on the national debts of each country would continue to be assessed separately, and debts incurred after the Act of Union would be provided for 'in a just proportion, varying always with the means of each'. Free trade would exist between the two countries 'except as far as to countervail a difference in internal or import duties'. No decision had been taken about the mode of negotiating the details of the Anglo-Irish union, but the Government were inclined to favour the appointment of parliamentary commissioners, after the precedent of the Scottish Union of 1707.

---

[1] Marshall to Castlereagh, 26 Sept. 1798 (*Castlereagh Correspondence*, i, pp. 378–80).

[2] There were in fact ninety-nine boroughs remaining after provision was made for the eighteen most considerable towns.

The most immediately controversial of these provisions concerned the Catholics, and it was this point which chiefly engaged the attention of the next envoy to go over from Ireland, the Lord Chancellor, Clare. Fortified by his own long-standing prejudices, and perhaps encouraged by the Protestant feeling which the rebellion had inflamed, Clare argued long and persuasively in his talks with the British ministers against incorporating any further concessions to the Catholics in the Union provisions. Cornwallis, who had gauged with some accuracy the strength of the Ascendancy's feelings on this issue, but who still placed great reliance in most matters on the Chancellor ('the most right-headed politician in this island'),[1] conceded that he would not insist on emancipation as an article of union; but he strongly advised Pitt that nothing irrevocable on the subject should be introduced into the Act.[2] However, when Clare arrived in London in mid October, he found Dundas away in Scotland—and Dundas, with his intimate knowledge of a non-Anglican British community, was the main advocate in Cabinet of Catholic concessions. It was Clare's advocacy which, by 16 October, had swung the inclinations of the British Cabinet against touching the question:

I should have hoped that what has passed would have opened the eyes of every man in England to the insanity of their past conduct, with respect to the Papists of Ireland; but I can very plainly perceive that they were as full of their popish projects as ever. I trust, and I hope I am not deceived, that they are fairly inclined to give them up, and to bring the measure forward unencumbered with the doctrine of Emancipation. Lord Cornwallis has indicated his acquiescence in this point; Mr. Pitt is decided upon it, and I think he will keep his colleagues steady. Most fortunately, we have a precedent in the Articles of the Union with Scotland, which puts an end to all difficulty on the only point insisted on by Lord Cornwallis, of which they are equally tenacious here. By one of the Articles, it is stipulated that every member of the Parliament of Great Britain shall take the Oath of Supremacy &c., on taking his seat, *unless it shall be otherwise provided for by Parliament*. So that it cannot admit of a question, that a similar provision should be made for Ireland, which Mr. Pitt is perfectly satisfied shall be done. He is also fully sensible of the necessity of establishing some

[1] Cornwallis to Pitt, 25 Sept. 1798 (P.R.O. 30/8/326).
[2] Same to same, 8 Oct. 1798 (ibid.).

effectual civil control over the Popish Clergy, which he thinks will be effected by allowing very moderate stipends to them, and obliging every priest to take a license from the Crown for performing ecclesiastical functions, on pain of perpetual banishment, if he shall officiate without it.[1]

The inclination of the British Cabinet to drop emancipation was soon communicated to the anti-Catholics in Dublin Castle, who approved this development as likely to win support to the cause of Union. 'If your Union is to be Protestant,' wrote Cooke to Auckland, 'we have 100,000 Protestants who are connected by Orange Lodges, and they might be made a great instrument.'[2]

Cornwallis, meanwhile, had been having second thoughts on this question, and on 17 October he dispatched to London the under-secretary for the Military Department, William Elliot,[3] a known liberal whose views might serve as a corrective to Clare. To Pitt, Cornwallis expressed his doubts '. . . whether a union with the Protestants will afford a temporary respite from the spirit of faction and rebellion which so universally pervades this island, and whether the Catholics will patiently wait for what is called their emancipation from the justice of the united Parliament'.[4] This he considered unlikely, especially if the British Opposition were to succumb to the temptation of fishing in these troubled waters. Castlereagh also wrote to Clare in the same vein, although by attributing the arguments for emancipation to Lord Cornwallis rather than espousing them as his own, he weakened any impression he hoped to make on the tough-minded Chancellor.[5] Elliot remained a month in London, taking part in ministerial discussions about Union, but he was unable to make much headway on the issue of religious tolerance, except with Dundas. Influenced by the majority

---

[1] Clare to Castlereagh, 16 Oct. 1798 (*Castlereagh Correspondence*, i, pp. 393-4).
[2] Cooke to Auckland, 22 Oct. 1798 (Add. MSS. 34455).
[3] M.P. for St. Canice, he had succeeded Edward Cooke on the latter's promotion to the civil department in 1796. Normally the Union negotiations would have been Cooke's preserve rather than Elliot's, but Cooke was required to help with advance publicity at that time, and besides, his views on the Catholic question were narrowly Protestant, although they were later to change under the influence of Castlereagh.
[4] Cornwallis to Pitt, 17 Oct. 1798 (P.R.O. 30/8/326).
[5] Castlereagh to Clare, 24 Oct. 1798 (Mt. Stewart MSS.).

of 'expert opinions' on Ireland, Pitt had determined to proceed 'on the *narrow* basis', without incorporating any hopes
of Catholic reforms in the Union provisions.[1]

Other leading Irish politicians were summoned to London. Sir John Parnell, whose attitude was uncertain, was
already there for the good of an invalid daughter's health.
A move was afoot to facilitate the return of Pelham as Chief
Secretary by persuading Parnell to exchange his office of
Chancellor of the Exchequer for Castlereagh's lucrative sinecure of Keeper of the Privy Seal, with a peerage as bonus.[2]
Parnell's habits as a financier had been a minor source of
anxiety to Camden during the crisis year of 1797, and it was
known that he was very friendly with the Speaker, John
Foster, whose dislike of Cornwallis and the Union was becoming notorious.[3] Eventually these negotiations fell through
because Pelham decided his health would not permit his
return to office, and Castlereagh was appointed his successor.[4] It does not seem that Parnell was much consulted on
the early stages of the Union, and in fact John Beresford, the
Chief Commissioner of the Revenue, had been the official
from whom the British Government had been collecting
financial and commercial information relevant to the Union.[5]
At the end of October, Beresford was summoned to London,
and the recalcitrant Foster, after some show of reluctance,
was also persuaded to come over.[6]

By now this notable migration of high officials to England
(and the leakages which seemed to be an inevitable feature
of Dublin politics) had aroused widespread speculation on
the possibility of a legislative union. During the first week of
November, the Dublin and Belfast newspapers ran paragraphs

---

[1] Elliot to Castlereagh, 24 Oct., 4, 9, and 23 Nov. 1798 (*Castlereagh Correspondence*, i, pp. 403, 426, 430; ii, p. 9); Pitt to Cornwallis 17 Nov. 1798 (P.R.O.
30/8/325).

[2] The transaction is alluded to in Marshall to Castlereagh, 26 Sept. and 29 Oct.
1798 (*Castlereagh Correspondence*, i, pp. 378, 415).

[3] 'Come,' said Foster to a dinner of 'near 20 persons', 'don't let's talk of him;
he is a damned silly fellow.' (Buckingham to Grenville, 10 Sept. 1798 (*H.M.C.
Dropmore MSS.* iv, p. 304).)

[4] Pelham to Castlereagh, 2 Nov. 1798 (*Castlereagh Correspondence*, i, pp. 419–21).

[5] Beresford to Auckland, 19 and 21 July, 2 Aug. 1798 (*Beresford Correspondence*,
ii, pp. 161, 163, 167). Beresford was not definitely informed of the Union until mid
October (Auckland to Beresford, 17 Oct. 1798, op. cit., p. 187).

[6] Cornwallis to Pitt, 7 Nov. 1798 (*Cornwallis Correspondence*, ii, p. 430).

asserting that the scheme was under consideration.[1] Politicians were already choosing their sides. 'The Union is
a subject now in every mouth,' wrote Colonel Ross, 'I am
clearly of opinion if it be on good terms, it will be the making
of Ireland.'[2] Francis Hardy, on the other hand, a good
opposition whig, exclaimed: 'A precious time, certainly, to
decide on the future of millions yet unborn', and added in
a letter to old Charlemont: 'When a proposition is intrinsic-
ally good, it cannot be too much unfolded in detail, when the
reverse, no detail should be entered into. The spirit of the
house evaporates, and time is given for the venal to sell
themselves.'[3] Pending definite information, however, some
of the Government's opponents such as Sir Laurence Parsons
cherished the hope that the scheme would be abandoned;[4]
but others, such as the able anti-Catholic lawyer, William
Saurin, were already considering steps for resistance, and
opposition was brewing among the Dublin lawyers some
little time before the official avowal of the project.[5]

The increasing ferment had not escaped Dublin Castle,
and on 1 November Cornwallis wrote to Pitt pointing out
that 'from the prejudices and the various interests of people
in this country, a considerable opposition to the Union must
be expected in the Irish Parliament', and urging the dispatch
of some definite news of the articles of union, which might
be shown to potential supporters.[6] In truth, the articles were
still in a fairly sketchy form,[7] and many important points of
detail had been left undecided—under the presumption that
they would be the topics of negotiation between two sets
of Commissioners, appointed by the Parliaments of Great
Britain and Ireland. It was not until 16 November that
Cornwallis received a draft of the articles from Portland, and

    [1] *Dublin Evening Post*, 2 Nov. 1798; *Belfast Newsletter*, 2 Nov. 1798; the latter
doubted the likelihood of the rumour, but thought that a report of the summons of
parliament for 20 Nov. had increased its strength.

    [2] Ross to Downshire, 6 Nov. 1798 (Downshire MSS.).

    [3] Hardy to Charlemont, 6 Nov. 1798 (*H.M.C. Charlemont MSS.*, ii, p. 338).

    [4] Parsons to Charlemont, 5 Nov. 1798; ibid., pp. 337–8.

    [5] Cooke to Castlereagh, 8 Nov. 1798 (*Castlereagh Correspondence*, i, p. 429).

    [6] Cornwallis to Pitt, 1 Nov. 1798 (P.R.O. 30/8/326).

    [7] Grenville to Buckingham, 5 Nov. 1798 (Buckingham, op. cit. ii, p. 411).
I shall deal with the development of the provisions of the Union in a subsequent
chapter.

by that time agitation on the Union was beginning to spread.[1] To give rise to so much public discussion, before any move had been made to ease the passage of the measure through Parliament, was not good policy on the part of the Castle. As Sheffield commented: 'That difficulties must attend so great a measure is a matter of course, but these difficulties are greatly increased by letting it come out to public consideration before the measure was perfectly well weighed, the detail of it arranged, and leading men and interests managed. . . .'[2] Later, when opposition to the Union seemed to be gaining ground, he elaborated the theme to Lord Auckland: 'If you or Lord Malmesbury or some man (if we have another well dispos'd and fit to send) of business and address had gone there before the measure had been divulged, and instead of sending for, had been sent to converse with the leading men of the country, and to enable those men *to talk to their friends*, the business might have gone on tolerably smooth. . . .'[3]

Even within Dublin Castle there was a consciousness that more might be done in the way of parliamentary management. Cooke, whose appreciation of this factor was so acute as sometimes to blind him to other considerations, had already said as much:[4] and even the relatively inexperienced Castlereagh ventured a similar diagnosis:

I am confirm'd in the opinion we entertain'd that Ld. C.[5] is rather inattentive to parliamentary management, and that from habits either purely military, or form'd in the administration of a different system, he is disposed to underrate the embarrassment which may arise in a popular assembly. It will be difficult to meet the popular opposition which must be expected to the Union, particularly if the leading members of the Govt. are only passive. . . . In proportion as difficulties multiply it will require exertion to keep certain of them from partaking in the politics of John Lees's[6] shop. I shall endeavour to impress on

---

[1] Portland to Cornwallis, 12 Nov. 1798 (H.O. 100/79). For evidence of public interest, cf. Cooke to Castlereagh, 8 and 9 Nov. 1798 (*Castlereagh Correspondence*, i, pp. 429, 431) and a long anonymous letter from Cork, 12 Nov. (ibid., p. 436).

[2] Sheffield to Auckland, 13 Nov. 1798 (Add. MSS. 34455).

[3] Same to same, 30 Dec. 1798 (ibid.).

[4] Cooke to Auckland, 2 Nov. 1798 (ibid.).   [5] Cornwallis.

[6] John Lees (d. 1811), created a baronet in 1804, was secretary to the Post Office. He had been an expert adviser to previous Viceroys on patronage matters, particularly in the period between 1767 and 1783. Cf. the remarks about him in the

Ld. C's mind when I return the necessity of withdrawing himself a little more, at least till the measure in question is fairly established, from military detail, and giving more of his time to civil communications.[1]

This early letter of Castlereagh's points to a desire to avoid the indiscriminate jobbery and peerage-mongering which had been characteristic of earlier régimes and which was soon to become so famous a feature of the Union controversy. The Government's position, however, was not strong enough to afford such abstinence. Cornwallis had courted neither the Castle clique nor the old opposition. 'The principal persons here', he had written, '. . . are not satisfied with me, because I have not thrown myself blindly into their hands . . . and I have shown no marks of confidence to any other set of men, and have particularly given no countenance whatever to those who opposed the former Government.'[2] Not that whig support would have strengthened the régime. Grattan, ill and in England, was an object of constant vituperation from the ultra-Protestants, and had been struck off the Privy Council at the King's desire.[3] The Ponsonbys had ceased to attend Parliament, and their conduct during the rising had been described by a ministerialist as 'purchasing a degraded security by their inaction'.[4] Courting their support would, in 1798, have provoked more trouble and promised less benefit to Cornwallis than Fitzwilliam had incurred three years earlier.

Until the plan of the Union had been received from London, Castlereagh confined himself to making contacts with a few leading public men. As early as 4 November he had, with rare virtuosity, communicated with two prominent Catholic noblemen and two of the most violent Protestant

---

Introduction to Dr. E. M. Johnston's article: 'The Irish House of Commons in 1791' (*Proc. Royal Irish Academy*, Mar. 1957).

[1] Castlereagh to Elliot, 9 Nov. 1798 (machine copy, Mt. Stewart MSS.).

[2] Cornwallis to Portland, 16 Sept. 1798 (H.O. 100/78). Matters had not improved two months later: on 8 Nov. Colonel Robert Ross, the Blimpish M.P. for Newry, wrote to Downshire: 'For heaven's sake do not let poor Ireland fall a sacrifice to the madness and dotage of a very silly old Indian bitch' (Downshire MSS.).

[3] Wickham to Castlereagh, 29 Sept. 1798 (*Castlereagh Correspondence*, i, p. 382); Cornwallis to Portland, 6 Oct. 1798 (H.O. 100/78).

[4] Henry Alexander to Pelham, 10 June 1798 (Add. MSS. 33105).

members, all four of whom gave opinions favourable to the Union. Lords Fingall and Kenmare, two of the few Catholic peers, promised the Government every assistance, and seem to have been content that the question of emancipation should be kept back for the time, so long as some provision was made for the clergy.[1] The ultra-Protestant Dr. Duigenan, on the other hand, was 'ready to go all lengths in its support', as was George Ogle, M.P. for Dublin city, 'understanding it is proposed on Protestant principles'.[2] It was not until 19 November that any further exploration could be made. On that day, Castlereagh wrote to Elliot: 'The Lord Lieutenant has received his brief, and is to proceed to business tomorrow. He begins with Lord Shannon. In a few days the measure must be declared, and we may expect a political beanfeast.'[3] Many individual members of the Irish Parliament were sounded by conversation or letter during the next two weeks, and a fairly hopeful picture began to emerge. Within the ranks of the Irish Cabinet, however, there was a serious lack of unanimity.

The most intractable opponent of the scheme was the Speaker, John Foster, whose knowledge of commercial principles and length of service in the Commons gave him a weight much beyond that which he might be expected to derive from electoral influence alone.[4] It had been hoped that, if compensated by a life pension and an English peerage, he would not obstruct the measure.[5] But Pitt, in a series of interviews lasting through November, was able to make

[1] These opinions are recorded in an unsigned document summarizing the views of leading politicians and the dates on which they were given. It is included in the Lord Lieutenant's *Union Correspondence*, vol. i (National Library of Ireland). Unlike many of the documents in this collection, this seems to be an original: the paper is watermarked 1797, and the handwriting is possibly Cooke's. Lord Kenmare was also stated to desire an earldom, which had been forfeited by his Jacobite ancestors.

[2] Ogle, formerly M.P. for co. Wexford, had been returned at a by-election for Dublin city, with a band playing 'The Protestant Boys' (Johnson to Downshire, 24 [July] 1798 (Downshire MSS.)). 'I am induced to hope that you may feel the importance of incorporating our representation with the protestant legislature of Great Britain' wrote Castlereagh to Ogle, 4 Nov. 1798 (Mt. Stewart MSS.).

[3] Castlereagh to Elliot, 19 Nov. 1798 (ibid.).

[4] He had been M.P. for the family seat of Dunleer 1761-8, and co. Louth since 1768; he also had some influence in Meath.

[5] Pitt to Cornwallis, 17 Nov. 1798 (P.R.O. 30/8/325).

no change in his outlook. He especially doubted the wisdom
of broaching the measure at so disturbed a time as the aftermath of the rebellion, and his attitude hardened when it
became plain that there would be a considerable body of
opinion against the proposal.[1] The other financial experts of
Dublin Castle were also less than enthusiastic: 'Beresford
and Parnell do not say much on the general measure, but I
think both, or at least the former, against trying it, but both
disposed to concur when they understand it is finally resolved
on.'[2] Pitt was mistaken: it was Beresford who, not without
grumbling at the strong opposition likely to be aroused,
eventually came down on the side of the Union, while
Parnell, who for many years had perfected the art of fence-
sitting in times of difficulty, managed to convey the impression of being adverse but not irreconcilable.[3] A hostile
combination of Foster with Parnell—which was rendered
probable by ancient friendship and common financial views—
raised a formidable obstacle to the Union's prospects. Under-
Secretary Elliot, who himself was inclined to resign his
post because of the abandonment of Catholic emancipation,
thought that the measure might have to be dropped in the
face of such strong hostility.[4] Castlereagh, however, was
cheered by the support of Isaac Corry, M.P. for Newry,[5]
who acted as Parnell's deputy in the House of Commons,
and opined that 'we must make use of him to keep Parnell in
order'.[6] Relations between the Chancellor of the Exchequer
and his subordinate were not of the best, but this sort

---

[1] Finding him hostile, Castlereagh wrote to him personally appealing for his aid
with the commercial details, and noting: 'The citizens are disinclined to the measure,
but some of their oracles are favourable to it as the only means of preserving the
Protestant State against the Irish Papists and *their English* supporters . . .' (Castlereagh to Foster, 24 Nov. 1798 (*Castlereagh Correspondence*, ii, p. 17)).

[2] Pitt to Cornwallis, 17 Nov. 1798 (P.R.O. 30/8/325).

[3] Parnell to Cornwallis, 1 Dec. 1798 (Mt. Stewart MSS.).

[4] Elliot to Castlereagh, 23 Nov. 1798 (*Castlereagh Correspondence*, ii, p. 9); cf.
Clare to Auckland, 26 Nov. 1798 (Add. MSS. 34455).

[5] Born 1755; son of Edward Corry, M.P. for Newry 1775–6; himself M.P. for
Newry 1776–1800 and 1802–6; Dundalk 1801–2; Newport (Isle of Wight) 1806–7;
originally an adherent of the Antrim liberal, Lord O'Neill, and like Castlereagh, had
some connexions with the Presbyterians and the commercial interests of Ulster;
equerry to duke of Cumberland 1780; Surveyor-General of Ordnance 1788; Commissioner of Revenue 1789–98; Surveyor of Crown Lands 1798–9; Chancellor of the
Irish Exchequer 1798–1804; died 1813.

[6] Castlereagh to Camden, 28 Nov. 1798 (Mt. Stewart MSS.).

of discipline was a two-edged weapon to be employed by an inexperienced Chief Secretary.[1] If the financial advisers of the Castle were doubtful, little better could be reported of the men of law. Toler and Stewart, the Attorney-General and Solicitor-General, had no hesitation in expressing their Unionist sentiments. But Lord Chief Justice Kilwarden[2] although 'convinced of the impracticability of the present system' was extremely cautious of committing himself, for fear of popular unrest; and the Prime Serjeant, James Fitzgerald,[3] although allegedly undecided was influenced adversely by the growing hostility of the Dublin Bar.[4]

However, the parliamentary prospects of the Union looked as if they would be strengthened by the adhesion of most of the borough-owning magnates. It was believed that the Government could count on the Primate, the Chancellor, the marquesses of Abercorn, Hertford, and Waterford, the earls of Shannon, Londonderry, Lucan, Darnley, and Fingal, and Lords Caledon, Clifden, Glentworth, Gosford, Kenmare, Longueville, O'Neill, and Yelverton, as well as Sir Henry Cavendish and twenty-three other members of the House of Commons. The Castle also mistakenly included in its list of supporters the marquess of Downshire ('undecided in his opinion, but apparently not inclined to oppose Govt. if the measure shd. be proposed')[5] and the earls of Erne and Ely, of whom the latter professed a spurious enthusiasm for the measure, 'relying on the favour of the Crown in an object personal to himself'.[6] The parliamentary following represented in this list came to between 90 and 100 members, against whom the Opposition was reckoned in much less impressive terms. For although there was reason to expect the

---

[1] Cf. Johnson to Downshire, 20 Oct. 1798: 'Parnell does not like Corry, and takes every opportunity of his absence to go thro' the business, and for this purpose puts me in the chair.' (Downshire MSS.) Castlereagh and Corry had in common an intermittent rivalry with the marquess of Downshire over patronage matters, the one in co. Down, the other in the borough of Newry.

[2] Formerly the Attorney-General Arthur Wolfe, he was promoted in June 1798.

[3] Born 1743; M.P. for Fore 1776–83, Tulsk 1783–97, Kildare borough 1797–1800, Ennis 1802–18; Third Serjeant 1779–82; Privy Councillor 1784; Prime Serjeant 1787–99; his wife a baroness 1826; died 1835.

[4] [? Cooke], memorandum in the Lord Lieutenant's *Union Correspondence* described in footnote 1, p. 151.

[5] Ibid.

[6] Cornwallis to Portland, 27 Nov. 1798 (H.O. 100/79).

hostility of the Ponsonbys and the two dozen members attached to them, the remaining anti-unionists—the duke of Leinster, the earl of Charlemont, the archbishop of Cashel, Pery, Foster, Parnell, and Sir Hercules Langrishe—were not at the head of any of the big battalions in the House of Commons.[1] In fact the archbishop of Cashel's influence[2] as head of the Agar family was to some extent vitiated by the unionist sentiments of his nephew Lord Clifden, with his four members; and the aged ex-Speaker Pery, although personally respected, lacked the active influence of his unionist nephew Glentworth. Besides there were some undecided politicians whose support might be won for the Union; such noblemen as the earl of Longford, who 'saw the difficulties of our situation, and the necessity of a change: had no particular objection to a Union; but desired not to be considered as pledged', or even the more dubious earl of Belmore who at any rate 'was for putting the question in a train of enquiry—wo.d vote for Commissioners and reserve himself for the plan when completed'.[3]

Meanwhile, the general public was to be introduced to the scheme. 'The opponents of the Union only wait for the Government to take the first step', wrote Castlereagh on 19 November, 'we shall endeavour to have this question stated to the public in such a way, as will give a tone to our friends and literary advocates.'[4] The composition of an anonymous pamphlet, setting forth 'arguments for and against an Union', with a strong bias in favour of the affirmative side was entrusted to Castlereagh's Under-Secretary Edward Cooke. The draft of this pamphlet—which came to fifty-six pages of close print, and went into seven editions in as many months—was complete by the 22nd, and distribution had begun by the end of the month.[5]

---

[1] *D.N.B.* erroneously claims Leinster as a unionist. Langrishe, although expected to oppose, in fact became a unionist.

[2] In writing to the archbishop on 19 Nov. Cornwallis apologized for not having notified him of the Union project before his recent departure from Ireland, and somewhat disingenuously suggested that the intention had only recently been notified by the British ministry (*Cornwallis Correspondence*, ii, pp. 440–1).

[3] [Cooke ?], memorandum (Lord Lieutenant's *Union Correspondence*).

[4] Castlereagh to Wickham, 19 Nov. 1798 (*Castlereagh Correspondence*, ii, p. 8).

[5] A friendly critic's comments on the manuscript are conveyed in Buckingham to Cooke, 22 Nov. 1798 (P.R.O.I.; C.S.O. 513/73/1). By 1 Dec. Castlereagh was

Counter-pamphlets were soon produced, one of the earliest being Joshua Spencer's *Thoughts on an Union*, which ran to four editions before the end of the year.[1] 'Surely all Bedlam, not Parnassus, is let out', wrote one of Lord Castlereagh's secretaries after a fortnight of this paper war.[2] The anti-unionist pamphlets which have survived far outnumber those supporting the measure, but neither side avoided a good deal of repetitiousness.[3]

The crux of the anti-unionist case was that an Irish Parliament was incompetent to annihilate itself by voting for a merger with the British legislature. It is difficult to find any strictly constitutional basis for this reasoning, especially after a precedent had been set by the Anglo-Scottish Union of 1707. However, the concept of an unalterable Irish constitution was acceptable to the nationalism which had been aroused in 1782, and this point was eloquently laboured by the anti-unionists. Tactically this argument had the great advantage of whipping up public feeling on the issue before Dublin Castle had time to complete its arrangements for the parliamentary management of the question, or even to put forward definite outlines of a plan which might permit of discussion and conversion.[4] The first organized protest emanated from the Dublin Bar. It was possible to claim that the majority of lawyers were hostile because Union might deprive them of the opportunity for a parliamentary career.[5] Once Dublin lost its status as a capital, there would also be a decrease in the amount of legal business arising out of commercial, land, and governmental transactions.[6] Besides

sending a copy to a friend in Londonderry for reprinting and local distribution (Castlereagh to Sir George Hill, 1 Dec. 1798 (*Castlereagh Correspondence*, ii, p. 33)).

[1] Joshua Spencer, *Thoughts on an Union* (4th ed., 1798). Other productions in the first half of Dec. included Richard Jebb's *A Reply to a Pamphlet* . . . ; Charles Ball's *An Union neither Necessary or Expedient for Ireland* . . . ; and the anonymous *Cease Your Funning*, or *The Rebel Detected*, attributed to Jonah Barrington or to Charles Kendal Bushe.

[2] Alexander Knox to Castlereagh, 15 Dec. 1798 (*Castlereagh Correspondence*, ii, pp. 44–45).

[3] Of some 50 pamphlets enumerated by McDowall in the bibliography to *Irish Public Opinion, 1750–1800*, not more than ten are written in favour of Union.

[4] Cornwallis to Portland, 5 Dec. 1798 (H.O. 100/79). Cf. Hardy to Charlemont, 6 Nov. 1798 (*H.M.C. Charlemont MSS.* ii, p. 338).

[5] Richard Annesley to Castlereagh, 12 Dec. 1798 (Mt. Stewart MSS.).

[6] Bishop Percy of Dropmore to his wife, 21 Jan. 1799 (Add. MSS. 32335):

these motives of self-interest the Dublin Bar had a long and respected tradition as a mouthpiece of educated opinion. Its own militia group, instituted during the Volunteering days of 1780 and revived to combat invasion and insurrection, had a lively, if at times verbose, sense of patriotism. There was also a fairly strong liberal element among them. In the dark days of April 1797, seventy barristers had been found to pass resolutions on the necessity of Catholic emancipation, reform, and the replacement of coercion by conciliation.[1]

As early as 8 November, William Saurin, a respected ultra-Protestant barrister, was believed to be planning an anti-unionist demonstration,[2] and it was at first his intention to convene a parade of the Lawyers' Infantry Corps on 2 December. At the last moment the parade was postponed, in order to avoid the impropriety of discussing political subjects in the character of a military unit—a step which would have exposed them to discipline by Cornwallis in his capacity of Commander-in-Chief.[3] Instead a general Bar meeting was summoned for Sunday, 9 December, on the signed request of twenty-seven barristers.[4] So numerously was it attended that the Chancery Chamber was found inadequate for the purpose, and the meeting adjourned to a larger building. Here Saurin proposed the motion: 'Resolved, that the measure of a Legislative Union of this kingdom and Great Britain is an innovation, which it would be highly dangerous and improper to propose, at the present juncture, to this country.'[5] In a closely argued and temperate

---

'. . . Against the Union are the local advantages of the City of Dublin, and the personal interests of all the lawyers, who hope to make their fortunes by spouting in Parliament rather than at the Bar. . . .'

[1] *Dublin Evening Post*, 20 Apr. 1797.

[2] Cooke to Castlereagh, 8 Nov. 1798 (*Castlereagh Correspondence*, i, p. 429). Buckingham believed Lord Charlemont, through Plunket, was at the back of this idea of 'Volunteer' pressure (Buckingham to Grenville, 7 Nov. 1798 (*H.M.C. Dropmore MSS*. iv. p. 367)).

[3] Cornwallis to Portland, 5 Dec. 1798 (H.O. 100/79). Notices of meeting and postponement are reproduced in *Cornwallis Correspondence*, iii, p. 5.

[4] Among them Charles Bushe, M.P. for Callan; W. C. Plunket, M.P. for Charlemont; W. P. Ruxton, M.P. for Ardee; William Saurin, Peter Burrowes, and Richard Jebb.

[5] This and all following extracts from the discussion are taken from *A Report of the Debate of the Irish Bar Sunday the 9th of December 1798, on the Subject of an Union of the Legislatures of Great Britain and Ireland* (Moore, Dublin, 1798).

speech Saurin avoided the argument of Parliament's incompetence to consider the measure, and confined himself to the inexpediency of the measure at the present time 'at the end of an alarming rebellion, when a foreign army of 40,000 men were in the country, and military law scarcely yet superseded'.[1] He suggested that the interests of Ireland would be unduly neglected in a Parliament of 500 British and 100 Irish members sitting at Westminster. As for the financial prospects of Union, Ireland was now rising to an enviable degree of prosperity, and if the burdens of the British public debt were distributed evenly throughout the empire, Ireland's load would increase to a greater proportion than had been the case in the period of autonomy. He was supported by the pamphleteer Joshua Spencer, and opposed by St. George Daly, M.P. for Galway town, and John Jameson, who moved the adjournment of the motion for a month so that the terms offered by Britain might be more precisely determined and maturely considered.

The subsequent debate lasted six hours. The majority of speakers sided with Saurin. Some followed his example in soberly enumerating the disadvantages expected of Union and the dangers of political agitation so soon after the rebellion and invasion. Others, carried away by their own professional tendencies to rhetoric, shifted on to more dangerous ground. A Mr. Barnes reminded the assembly that only the King, Lords, and Commons of Ireland could govern that nation: 'Bred as he was to the use of arms, he would not tamely surrender that right to the cunning or the insolence of that serpent and political apostate, Mr. Pitt.' While Thomas Goold, who had hitherto had the name of a fairly conservative disciple of Burke, was even less restrained: 'There are forty thousand troops, in British pay, in Ireland; yet, with forty thousand bayonets at my heart, I would tell the British Minister he shall not, cannot plant another Sicily in the bosom of the Atlantic. . . . The great Creator of the World has given unto our beloved country the gigantic outlines of a kingdom, and not the pigmy features of a province. God and Nature, I say, never intended that Ireland shall be

---

[1] Military law had existed concurrently with civil justice until the advocate Curran had successfully sought a stay of execution on Wolfe Tone on 12 Nov.

a province, and, by God, she never shall.' (General applause.)
Nor was this great-hearted advocate allured by talk of commercial advantages: 'On a great constitutional question, my
mind recoils from the stupid and unfeeling work of calculation. On a great constitutional question, my mind disdains
to be governed by the rules of vulgar arithmetic.' Against
such a feeling, the arguments of the unionists—which mainly
went no further than requests for time to consider the issue
fairly before arriving at an over-hasty verdict[1]—failed to hold
their own. It was all very well for a Castle official to comment
that the anti-unionist speeches were 'all empty declamations,
void of argument, but replete with passionate and mischievous irritation',[2] or for a unionist lawyer, McClelland, to
excuse his want of effect by saying that 'some desultory
speeches afterwards drove away many who would have voted
with us',[3] but it was nevertheless an unpleasant shock and
a setback when St. George Daly's motion for the adjournment was rejected by so wide a margin as 166 votes to 32,
and Saurin's original resolution carried with acclamation
immediately afterwards.[4]

This division seems to have reflected opinion in the profession fairly accurately. The taste of the Irish gentry for
litigation, combined with the contemporary notion that law
was the only civilian calling fit for a gentleman,[5] overstocked
the Irish Bar. Lack of employment increased the tendency
of the Bar to oppose the Government at all times. Moreover,
the Irish Parliament—whose independent existence was now
threatened—provided a career for many aspiring lawyers.

[1] One bold unionist, Thomas Grady, attacked the corrupt features of the Dublin
Parliament, which he said was the legislature of 'an arrogant aristocracy, who while
they hold the Sovereign in shackles, trampled upon his people'. Under the old
system, law preferment had been given to timeservers of the Protestant Ascendancy.
The Union might promote reforms: it was favoured by the commercial and Catholic
interests of Munster and Connaught. His arguments, which must have been as
embarrassing to his own side as they were to the anti-unionists, provoked considerable interruption.

[2] Alexander Knox to Castlereagh, 10 Dec. 1798 (Mt. Stewart MSS.).

[3] McClelland to Isaac Corry, 9 Dec. 1798 (*Castlereagh Correspondence*, ii,
pp. 37–39).

[4] Cornwallis to Portland, 15 Dec. 1798 (H.O. 100/79).

[5] Francis Dobbs remarked: 'I will venture to assert there is not a family in Ireland of £1,000 a year, that has not a near relation at the Bar' (*Parl. Reg.*, 22 Jan.
1799, p. 113).

There were sixty-seven barristers in the House of Commons at that time, of whom forty-two were in active practice.[1] Many of them had purchased a seat, if they could not find a patron to present them with one, in the hope that their talents would show to such advantage in the Commons that the Government would help them to speedy and spectacular preferment. As a rule these lawyers began their careers in opposition, which allowed more scope for facile eloquence and left the way open for the Government to persuade them to its side when a suitable vacancy occurred. Even John Fitzgibbon, who as Lord Chancellor Clare was viewed as the bulwark of reaction, had begun his career as an assailant of the hapless Lord Lieutenant Buckinghamshire. It was not known at this stage whether any of the Irish courts were to be abolished, and here, as in so many other respects, the indefinite nature of the Union scheme fanned nationalist suspicions and engendered an inclination to play safe by having nothing at all to do with the idea.

The example of the lawyers was followed by the Dublin merchants. Castlereagh had hoped that this might be offset to some extent by the adhesion of the members for the city, one of whom, George Ogle, had already declared himself in favour of Union, and the other of whom, John Claudius Beresford, was a member of a clan noted for its support of the Castle. Much was hoped of a former Lord Mayor, Alderman William James, 'who has great weight, not only in the Corporation, but particularly in the Orange Lodges'.[2] On 4 December, however, a strong unofficial hint of Dublin sentiment was revealed at the meeting of the Aldermen of Skinners' Alley, an influential loyalist pressure-group, of whom Beresford was Governor. He thus reported its proceedings to Castlereagh: '. . . the universal opinion of every person was against the measure, and violently against it, except one Alderman James, who said nothing openly, but whispered me that he thought it the only chance the Protestants had: the other citizens of Dublin, that is, I mean,

[1] *Belfast Newsletter*, 15 Jan. 1799. I believe this to be a fairly accurate estimate: it is a little difficult to trace all the Irish M.P.s who had been bred to the profession in youth, but no longer practised.

[2] Castlereagh to Wickham, 23 Nov. 1798 (*Cornwallis Correspondence*, iv, p. 447; H.O. 100/79).

the bankers and merchants whose business keeps them out of the way of these clubs, and who have not the same inducements to attend them that I have, are about to declare their sentiments in a more open manner. . . .'[1] A fortnight later, on 18 December, 'a numerous and respectable meeting of the bankers and merchants of Dublin' met at the Mansion House, with the Lord Mayor presiding. Unlike the Bar, this meeting wasted little time on declamation. Five resolutions were proposed, of which the gist was stated in the fourth: 'Resolved that, impressed with every sentiment of loyalty to the King, and affectionate attachment to British connexion, we conceive that to agitate in Parliament a question of Legislative Union between this kingdom and Great Britain would be highly dangerous and impolitic.'[2] After speeches against the measure by Beresford and the banker Digges Latouche, the resolutions were passed unanimously.

This mobilization of anti-unionist opinion in the capital had its effect even on the conservative Corporation of Dublin, who passed hostile resolutions on 17 December. The Orange Lodge of Dublin was, according to J. C. Beresford, 'mostly adverse to the measure'[3] and the utmost which could be achieved by the Government's friends was an agreement that the Orangemen should abstain from passing resolutions or canvassing on the issue.[4] In Londonderry Protestant opinion was inclined to baulk over an implication on Cooke's pamphlet that the United Parliament might at some time consider a repeal of the Test Laws. Sir George Hill, a son-in-law of John Beresford, who was much in contact with the Orangemen of Londonderry, thought that opposition could be avoided only if Union was seen as 'a final barrier to catholick pretension'.[5] As for the Catholics, their leaders Fingall, Kenmare, and Dr. Troy[6] were inclined to favour the measure:

---

[1] J. C. Beresford to Castlereagh, 12 Dec. 1798 (*Castlereagh Correspondence*, ii, p. 41).   [2] Reproduced in ibid., p. 48.

[3] J. C. Beresford to Castlereagh, 12 Dec. 1798 (ibid., p. 42). Beresford was anxious to discourage the development of clubs as organized pressure-groups, for which practice he felt the French Revolution had set a bad precedent.

[4] Duigenan to Castlereagh, 20 Dec. 1798 (ibid., p. 53).

[5] Sir George Hill to Castlereagh, 9 Dec. 1798 (Mt. Stewart MSS.).

[6] Dr. John Thomas Troy (1739–1823), titular archbishop of Dublin, is the subject of a D.Phil. thesis by the Revd. Edward Peel, of the University College of Cork.

as Cooke observed, 'many thought it foolish to oppose a
measure which was opposed by their enemies, the Orangemen'.[1] Yet in the absence of any specific promise of concessions, the Catholics as a body were not eager to commit their
support. Sitting on the fence seemed a better tactical position
for future negotiations. A meeting of thirty-seven Dublin
Catholics held at Lord Fingall's house on 15 December
failed to reach any agreement. After a week's adjournment,
a second larger meeting formed the view that '. . . the
Catholics, as such, ought not to deliberate on the Union as
a question of Empire, but only as it might affect their own
peculiar interests as a body; and on this it was judged inex-
pedient to publish any resolution or declaration at present;
wherefore neither of any kind was proposed or suggested,
and the meeting adjourned *sine die*.'[2] This revealed a lack of
unanimity in the Catholic ranks, but it also left them in a
bargaining position of some flexibility. Despite the inability
of Catholics to sit in Parliament, Cornwallis regarded their
influence as of some importance:

What line of conduct they will ultimately adopt when decidedly
convinced that the measure will be persevered in on a Protestant principle, I am at present incapable of judging. I shall endeavour to give them
the most favorable impression, without holding out to them hopes of
any relaxation on the part of Government, and shall leave no effort
untried to prevent an opposition to the Union being made the measure
of that party; as I should much fear, should it be made a Catholic
principle to resist the Union, that the favorable sentiments entertained
by individuals would give way to the party feeling, and deprive us of
our principal strength in the South and West, which could not fail, at
least for the present, to prove fatal to the measure.[3]

As yet, however, little was known of the reactions of the
country districts to the Union proposals. It was hoped that
the hostility of Dublin would be offset by the unionist sympathies of rival ports, Limerick, Belfast, and especially Cork,
whose trade might hope to profit in the event of Ireland's
admission to commercial equality with Great Britain. Except

[1] Cooke to Castlereagh, 17 Dec. 1798 (*Castlereagh Correspondence*, ii, p. 46); cf.
Buckingham to Grenville, 2 Jan. 1799 (*H.M.C. Dropmore MSS.* iv, pp. 435-6).
[2] Troy to Castlereagh, 24 Dec. 1798 (*Castlereagh Correspondence*, ii, p. 61).
[3] Cornwallis to Portland, 2 Jan. 1799 (H.O. 100/85).

in the county of Dublin, where a meeting had been summoned for 4 January, and where the attitude towards Union
could be foreseen as unfriendly, no steps had been taken to
sound opinion on the Union in any of the counties. Those
who were likely to express decided opinions on the Union
were not the forty-shilling freeholders—very often political
ciphers in the hands of their landlords—still less the common
peasantry, with little inclination or time to argue political
issues about which they were not thought worth consulting.
In the contest which was to seek to mobilize public opinion
over the Union, both the Government and its opponents
appealed in the main to those with a stake in the country,
respectable men of property, or at least those middle classes
in town and country who had risen above the subsistence
level of the majority. At the end of 1798, however, except
around the metropolis no concerted effort had been made
by either side to elicit public opinion, and thus to influence
the conduct of Members of Parliament. Many doubted
whether the country, newly emerged from rebellion and still
threatened by invasion, could sustain the excitements of a
full-scale political campaign. It must be remembered that the
Irish nation whose future was debated during the Union
controversy was not to be identified with that section of the
Irish people who had risen in Wicklow and Wexford in May
1798; and it was to be found that the governing minority
could be divided temporarily into the most unexpected
alliances and alignments, without the slightest effect or
interest on the part of the submerged peasantry.

IV

UNION DEFEATED, JANUARY 1799

Yet he (Dr. Johnson) had a kindness for the Irish nation,
and thus generously expressed himself to a gentleman
from that country, on the subject of an UNION which
artful Politicians have often had in view—'Do not make
an union with us, Sir. We should unite with you, only to
rob you. We should have robbed the Scotch, if they had
had any thing of which we could have robbed them.'

JAMES BOSWELL[1]

ON 12 November 1798 the Home Government dispatched to Cornwallis a set of nine draft articles of
Union, compiled after taking advice from a number
of experts on Ireland. Of these the first and third were matters of little controversy. These provided that the kingdoms
would be joined under the name of 'the United Kingdom of
Great Britain and Ireland', that the succession laws would
remain unchanged, and that the privileges of Irish peers
would be modelled on the Scottish precedent. The second
article, concerning the structure of the United Parliament,
was less easy. There was no trouble in deciding that the
British part of both Houses should continue as before, members returned at the 1796 election continuing to act until the
next ordinary general election. The Irish part would 'consist
of Spiritual Lords, Temporal Lords, and Commons, to be
chosen according to an Act to be passed in the Parliament of
Ireland'. But how many of each? Very early in the calculations it was estimated that there were about four million
inhabitants of Ireland to ten million in Great Britain, on
which basis about 108 Irish peers and 223 commoners
should be added to the British Houses—an increase of some
40 per cent.[2] However, putting the Irish population against
the one and a half million of Scotland, it could be argued that

---

[1] J. Boswell, *The Life of Samuel Johnson Ll.D.*, London (Everyman ed.), 1949,
ii, p. 291.
[2] 'Points to be considered . . .' (Lord Lieutenant's *Union Correspondence*).

as Scotland returned 16 peers and 45 commoners, Ireland in proportion might be satisfied with 45 peers and 120 commoners. Even this was considered too great an influx, and the British Cabinet eventually determined that Ireland should be represented by 32 peers (6 of them spiritual) and 100 commoners; although in suggesting these numbers, the Duke of Portland fatuously hoped that the Irish might show their confidence in Britain's good intentions by being contented with less.[1]

This whittling down of the proposed Irish representation was not merely due to a wish to enfeeble Ireland. The Government had good reason to fear that even the introduction of 100 new members into the House of Commons would meet with resistance from their own supporters in Great Britain. The veteran parliamentarian, Lord Liverpool feared (and cited Burke in support of his view) 'that so great an addition to the House of Commons and (what must, I think, be the consequence) a larger room for them to meet in, might have the effect in some degree, of changing the character of our government, by increasing or diminishing the powers of those who now deliver their opinions and take a share in it . . .'.[2] Lord Sheffield was even more bluntly against 'the admission of 100 wild Irish. The intrusion of eighty is rather too much, 75 would be sufficient, the present House of Commons is very trumpery and bad enough. I do not think any of our country gentlemen would venture into parliament if they were to meet 100 Paddies.'[3] On the other hand, the Opposition suspected that the hundred Irish members would swell the influence of Court and minister, becoming a larger edition of Dundas's 'Scotch pack'; and for that reason, they too urged a reduction in the number. Beset from both sides, Portland frequently reminded Cornwallis and Castlereagh that on no account must the Irish representation in the Commons exceed 100.

The selection of this hundred involved much complex calculation. Adequate representation had to be secured for thirty-two counties and 118 boroughs. The simplest

[1] Portland to Cornwallis, 25 Nov. 1798 (H.O. 100/79).
[2] Liverpool to Portland, 16 Nov. 1799 (Add. MSS. 38311).
[3] Sheffield to Auckland, 13 Nov. 1798 (Add. MSS. 34455).

procedure was for each of these constituencies to return one
member to the United Parliament, in lieu of two to the
Dublin legislature, but this was inadmissable as inflicting
150 Irishmen on Westminster. Under-Secretary Cooke's
plans were surprisingly liberal; 'let fifty of the most decayed
boroughs be struck off, and the other one hundred places
send a member each, and where the charters run to sovereign
and burgesses only, extend them to freemen and free holders
of the vicarage'.[1] This idea foundered on Portland's insistence that the Union arrangements should on no account be
made the means of introducing novel schemes of parliamentary reform. The plans considered by the Government in
November 1798 all started from the assumption that each
of the 150 constituencies would return one member each.

Members representing the thirty-two counties and eighteen biggest towns would always sit in the Commons; the
other hundred representatives would select fifty of their
number by ballot, lot, or a system of delegation. Buckingham,
who was in close touch with Grenville, urged that the whole
100 should be chosen at the commencement of each session
by ballot from among the 150, with power of exchange by
consent with those left out. The remaining fifty would be
employed in Ireland on committees on private bills, contested election returns, and other matters not worth the
expense of reference to Westminster. This scheme appeared
to meet the objection that Union would increase administrative costs, and the Government endorsed it as acceptable.
Castlereagh, however, in a sketch put out for public information in January, advocated two members each for
Dublin and Cork, one for eight other large towns and the
thirty-two counties, with the other 108 boroughs each sending one member to alternate Parliaments. He particularly
wished to conciliate Dublin by allowing it two members, and
this point Portland was inclined to concede. The Scottish
precedent of grouping the smaller boroughs by twos or
threes into single constituencies was thought inadvisable,
because the variation in their franchises raised difficulties
over compensating the proprietors.

Scottish precedent also seemed inappropriate for the

[1] Cooke's memorandum (Add. MSS. 34455).

Lords. So many Irish peerages were of recent creation, limited to male heirs and so liable to early extinction, that it was feared that the return of Irish members to the House of Lords might fall into the hands of a small junta: especially if the Scottish custom was observed of electing representative peers at a meeting of all the nobility before each Parliament. On 18 December the British Cabinet decided that the Irish lords should elect their representatives for life. To avoid lobbying and intrigue, vacancies would be filled not by a meeting in Dublin but by postal poll, conducted by the Chief Secretary. Irish peers not elected to the Lords could continue to stand for the House of Commons, although this right would not be extended to Irish seats where their influence might overshadow that of the untitled gentry. As over forty Irish lords were already peers of Great Britain, their representation was not inadequate. The Church of Ireland would be represented by one archbishop and three bishops, chosen in rotation for a term of one year only. Any more permanent tenure might give rise to the evils of absenteeism. The ambitious archbishop of Cashel would have preferred that Ireland should be presented by the four provincial archbishops alone, but he received little encouragement.

These arrangements probably contributed largely to the defeat of the Union proposals in January. County members could scarcely welcome a plan which halved their numbers and exposed them to keener contests at future general elections; and borough proprietors faced a diminution of the value of their property, into which many of them had invested hard cash, and for which they might expect improved prices with the return of stability. It was one of the facts of Irish political life that boroughs were regarded as property, and no provision for compensation was adumbrated in the Union proposals. As Cornwallis wryly told Pitt: 'That every man in this most corrupt country should consider the important question before us in no other point of view than as it may be likely to promote his own private objects of ambition or avarice, will not surprise you. . . .'[1] Some doubted whether 32 lords and 100 commoners were enough to serve

[1] Cornwallis to Pitt, 7 Dec. 1798 (P.R.O. 30/8/326).

Irish interests. There was no convincing answer, apart from English prejudice, to Lord Downshire's view that, on a population basis, 100 lords and 300 commoners were more suitable.[1] Unable to foresee the party discipline of the nineteenth century, many anti-unionists professed themselves fearful that the Irish would have no influence in a House of Commons totalling 658. In the first Union debates Francis Hardy suggested that the 100 Irish members might be further reduced by the ill will of English and Scottish interests in the United Parliament, and skilfully quoted *King Lear* as an analogy to remind his hearers how the hundred knights of that potentate were soon diminished in number.[2] No serious attention seems to have been devoted to the schemes envisaging the separation of Irish members into a first-class category with seats at Westminster, and a second-class group at Dublin, occupied with minor local business of a closely specified description. Nor was much thought given to a federal union between Great Britain and Ireland. This was the more surprising because the American example was frequently cited by unionists as a model of the advantages of closer political ties. One of the most thoughtful anti-unionists, Richard Jebb, advocated limiting the Irish Parliament's powers to local and municipal affairs, and in England Lord Sheffield tentatively suggested something similar, with the Irish Parliament sending seventy or seventy-five delegates to Westminster 'to take part in the great affairs of Empire'.[3] No such arrangement was officially considered; perhaps the British ministry feared that the Opposition would intrigue with even the most circumscribed Dublin legislature.

The fourth and fifth draft articles dealt with religion. All members of the United Parliament were to take the oaths required by law in Great Britain, but subject to such changes as might be made by the United Parliament. This formula skirted Catholic claims without discouraging them; however, the fifth article stated the continuance of the existing Church Establishment to be fundamental. Pitt's British advisers

---

[1] Pitt to Castlereagh, 26 Nov. 1799 (*Castlereagh Correspondence*, iii, p. 11).

[2] *Parl. Reg.*, pp. 58–59.

[3] Richard Jebb, *A Reply to a Pamphlet entitled Arguments for and against an Union*, 2nd ed., Dublin, 1799; also Buckingham to Cooke, 22 Nov. 1798 (C.S.O. 513/73/1), and Cooke to Castlereagh, 18 Dec. 1798 (*Castlereagh Correspondence*, ii, p. 50).

attempted in this article to devise a formula for the commutation of tithes, with compensation to the Church of
Ireland. It was suggested that compensation should be computed on current rent prices, with payment conditional on
the continued residence of the clergy in Ireland, if necessary
under legal compulsions to back the authority of the bishops.
The continuance of a state provision for the Dissenting
clergy, as established by Charles II, and the establishment
of a similar fund for the Roman Catholic priesthood would
not be guaranteed under the articles of union, but left
subject to the goodwill of the Crown, and hence to the good
behaviour of the recipients. None of these speculations
about the post-Union religious settlement was communicated
to Dublin Castle, and the subject formed little part of the
Union debates.

'The greatest difficulty', wrote a Dublin official early in
the discussions, 'seems to arise from the impossibility of
equalizing the systems of Commerce, Revenue, and Debt
in the two countries.'[1] If import duties and excise were
equalized, Ireland's burden would be greatly increased; but
if duties remained on their current footing, English tariffs on
imports from Ireland, one of the long-standing grievances
which Union was designed to obviate, would still continue.
Yet Irish industry called for protection. The unlucky history
of the 1785 commercial propositions had impressed authorities with the difficulty of satisfying all parties. It was a
'luminous' suggestion by Cooke which led to the adoption
of the French tariff of 1786 as the model on which future
Anglo-Irish commercial relations should be based.[2] This was
one ground for Foster's dislike of the Union '. . . for that it
was notorious Lord Auckland had overreached the French
ministry; but that, if a Union were to take place, the propositions of 1785 should be taken as the basis of the commercial arrangement, as the objections in Ireland to the
propositions were only on the score of the constitution, and
not on any inequality of arrangement.'[3]

---

[1] 'Points to be considered . . .' (Lord Lieutenant's *Union Correspondence*).
[2] Castlereagh to Camden, 21 Nov. 1798 (Mt. Stewart MSS.).
[3] Memorandum by R. J. (probably Robert Johnson) in the Mt. Stewart MSS.
(printed in *Castlereagh Correspondence*, iii, p. 180).

The defection of Foster and Parnell from the Administration threw the main burden of shaping the commercial arrangements and piloting them through Parliament on Castlereagh, with some preparatory assistance from Beresford. Pitt's disciple in assuming that 'perfect freedom of trade is an object to contend for',[1] Castlereagh aimed at retaining duties only where required as countervailing tariffs on articles subject to internal duty in Great Britain. Some exception had to be made for such articles as cottons, woollens, silk, and iron manufactures, where the Dublin Parliament had imposed protective tariffs on the import of English produce. To allay the impact of increased competition on Irish manufacturers, Castlereagh planned the retention of protective duties for not more than twenty years from the establishment of the Union; but the maximum duty would be 10 per cent., which, together with the cost of freight over the Irish Sea, was considered sufficient protection for any local industry. As for public revenue, the national debts hitherto incurred would be borne by the respective countries—a point often ignored by the anti-unionists, who claimed that a prosperous Ireland would be obliged to assume Great Britain's vast accumulation of debt. Future expenditure over the next twenty years would be levied in the proportion of 15 : 2 as between Great Britain and Ireland. This proportion was arrived at by comparison of the exports, imports, war-time and 'normal' government expenditures of the two countries.

The British Cabinet had determined that the measure should be introduced into the British and Irish Parliaments simultaneously. The British House of Commons had been adjourned to 22 January 1799, on which day the Irish legislature was also to meet. Identical messages from the King to the British Parliament and from the Lord Lieutenant in his speech from the Throne would recommend the necessity of strengthening Anglo-Irish relations. No specific mention would be made of Union: 'The answer to the communications should be in the first instance quite general', wrote Portland, 'and a day should be fixed for taking the subject into consideration.'[2] On that day, probably 5 February, it was hoped

---

[1] Undated memorandum by Castlereagh (ibid., pp. 188–93).
[2] Portland to Cornwallis, 24 Dec. 1798 (H.O. 100/79).

that joint addresses from both Houses would be procured in each kingdom, requesting the appointment of commissioners to devise a plan of Union. This would follow the successful example of Scotland in 1707; and within six weeks, conferences would begin between the commissioners. From a desire not to deprive the Castle of its few able men of affairs, and from deference to Irish susceptibilities, a delegation from Great Britain would visit Dublin, and on the basis of the plans already outlined work out the articles of union for submission to the two legislatures. Hobart, Pelham, Auckland, and Douglas were mentioned as likely commissioners for Great Britain, and the marquess of Buckingham made no secret of his desire for employment. But these plans were working on the assumption that the draft articles of Union were known only in official circles. As it happened, Irish politicians visiting London found little difficulty in viewing a copy; Robert Johnson, one of Lord Downshire's members, commented derisively: 'I have seen their plan. It goes to scarcely anything. Almost as good a one could be drawn with a burnt stick on a wall.'[1] Because of the difficulty of welding together acceptable compromises on debatable points such as the Catholic question, tithes, and the Irish representation in the United Parliament, there were many loose ends which offered ample scope for anti-unionist propaganda.

As the probable strength of opposition revealed itself in Dublin, many politicians lost their first enthusiasm for Union. As Cornwallis observed: '. . . if those who possess the borough interest believe that the British Government are determined to persevere in the measure of the Union, and that they will be able to carry it, they will afford them the most hearty support; but if they should entertain doubts on either of these points, they will contend for the merit of having been the first to desert.'[2] The beginning of January found the Castle with remarkably little idea of feeling throughout the country. To offset the vocal opposition of Dublin, it was believed that the measure would be supported in the Catholic south and west, both on religious and commercial expectations; although Clare, with his usual bias, believed that the

---

[1] Johnson to Downshire, 6 Dec. 1798 (Downshire MSS.).
[2] Cornwallis to Portland, 24 Dec. 1798 (H.O. 100/79).

Catholics of Limerick had instructions to oppose.[1] Support was also expected from the Presbyterians of Belfast and Londonderry, who in a time of growing prosperity were shifting away from radicalism.[2] The border counties of Ulster, however, where tensions festered from a fairly even balance of Protestants and Catholics, were strongly influenced by Orange Lodges who objected to the prospect of losing the Protestant-dominated Dublin legislature.

Prompted by the influence of Lords Longueville and Donoughmore, the common council of Cork passed resolutions in favour of the Union on 8 January, and addressed a petition 'approved by a great number of the principal residents' to the Government.[3] This provided the Castle with a welcome (and frequently cited) counter to the increasing anti-unionist agitation in the metropolitan area. Dublin county had met on 4 January under the chairmanship of the Sheriff, Alderman Kirkpatrick: 'I do not understand that the attendance was very respectable', commented Castlereagh;[4] but there was no sign of any counter-demonstration. Nor could the Administration produce propaganda as appealing to Dublin public opinion as *The Anti-Union*, a publication modelled on the *Anti-Jacobin*, whose spirited attacks on the scheme appeared three times a week after the middle of December.[5] The anti-unionists scored again at a meeting

[1] Castlereagh to Portland, 9 Jan. 1799 (H.O. 100/85).

[2] Cf. A. T. Q. Stewart, 'Presbyterian Radicalism in Ulster' (M.A. thesis, Queen's University of Belfast). 'Belfast has shown no disinclination, at which some of the violent party in Dublin are not less surprised than indignant' (Cornwallis to Portland, 2 Jan. 1799 (H.O. 100/85)).

[3] Longueville to Castlereagh, 10 Dec. 1798 and 5 Jan. 1799; Donoughmore to Castlereagh, 10 Jan. 1799 (Mt. Stewart MSS.); the latter encloses a copy of the resolutions.

[4] Those present included Sir John Jervis (later a unionist); Robert Leeson, 'a mad and democratic brother of Lord Miltown's'; Arthur Guinness, the brewer; and Joshua Spencer, who had seconded Saurin's motion at the Bar meeting. Henry Grattan was expected, but did not attend (Castlereagh to Portland, 5 Jan. 1799 (H.O. 100/85)).

[5] The whigs had not been hopeful of achieving much publicity. Late in 1798 Grattan wrote to the Revd. Edward Berwick: 'The state of the press is a reason against departing from the principle of secession on the subject of Union. That question will never come before the Parliament of Ireland until it be carried; and if ever there was a mock debate in the Irish Senate, it will be on the subject of Union— no press to publish—a garrison without—and a court majority within' (Grattan, *Life*, iv, p. 420).

of freeholders convened on 14 January in the county of
Louth, immediately north of Dublin, an area where Foster's
influence was great.[1] Here a son-in-law of the earl of Enniskillen, the young lawyer Blayney Balfour concluded a rousing
speech by successfully moving a strong set of anti-unionist
resolutions, allegedly framed by Foster himself. Besides the
customary arguments about the tranquillity of the country
under the existing régime, the likely increase of taxation and
absenteeism under Union, and the incompetence of Parliament to pass such an Act, these resolutions included the
rather ominous assertion: '. . . that if an Union be enacted
by the legislation of this Kingdom, either contrary to or
without the advice of the assembled freeholders and burgesses,
the submission of the people of Ireland thereto will be a
matter of prudence, and not of duty.'[2] Because of Foster's
influence, the result of this meeting was a foregone conclusion; but it had been necessary to call it in order to make
up the mind of his colleague for the county, William Charles
Fortescue. Believing the available information about the
terms of Union to be insufficient, Fortescue had announced
his intention of modelling his conduct on the instructions of
his constituents.[3] In several other counties, although the
local members had declined to express definite opinions on
Union until they could 'consult their friends' it was decided
—as in Armagh and Longford—to defer public discussions
until the outcome of the struggle in Parliament was known.[4]

By now it was time to marshal parliamentary support. On
7 January Castlereagh sent a circular letter to all members of
the Irish House of Commons: 'I am directed by my Lord
Lieutenant to acquaint you that business of the greatest
importance will be submitted to Parliament on the first day
of the session, and his Excellency trusts that it will suit your

---

[1] Cornwallis to Portland, 26 Dec. 1798 (H.O. 100/85). Foster built up his
standing in Louth by use of his patronage as Speaker. The anti-unionist meeting
was convened by McClintock, Serjeant-at-Arms to the House of Commons, whose
deputy, Henry Coddington, was co-proprietor of the borough of Dunleer with
Foster.

[2] Resolutions included in Castlereagh to Portland, 16 Jan. 1799 (H.O. 100/85).
Buckingham to Grenville, 18 Jan. 1799 (*H.M.C. Dropmore MSS*. iv, p. 445).

[3] Fortescue to Castlereagh, 4 Jan. 1799 (Mt. Stewart MSS.).

[4] The Revd. Nathaniel Alexander to Castlereagh, 17 Jan. 1799; Longford to
Castlereagh, 10 and 19 Jan. 1799 (ibid.).

convenience to be in town previous to that time when I shall hope to have an opportunity of communicating with you upon the measures to be brought forward.'[1] This sort of government whipping-in was a portentous innovation, and although intended to cement the solidarity of the Government's supporters, probably had an opposite effect. Several independent-minded members felt restive at being committed in advance. Prudent magnates and members, reflecting that this would be the last opportunity ever of exercising their parliamentary influence to procure favours and titles, became shy of giving themselves away too cheaply. No more sensitive barometer of parliamentary fortunes could be found than that accomplished trimmer the earl of Ely, head of a numerous and parsimonious family, whose inadequate estates in Wexford and Fermanagh were eked out with the proceeds from the judicious management of a ten-man phalanx in the House of Commons. In November the earl had been an enthusiast for Union, 'relying on the favour of the Crown in an object personal to himself'.[2] A month later he went to London, and at the end of the year, Portland reported: 'He professed to have formed no opinion respecting the Union, *of course*, intimated many doubts, and affected ignorance; and I am certainly not authorized to say more than that he is not averse from being *convinced* of the propriety of the measure.'[3] On 7 January Ely wrote to Castlereagh (and subsequently informed the duke of Portland in conversation) that he had not heard one argument for the utility or necessity of Union, and piously remarked: 'God grant that his mad scheme may not go too far for all the projectors of it to appease!'[4] It was also reported that he intended to return Henry Luttrell for a vacancy at Clonmines. Luttrell, like his father the earl of Carhampton, was a vociferous anti-unionist.[5] Cornwallis

---

[1] *Castlereagh Correspondence*, ii, p. 82.

[2] Cornwallis to Portland, 27 Nov. 1798 (H.O. 100/79).

[3] Portland to Castlereagh, 31 Dec. 1798 (Mt. Stewart MSS.).

[4] Ely to Castlereagh, 7 Jan. 1799 (Mt. Stewart MSS.).

[5] (Ibid.); Cornwallis to Portland, 11 Jan. 1799 (H.O. 100/85). The vacancy at Clonmines had arisen when Ely quarrelled with his niece's husband, Luke Fox, M.P. since 1797, and had compelled him to vacate his seat by accepting an escheatorship (Ely to Castlereagh, 9 Jan. 1799 (Mt. Stewart MSS.)). Jonah Barrington (*Rise and Fall of the Irish Nation*, 1834 ed., pp. 297–9) claims that Fox attended the first night of the Union debates, found himself inadvertently on the anti-union side during

wrote Ely a letter 'to explain very clearly to him that he will not be allowed to shuffle on this occasion',[1] and urbanely informed that shifty nobleman: '. . . your opposition to a proceeding so reasonable in itself . . . would be considered by the King's servants in both countries as an absolute separation on the part of your Lordship and your friends from all connection with His Majesty's Government—an event which would be an equal subject of regret to me in my private and public situation.'[2] This ultimatum was sent to Portland, to be communicated to Ely if he remained uncommitted; but it is uncertain whether it ever reached him. His vacillations in a crisis were well known to such old acquaintances as John Beresford, who commented: 'By his discourses I conceive him hostile, but he is to be come at in the old way.'[3] Camden, who knew his Irish politicians, secured Ely two interviews with Pitt; and when on 17 January Ely set out for Ireland, the latter reported that 'he professes to go *quite unprejudiced*, but is apparently very well disposed; and, I rather hope, has made up his mind to support'.[4] It seemed that Ely would certainly favour the initial question, that of taking the subject of Union into consideration, even though his subsequent conduct would be less predictable.[5] In the event, even this was to prove too great a strain on his reliability.

Another uncommitted element was the eight-member following of the marquess of Downshire. Almost constantly resident in England, Downshire had visited Ireland only once in the three years before the Union debates—for one week in December 1798—and his information about Irish affairs was mainly derived from such sources as his agent

a division, and, to avoid voting against the Government, said he had taken the escheatorship; which he was subsequently granted, in order to cover his story. Lecky repeats this yarn. Unfortunately it can be completely disproved by the evidence: Fox's escheatorship was promised a fortnight before the opening of Parliament. The story does not appear in the 1809–13 edition of Barrington's work; instead there is a panegyric on Fox's ability and honesty (p. 19).

[1] Cornwallis to Portland, 13 Jan. 1799 (H.O. 100/85).

[2] Cornwallis to Ely, 13 Jan. 1799 (*Cornwallis Correspondence*, iii, p. 37).

[3] Beresford to Auckland, 12 Jan. 1799 (Add. MSS. 34455).

[4] Camden to Castlereagh, 15 Jan. 1799 (*Castlereagh Correspondence*, ii, p. 111): 'I collected from Mr. Pitt that he gave Lord Ely to understand his objects would be attended to.' (Cf. Pitt to Castlereagh, 17 Jan. 1799 (op. cit. ii, p. 116).)

[5] Beresford to Auckland, 19 Jan. 1799 (Add. MSS. 34455).

Thomas Lane, and his M.P.s, particularly Colonel Robert Ross and Robert Johnson.[1] These men were bigoted Protestants, bitterly critical of Cornwallis's policy of lenity, and given to alarmist reports of unrest and discontent. Downshire had no great cause for friendship with Castlereagh. The latter had entered politics by opposing him for county Down in 1790; there had been some difficulty between them over a monetary transaction early in 1796;[2] and even after Camden had persuaded them to co-operate, their relations were polite rather than cordial. It was hardly surprising that Downshire showed great reluctance to support a measure which would curtail his patronage.[3] For the moment, however, he confined his opposition to criticizing the untimeliness of Union: 'I confess I can see nothing but dire confusion and calamity to arise from the pushing it at this moment, far greater than any advantage that can result from the measure. I believe the Govt. are very little aware of our situation. . . .'[4] In this opinion he continued throughout the three weeks preceding the Union debates, and not even the persuasion of Pitt could shake him from the notion that the measure was ill-timed: 'I look for rebellion or separation as the consequence', he wrote to Castlereagh, 'which God forbid, but these are not times for speculative experiments to be made in Ireland.'[5] Constant reports of the inertia of the Government and the strength of the Opposition reached him from Johnson, although the M.P. for Hillsborough was against trying to block the measure, on the grounds that 'it cannot be done without assistance here probably more formidable as friends than as enemies'.[6] As yet Downshire refrained from coming to Ireland or giving his members any instructions about their votes. But Castlereagh took assurance from Camden, who

---

[1] Downshire MSS., *passim.*

[2] Lane to Downshire, 16 Feb. 1796 (Downshire MSS. 608/635). The details of the contretemps are meagre, but it appears that Castlereagh had borrowed £1,000 from the Downshire estate; and when Downshire's agent wished to raise the interest to 6 per cent., Castlereagh insisted on six months' notice before consenting.

[3] Cooke to Auckland, 15 July 1799 (Add. MSS. 34455).

[4] Downshire to Castlereagh, 30 Dec. 1798 (Mt. Stewart MSS.).

[5] Same to same, 14 Jan. 1799 (ibid.).

[6] Johnson to Downshire, 5 Jan. 1799; cf. same to same, 8, 12, and 13 Jan. 1799, and Richard Annesley to Downshire, 5 and 12 Jan. 1799 (Downshire MSS.).

H

wrote: 'I hear his conversation is hostile, and yet, when he understands that Ministers make a point of carrying the question, I doubt not he will support them.'[1]

No good was done for the prospects of Union by the wavering of Ely and Downshire, two magnates whose support of the Government was normally unquestioned. On 11 January, Cornwallis wrote to Portland: '. . . a very unfavourable impression has been made within the last two days against the Union, partly by the arrival of the Speaker, but still more by its being generally circulated and believed in town that both Lord Downshire and Lord Ely are adverse to the measure. . . . It not only transfers 18 votes in the Commons to the Opposition, but strikes a damp among the supporters of the measure which may operate in a fatal extent against us.'[2] In fact the defection of major interests from the Government was greater than this. As Beresford subsequently pointed out, there was no reason to expect the adherence of such ultra-Protestant noblemen as Enniskillen, Belmore, and Kingston, who had taken offence at the conduct of Cornwallis's Government during and after the insurrection.[3] Doubt also surrounded the interest of the marquess of Donegall. Equally dominated by a young wife of pronounced Opposition views and an agent, Sir Charles Talbot, whose gratitude had recently been earned by Camden with the promise of an English baronetcy, Donegall had the largest rent-roll of any peer in Ireland and influenced at least three Members of Parliament. His death on 15 January 1799 increased the uncertainty, but there is some slight evidence to suggest that Castlereagh expected his members to support.[4]

If the Castle's relations with major borough owners were in so uncertain a condition, they were no better equipped to manage the smaller fry. Pelham in his last year or two of

---

[1] Camden to Portland, 15 Jan. 1799 (*Castlereagh Correspondence*, ii, p. 111).

[2] Cornwallis to Portland, 11 Jan. 1799 (H.O. 100/85).

[3] Camden to Portland, 2 Jan. 1798; Portland to Camden, 8 Jan. 1798 (H.O. 100/75); cf. *H.M.C. Rep. XIII*, appendix iii, p. 566.

[4] In no calculations prior to 22 Jan. are Lord Donegall's members included among those likely to oppose. It is certain that Castlereagh expected the support of William Skeffington, M.P. for Antrim borough, with whom Donegall was believed to have influence (Pole to Mornington, 20 Mar. 1799 (Add. MSS. 37308)).

office had been too much occupied with maintaining the peace of the country to worry about maintaining a good name in patronage matters, and Cornwallis and Castlereagh had done nothing to recover the ground lost. As Beresford grumbled: 'Where there was no sort of communication, either convivial or on business, with gentlemen previous to bringing forward this measure, how could it be expected that there could be an advantageous commencement of negotiation in the first instance, and that, too, carried on by two men neither of whom are well adapted for the purpose?'[1] Now that the Government found itself in need of votes, it was at the mercy of every petty politician with an axe to grind. 'The demands of our friends rise in proportion to the appearance of strength on the other side', Cornwallis observed shortly before the opening of Parliament.[2] Among the replies to his circular requesting the attendance of members, Castlereagh was to receive answers such as that of Henry Coddington, M.P. for Dunleer. Emphasizing that he was as yet undecided over the consequences of Union for Ireland, Coddington continued: 'I shall take an opportunity of waiting on you according to your desire, but at the same time cannot help expressing my surprize that any degree of attachment to Administration should be expected from a man who after having showed such unremitting attention as I and my son have done for upwards of sixteen years, was refused so small a favor as the reversion of a living of £400 a year for my son.'[3] Coddington had supported the Government since 1783; but as Deputy Serjeant of Arms he owed something to the patronage of his neighbour in county Louth, the Speaker, and he turned anti-unionist. Sir John Tydd, Paymaster of Corn Premiums, was aggrieved because the Government had not fulfilled an old promise made in Lord Westmoreland's time to return him for their borough of Clogher, but had instead left him to purchase a seat at Fore.[4] He pointedly absented himself throughout the Union debates. Lord Cahir excused his opposition 'being well aware

---

[1] Beresford to Auckland, 6 Feb. 1799 (*Beresford Correspondence*, ii, pp. 211–12).
[2] Cornwallis to Ross, 21 Jan. 1799 (*Cornwallis Correspondence*, iii, p. 39).
[3] Coddington to Castlereagh, 6 Jan. 1799 (Mt. Stewart MSS.).
[4] Tydd to Pelham, 11 May 1798 (Add. MSS. 33105).

of what every man in my situation must give up, should it be carried'.[1]

For every politician who considered the Union in terms of national interest, there were others—not surprisingly in Ireland at the close of the eighteenth century—who translated its effects into terms of personal benefits; and for such it was necessary for Cornwallis and Castlereagh to dabble in 'patronage'. Not without distaste, Cornwallis secured from Portland late in December a free hand to enter into 'any engagements deemed necessary or expedient to carry the Union', for it was stated that 'the conduct of individuals upon this subject will be considered as the test of the disposition to support the King's government'.[2] The extent of the Government's use of influence to pass the Union was the subject of excited comment from Jonah Barrington as early as the first night of the parliamentary session (22–23 January). Of Castlereagh, he claimed that 'corrupt and unconstitutional means had been used by the noble lord to individuals of the Irish Parliament', and went on to assert: 'Peerages (as was rumoured) were bartered for the rights of minors and . . . if this was true, it encroached the Constitution, and if the Executive overstept its bounds, the people are warranted to do the same on their part. . . .'[3] The charge was echoed by Plunket: '. . . within these last six weeks a system of black corruption has been carried on within the walls of the Castle which would disgrace the annals of the worst period of the history of either country. . . .'[4] The assertion that peerages were used to buy votes has been made frequently since. But family traditions have exaggerated the size of the inducements offered to anti-unionists for changing sides. Thus it is related that Arthur French (M.P. for county Roscommon) and Charles Kendal Bushe (M.P. for the boroughs of Callan and Donegal) refused earldoms for their vote and that

---

[1] Cahir to Castlereagh, 19 Jan. 1799 (Mt. Stewart MSS.).

[2] Portland to Cornwallis, 24 Dec. 1798 (H.O. 100/79).

[3] *Parl. Reg.*, 22–23 Jan. 1799 (p. 28). Barrington's assertion that 'peerages were bartered for the rights of minors' is nonsense. There were two borough-owning minors in Ireland at that time, Lord Riversdale (whose trustees sold the seats for Rathcormuck) and Henry Bruen, Junior (whose mother returned the members for Duleek and Taghmon). Neither received any honours or emoluments for their family's support of the Union.

[4] Ibid., pp. 48–49.

Viscount Powerscourt could have been promoted to marquess.[1] Yet it was a settled rule of George III's ministers that nobody should be advanced more than one step in the peerage at any time; and the rule was strictly maintained throughout the whole of the struggle to pass the Union.[2] Besides, common sense would suggest that if earldoms were to be bestowed for individual unionist votes, most members would demand one and the honour would be inordinately cheapened.

In the generation before 1799 most Irish peerages granted for parliamentary services went either to the owners of boroughs or to county members of long standing and good estate. Not even at the times of greatest crisis, such as 1780, 1782, or 1789 had Dublin Castle bought individual votes with peerages. If only from self-interest, it was Government policy to keep up the value of honours as much as possible.[3] During the winter of 1798–9, there is definite evidence for the promise of two peerages, and circumstantial details suggesting the offer of two others; and this is all. Castlereagh, who as Chief Secretary handled patronage dealings for the Castle, was sanguine of a decisive victory in Parliament, and in such circumstances there was no need for the Government to be prodigal of honours. Sir John Blaquiere, who had settled in Ireland after a successful term as Chief Secretary (1772–7) had no borough influence, but his reputation as a good host made him a most useful contact man for the Government. He had recently taken a foremost part in dissuading the English militia units from withdrawing from voluntary service in Ireland, and it was for this as much as for 'the hospitable meetings of Members at his house'[4] that Cornwallis recommended his wife for a peerage. Henry

---

[1] *Cornwallis Correspondence*, iii, p. 50; footnote by the editor C. Ross; E. Œ. Somerville and M. Ross, *An Incorruptible Irishman*, London, 1938, p. 106.

[2] Baroness Dufferin (mother of Sir James Blackwood, M.P. and owner of Killyleagh borough) 'solicited to be created originally a Viscountess, which was declined, as it was not intended to recommend any person for two steps in the first instance— No promise was give as to future promotion and this fact is only here stated in case her Ladyship should hereafter desire that her claim may be considered'. (Memorandum on honours in Lord Lieutenant's *Union Correspondence*, Nat. Lib. Ireland.)

[3] Camden to Portland, 8 July 1797 (H.O. 100/70). Grenville to Carysfort, 7 Jan. 1799 (*H.M.C. Dropmore MSS.* iv, p. 436) indicates that only two Irish lords were intended to get English peerages.

[4] Cornwallis to Portland, 4 Jan. 1799 (H.O. 100/85).

Moore Sandford, who owned and represented Roscommon borough, offered the second seat for that constituency to a nominee of the Lord Lieutenant 'if a request lately made should be complied with'. The vacancy was created by the retirement of his brother George Sandford, who had gone to reside permanently in England; and it was suggested that George Sandford's employment as Barrack-Master of Dublin could profitably be conferred on Thomas Newenham, one of Lord Mount Cashel's members, who was believed to differ from his anti-unionist patron.[1] The Government put up for the seat William Johnson, one of the few lawyers whose pen and tongue were employed on the side of Union.[2] In July 1800 the owner of the borough was created Baron Mount Sandford with remainder to his brothers, as he had desired.

Although there is no evidence for it in the official records, family tradition asserts that a peerage was offered to Sir John Blackwood, M.P. and owner of the borough of Killyleagh. It was a fair try, as Sir John, after almost thirty years of constant opposition, was known to have asked some years earlier to be created a viscount.[3] As he was a borough owner, there is perhaps less reason to reject the story than others of the same nature.[4] The same consideration applies to John

---

[1] H. M. Sandford to Castlereagh, 12 Jan. 1799; the nature of the request is elicited in Cornwallis to Castlereagh, 16 Jan. 1799 (Mt. Stewart MSS.). In the latter, Cornwallis says: 'I promised Mr. Sandford to let him know whether there was a possibility of his getting the peerage in the manner he desired (viz. for himself with remainder to his two brothers) before the meeting of Parliament. May I venture to give him reason to expect it? after the scolding I have received about Blaquiere, I am afraid of being again reprehended for exposing the weakness of Government.' This sounds as if Blaquiere and Sandford were the only two members recommended for peerages before the Union debates.

[2] He was brother to Robert Johnson, Lord Downshire's M.P. for Hillsborough; Third Serjeant 1813; Second Serjeant 1814; Prime Serjeant 1816; Justice of Common Pleas 1817.

[3] Hobart to Hillsborough, 3 Apr. 1790: 'Sir John Blackwood's Viscountcy is totally impossible' (Downshire MSS., D.O.D. 607/335a).

[4] Sir Jonah Barrington (op. cit., p. 294, 1834 ed.) and Henry Grattan, jnr. (*Life*, iv, p. 432) have got hold of a story in which Castlereagh tempts Sir John Blackwood and is kicked out of the house by the irate baronet. Lyall (op. cit., p. 3.) writes: ' "Your crest", said an emissary from the Castle, who was examining the plate on his dinner table, "is a very pretty one, but would be improved by a coronet." "The motto", replied Sir John, "*per vias rectas*, has escaped your notice." ' Lyall, however, also asserts that Blackwood died in the act of setting out to vote against the Union: his death was on 27 Feb. 1799, five weeks after the divisions.

Bingham, owner and member for Tuam, whose barony was forecast at least as early as February 1799.[1] But the ennoblement of borough proprietors such as Sandford, Blackwood, and Bingham, or a veteran supporter like Blaquiere was much more in keeping with contemporary practice than the 'black corruption' hinted (but never specified) by Plunket and Barrington and subsequently accepted by nationalist historians. It was only after the defeat of January 1799, when the difficulty of securing a majority became apparent, that the scramble for emoluments began.

Meanwhile, the Administration needed to discipline the faltering among its own ranks. With Foster hostile, Parnell very uncertain, and Beresford still absent in England, a lukewarm attitude to Union was especially noticeable in the Boards of Treasury and Revenue, where the conduct of Ely and Downshire was giving rise to defeatism.[2] Cornwallis determined to proceed first with the Chancellor of the Exchequer, Sir John Parnell. After delaying his return from England, Parnell still tried to sit on the fence: the line he took with Cornwallis was that 'of withholding . . . his approbation from the principle of the measure, and merely promising acquiescence in case every thing went smooth'.[3] Accordingly on 15 January the Chancellor of the Exchequer was dismissed, and his place given to Isaac Corry, M.P. for Newry. Six days later, it was the turn of the Prime Serjeant, James Fitzgerald. No other dismissals occurred before the opening of Parliament on 22 January, although doubts were entertained of Thomas Burgh, Secretary to the Treasury, and the Speaker's brother-in-law; John Claudius Beresford, Inspector-General of Imports and Exports; and George Knox and Thomas Foster, Commissioners of Revenue. Burgh eventually voted for the Union. The cases of Beresford

---

[1] Johnson to Downshire, 19 Feb. 1799: 'I hear a Mr. Bingham (Yelverton's son-in-law) is to be a peer. Bingham is a ruffian in his manners, so I wish your Lordships joy of him.'

[2] Cornwallis to Portland, 11 Jan. 1799 (H.O. 100/85). Johnson described John Monck Mason, a commissioner of the Treasury, as pessimistic and reported Toler, the Attorney-General, 'in some alarm, as he fears he will be obliged to speak almost alone' (Johnson to Downshire, 12 Jan. 1799; and cf. same to same, 13 Jan. 1799 (Downshire MSS.)).

[3] Castlereagh to Portland, 16 Jan. 1799 (H.O. 100/85). Cf. Cornwallis to Parnell, 15 Jan. 1799 (in possession of Parnell's descendant, Lord Congleton).

and Knox were particularly embarrassing to the Government, as each was connected with an important faction supporting the Union—respectively those of Lords Waterford and Abercorn. Consistency demanded their dismissal, but it would have been foolhardy to offend their patrons. Both officials within a few days handed in their resignations, and thus eased the dilemma of a Government with whose ideas apart from Union, they were mainly in sympathy.[1]

It was the measure of Castlereagh's inexperience that, on the day before Parliament assembled, he was still convinced that the Government had a clear majority on the Union question. As early as 5 January it had come to his knowledge that the Opposition were claiming that 113 members would be found to resist even a proposal for taking the measure into consideration. This number included the Speaker and three of the revenue commissioners.[2] Shrewd old John Beresford saw well enough what this meant. On 12 January he wrote to his friend Auckland: 'My letters say that the opposition to the Union brag that they have 114 pledged, if so we shall be beaten.' However, his own estimate was 133 for and 102 against Union.[3] Castlereagh seems mainly to have relied on that experienced aide Cooke, who put the margin wider, with the Union majority at 146 to 91.[4] On the eve of the opening of Parliament, Castlereagh informed the Home Secretary: 'I am not enabled to form a very accurate statement of numbers. There is a considerable body still undecided: we reckon from 160 to 170 with us, if they attend. Mr. Cooke thinks the Opposition can muster 100 certain, if they assemble. The Speaker is active and appears sanguine.'[5] Cornwallis, whose habitual caution at times reached downright pessimism, was more guarded: 'We think ourselves tolerably strong as to numbers, but so little confidence is to be placed in professions, and people change their opinions

---

[1] Cornwallis to Portland, 25 Jan. 1799 (H.O. 100/85); Beresford to Auckland, 25 Jan. 1799 (*Beresford Correspondence*, ii, p. 198).

[2] Castlereagh to Portland, 5 Jan. 1799 (H.O. 100/85).

[3] Beresford to Auckland, 12 Jan. and 24 Jan. 1799 (Add. MSS. 34455).

[4] Cooke to Auckland, 23 Jan. 1799 (ibid.).

[5] Castlereagh to Portland, 21 Jan. 1799 (H.O. 100/85). Castlereagh at first wrote that he expected '170 to 180' supporters, but deleted this figure for a slightly more modest estimate.

here with so little ceremony, that no man who knows them can feel quite at ease on that subject.'[1] Indeed, even on Castlereagh's estimate, an opposition of 100 members represented a more formidable desertion from the Administration than at any time since just after the Regency showdown. Yet his optimism prevailed even through the first long, heated debate of 22–23 January; just before the division at which the Government was to scrape home by a majority of one, he was heard to assure William Skeffington (who, incidentally, voted for opposition) that 'we should carry the division by 45'.[2]

On 20 January the anti-unionists assembled at the home of the aged and respected ex-Speaker Pery, and there planned their strategy. Pery advised against contesting the Address, but to await a more specific proposal of Union before showing their hand.[3] The younger members rejected this counsel, and strengthened by the return to Parliament of the Ponsonbys and their allies, prepared to do battle immediately Parliament met on the afternoon of 22 January. The Lord Lieutenant's Speech from the Throne made no mention of Union. Its phrasing ran:

> The unremitting industry with which our enemies persevere in their avowed design of endeavouring to effect a separation of this kingdom from Great Britain must have engaged your particular attention; and His Majesty commands me to express his anxious hope that this consideration, joined to the sentiment of mutual affection and common interest, may dispose the Parliaments in both kingdoms to provide the most effectual means of maintaining and improving a connexion essential to their common security, and of consolidating, as far as possible, into one firm and lasting fabrick, the strength, the power, and the resources of the British Empire.[4]

As soon as the Address had been read, attack was joined by that veteran parliamentary tactician George Ponsonby, who contended that Castlereagh should be made to vacate his seat and seek re-election, as by becoming Chief Secretary he had

[1] Cornwallis to Portland, 21 Jan. 1799 (H.O. 100/85).
[2] Wellesley Pole to Mornington, 14 Mar. 1799 (Add. MSS. 37308).
[3] Castlereagh to Portland, 21 Jan. 1799 (H.O. 100/85).
[4] *Reports of the Debate in the House of Commons in Ireland on Tuesday and Wednesday, 22nd and 23rd of January 1799, on the Subject of an Union* (Moore, 1799), p. 1. All extracts from this debate and that of 24–25 Jan. are from this text.

accepted an office of profit under the Crown. This objection was pursued over a debate of some hours, but since its main purpose seems to have been that of harassing the inexperienced Chief Secretary, Ponsonby at length withdrew without pressing for a division.

It was planned that the Address-in-Reply should be moved by two county members—the earl of Tyrone, one of the Beresfords, and Lord Shannon's follower, Colonel Robert Fitzgerald.[1] In hopes of avoiding any controversy on the Union on the first day of the session, Tyrone was careful to state, in moving an address of thanks to the Lord Lieutenant: 'The address does not pledge the House in its decision upon that great and important question which now so much occupies and interests the public mind. As to the measure of a Union between Great Britain and Ireland, I at present can give no opinion; it would be to prejudge and anticipate that which is of so much weight, nor can I fairly decide upon it until it shall come regularly in detail and discussion before the House. . . .'[2] The plea went unheeded. At once Sir John Parnell intimated the intention of the anti-unionists to secure the scheme's immediate rejection: '. . . the measure having been publicly avowed and introduced by a side wind into the speech, I shall oppose it *in limine* as being a question simple in its nature and on which no further information is necessary, than to show that we are called on to put an end to the existence of an Irish Parliament.'[3] In his speech Parnell argued the case against the Union with a common-sense cogency which was to be all too infrequent in the debate that followed. He deplored a constitutional change which would diminish the number of the people's representatives and submit them to a British majority with different local interests. It was, he maintained, fallacious to expect commercial benefits from Union. The trade lost to Dublin might go, not to Cork or Waterford, but to some English port such as Liverpool. The increased absenteeism of landlords and Members of Parliament would diminish the trade in luxury articles,

---

[1] Fitzgerald (1756–1808) was brother of Sir Thomas Judkin Fitzgerald, the notorious High Sheriff of Tipperary, and son-in-law of John Beresford; M.P. for co. Cork 1797–1806; member of the Board of Ordnance 1798–1801.

[2] *Parl. Reg.*, pp. 6–7.

[3] Ibid., p. 8.

and would not improbably lead to a fall in land prices, which had steadily risen over the last twenty years. Religious difficulties would not be solved: 'Will the Catholic and Protestant mind be satisfied by each party ceasing to have a Parliament within the reach of its approbation?' demanded Parnell, with adroit impartiality. As for the British connexion, it had always been supported by the loyalty of the Dublin Parliament; moreover, it had hitherto been the policy of the Government, of which he had long been a member, to eschew unnecessary change, especially at times of disturbance.

This keynote speech was followed up by George Ponsonby, who moved as an amendment to the Lord Lieutenant's address the addition of the following words to the paragraph about strengthening the Anglo-Irish connexion: '. . . maintaining, however, the undoubted birthright of the people of Ireland to have a resident and independent legislature, such as it was recognized by the British Legislature in 1782, and was finally settled at the adjustment of all differences between the two countries.' The ensuing debate, contrary to the intentions of the Government, centred exclusively on the Union and lasted sixteen hours. In the view of the ministerialists, its unprecedented turbulence was remarkable. Castlereagh wrote: '. . . the country gentlemen, as if they had been engaged in a fox-hunt, instead of a debate, on a most momentous question, seemed to contend who should indulge most loudly in an outcry, too frequently unconstitutional.'[1] While according to John Beresford, who had nearly forty years' experience of the House: 'I never was witness to such a scene: you would have thought that you were in a Polish diet. Direct treason spoken, resistance to the law declared, encouraged and recommended. I never heard such vulgarity and barbarism. I cannot bring myself to repeat what was said and done.'[2] From the report of the debate, which is abridged in places,[3] it would seem that the anti-unionists,

---

[1] Castlereagh to Portland, 29 Jan. 1799 (H.O. 100/85).

[3] Beresford to Auckland, 24 Jan. 1799 (*Beresford Correspondence*, ii, p. 195).

[2] Many of the less prominent speakers are reported in a very summary form, and there is some confusion in the arrangement. For instance, James Moore O'Donel refutes the Attorney-General's arguments from historical parallels some pages *before* the Attorney-General's speech (pp. 74–76 and 78–79). The reporters show a suspicion of anti-unionist bias. Castlereagh's speech is partly condensed into note

supported as they were by the majority of legal talent, had the more eloquent and effective spokesmen. Several of the uncommitted independent members, such as Richard Lovell Edgeworth, claimed to have made up their minds against the Union on the strength of the arguments adduced during the debate: so that Isaac Corry complained that 'towards the end, it became the fashion to run in to the opposition'.[1] Both sides went in for a good deal of repetition. From the anti-unionist speakers there were some fine, impassioned bursts of rhetoric on love of country; the unionists were always on the defensive, and less effective. For the most part their speakers refrained from advocacy of the measure, and merely requested that the House would give the question mature consideration before deciding whether to accept or reject it.[2]

Castlereagh's presentation of the unionist case was unfortunate. In reviewing the Anglo-Irish connexion established by the 1782 agreement, he employed language which, however realistic, was quite unpalatable to the fervent nationalist mood of many of his hearers:

What was the price of connexion at present with Great Britain? A military establishment far beyond our natural means to support, and for which we are indebted to Great Britain, who is also obliged to guarantee our public loans. You talk of national pride and independance, but where is the solidity of this boast? . . . the greater country must lead— the lesser naturally follow, and must be practically subordinate in imperial concerns—but this necessary and beneficial operation of the general will must be preceded by establishing one common interest.[3]

Ireland's reliance for defence on Great Britain was also stressed by Charles Coote,[4] while E. A. McNaghten argued that Union would make Great Britain more careful of

form (p. 45) and the concluding part of Denis Browne's speech is summarized (probably with justice) as 'some further observations on the subject not very remarkable for their novelty or application' (p. 108). Charles Osborne's speech is reported in three lines (p. 54) which nowhere mention arguments of his later dissected by the anti-unionist Francis Hardy (p. 55). Many of the speeches against the Union had full coverage (e.g. Plunket, Dobbs, Barrington, Hardy, Francis Knox *et al.*).

[1] Isaac Corry to Auckland, 24 Jan. 1799 (Add. MSS. 34455). R. L. Edgeworth, *Memoirs*, ii, p. 243 (ed. of 1820); cf. remarks of Francis Dobbs (*Parl. Reg.*, p. 37); and Griffith to Pelham, 24 Jan. 1799 (Add. MSS. 33106).

[2] e.g. Isaac Corry (p. 63); Sir Thomas Newcomen (p. 78); Richard Archdall (p. 80).

[3] pp. 43–45.   [4] pp. 65–66.

Ireland's interests.[1] Members from the Catholic west and south, such as the Knight of Kerry[2] and Richard Martin[3] expressed the hope that the United Parliament might be free from local prejudices and amenable to religious tolerance. All these arguments postulated a recognition of the shortcomings of the Irish Parliament, and this was precisely what the Opposition refused to concede. The Attorney-General, Toler, twitted the Ponsonbys for being so active in the defence of a legislature which two years previously they had left in disgust at its refusal to accept reform or to reflect adequately the national will.[4] To this George Ponsonby replied that his faith in the Dublin Parliament had been renewed by its unexpected spirit in resisting subversion by Great Britain.[5]

The central plank of the anti-unionist platform was a stark denial of the right of the Irish Parliament to negotiate the Union. It was held that by passing this measure, Parliament would dissolve the contractual basis of Irish polity. This was expressed most eloquently by Plunket: 'Sir, I in most express terms deny the competency of Parliament to do this act. I warn you, do not dare to lay your hand as you are, you pass this act, it will be a mere nullity, and that no man in Ireland will be bound to obey it . . . if you do so, your act is a dissolution of the Government, you resolve society into its original elements, and no man in the land is bound to obey you.'[6] Several speakers pertinently maintained that Parliament had received no mandate from the people to negotiate a Union, but this led to some inconsistency: for while Alexander Crookshank maintained that 'Parliament could not transfer its trust to another kingdom without permission of its constituents, expressly or implicitly given',[7] Francis Hardy took the view that '. . . if more than half the counties in Ireland petitioned in favour of a Union, I think that this House could not, consistently with its strict duty, attend to such petitions. The people have no right to demand the abolition of their own independent legislature, either totally or in part.'[8] Most of the speakers, such as Colonel Archdall, M.P. for co. Fermanagh[9] and John Egan, M.P. for Tallagh[10] dealt

[1] pp. 24-25.   [2] pp. 16-17.   [3] p. 73.   [4] p. 78.
[5] pp. 90-91; 105-7.   [6] p. 49.   [7] p. 21.   [8] p. 60.
[9] p. 27.   [10] p. 133.

with this point by claiming that their constituents would be adverse to Union, and that, until definitely requested by their electors, they would have no right to consider the scheme. John Claudius Beresford, however, who represented the city of Dublin, subscribed to the views expressed by Burke at Bristol: 'In my opinion', said Beresford, 'a member of parliament is by no means bound to an implicit obedience to the instructions he receives from his constituents.'[1] Nevertheless, he added, if he had been a unionist, he would have explained his sentiments to his anti-unionist electorate and then resigned his seat.

Burke was more usually cited by the anti-unionists to support their doctrine that the Irish Parliament was incompetent to relinquish its sovereignty.[2] The example of Scotland, which might appear to prove the contrary, was dismissed: 'I never desire to be annihilated by precedent', commented Francis Hardy.[3] Instead of impugning the constitutional validity of the Anglo-Scottish union, most speakers who touched this point concentrated on attacking the means by which it had been procured and the alleged disadvantages later suffered by Scotland—including two Jacobite rebellions. Late in the debate of 23 January, William Smith, a young lawyer hitherto prominent in opposition, but now a unionist, roundly asserted that 'Parliament is as competent to conclude an Union, as it is to enact a turnpike bill'.[4] But the anti-unionists continued to assert the changelessness of the constitution, and some argued that Parliament would be incompetent even to reduce the number of its members, let alone incorporate itself with another legislature.[5]

[1] *Parl. Reg.*, p. 68: 'for', Beresford went on, 'as soon as he is returned to Parliament by them, he ceases to become the member for the individual seat for which he is returned, but becomes a member for the legislative body of the nation at large, in which capacity he is not to consider the local interests of the nation: for, was the representative to recur in every instance to the constituent body, he would himself be but a cypher in the Parliament.' This doctrine was not so popular among the anti-unionists as some of the others taken from Burke.

[2] Both James Fitzgerald (p. 18) and Arthur Moore (p. 145) cited the passage from *Reflections on the French Revolution*: '. . . the House of Commons cannot renounce its share of authority. The engagement and pact of society, which generally goes by the name of the constitution, forbids such invasion and such surrender. The constituent parts of a state are obliged to hold their public faith with each other . . .' (p. 19, Everyman ed. 1953).

[3] p. 90.   [4] p. 87.   [5] p. 83.

Many anti-unionists appeared to think this abstract constitutional point of more importance than the financial and
commercial implications of Union: 'Perish commerce! but
live the liberty and constitution of Ireland', said James
Fitzgerald.[1] Yet it is a little hard to understand why more
was not made of the down-to-earth arguments of Sir John
Parnell and William Tighe, who doubted whether self-
interested British merchants would want to invest capital in
a disturbed Ireland whom they feared as a competitor, even
in the event of a Union.[2] Instead, 'the attack on the Constitution' supplied a pretext for oratory which ran away with
common sense. J. M. O'Donel informed the House that
'. . . if the Parliament of Ireland should be mean enough to
vote away the legislative independence of Ireland, the people
of Ireland would not be mean enough to submit to it, they
would assert their rights, die as freemen rather than live as
slaves . . . I have made up my mind what my conduct shall
be—I shall either live free or fall by Cut Six of some Hessian
sabre, or other foreign mercenary'.[3] He fell in September
1801 in a duel with Denis Bingham. And it was Lord
Charlemont's protégé Plunket, from 1803 the holder of high
legal office under Pitt and several later United Kingdom
ministries, who declared: 'For my own part, I will resist it
to the last gasp of my existence, and with the last drop of my
blood, and when I feel the hour of my dissolution approach-
ing, I will, like the father of Hannibal, take my children to
the altar, and swear them to eternal hostility against the
invaders of their country's freedom.'[4] Such talk was never
followed by action. It was wishful thinking for anti-unionists
to claim that the threat of Union was reviving the Volunteer
spirit of nationalism and eliminating social and religious rifts
in the community. Plunket, O'Donel, and the other anti-
unionist lawyers had served enthusiastically against the rebels
of 1798, and it was sheer bluff for them to pose as leaders
of an Irish war of independence. Their ardent oratory merely
convinced the British ministry of the impracticability of
dealing with an autonomous Irish legislature, and weakened

[1] pp. 16–17. He also suggested that the women of Ireland should apply the
methods of Lysistrata against the unionists.
[2] pp. 149–52.   [3] p. 76.   [4] p. 53.

the position of such moderate anti-unionists as the ex-ministers Fitzgerald and Parnell, who wanted to strengthen the Anglo-Irish connexion by means short of a legislative union. As George IV said to Charles Kendal Bushe in 1821: 'You made a great mistake in refusing to consider the question. You should have appointed commissioners and made your bargain, and then you would have got better terms.'[1]

The anti-unionists took it for granted that 100 Irish members would be an ineffectual pressure-group in the United Parliament. Their suspicions of Britain were reinforced by the reluctance of British ministries and commercial interests throughout the eighteenth century to make timely concessions until compelled by Irish strength. As the lawyer John Ball said of the proposed parliamentary representation: 'If then the proportion of one to six, which we are taught to expect, would be of no avail to protect us from the jealousies of the English merchant, or the rapacity of the English minister; let us not deceive ourselves by a name, but consider the projected Union to be what in fact it is, but an absolute subjection to the will and uncontrolled dominion of a superior.'[2] And he pointed out that, while almost any other act could be repealed by a subsequent parliament if found bad or faulty, there would be no way for Ireland to rid herself of the Act of Union, if its effects were less beneficial than had been promised. Another lawyer, Edward Lee, foresaw that the influence of the Crown would be immensely increased by the addition of an Irish phalanx to the House of Commons, and said of Pitt: 'With his 46 Scotchmen on one hand, his corps of seapoys (for even the Nabobs have representatives in that virtuous parliament to which you are called on to give up your interests) and his hundred hardy Hibernians as a corps of reserve, what may he not do, thus supported?'[3] The anti-unionist answer was that he would overload Ireland with taxation. It was stated by O'Donel that Pitt's maladministration of war-time finance had bled Britain white, and that Ireland was coveted as a new untapped source of revenue: 'Now that England has grown old, sinking under a debt of five hundred millions, and Ireland owing a debt of only

---

[1] E. Œ. Somerville and M. Ross, op. cit., p. 243.   [2] *Parl. Reg.*, p. 71.
[3] pp. 18–19.

fourteen millions, independent as she, possessing commerce, wealth and agriculture, she generously proposes a Union to rob us of everything that should be dear to a nation.'[1] The point was later developed by Arthur Moore, who reminded his hearers that the American Revolution had grown out of a dispute over arbitrary taxation, and that during the war these same Americans had rejected as unsatisfactory a British offer to admit a number of their representatives to Westminster.[2]

Late on the morning of 23 January, the division was called. Ponsonby's amendment was defeated by the narrowest possible margin: 105 votes in favour, 106 against. John Beresford commented:

The result was that, with a majority of one, it was impossible to proceed, and Castlereagh was obliged to say that he would not press the measure while the disposition of the House was such. Mr. Ponsonby pressed him to declare how far he meant to relinquish the measure, but Sir. J. Parnell interfered, and stated that, in Lord Castlereagh's situation, it was impossible for him to answer such a question. This pacified for the moment, but I fear that the Speaker has persuaded them to insist on a total relinquishment of the measure, and to oppose the Address on the Report, until such a declaration is made. . . .[3]

So it was that when the House of Commons met on 24 January, and Lord Tyrone brought up the Address in Reply, Sir Laurence Parsons at once moved for the deletion of the tenth paragraph. This, after repeating almost word for word the sentiments of the Viceroy's message about the need to foster common interests and to combat foreign designs by 'consolidating as far as possible into one firm and lasting fabric the strength, the power, and the resources of the British Empire', concluded: 'We shall not fail to give the fullest consideration to a communication of such momentous importance.'[4] Parsons had not spoken at length during the first debate. He now opened the attack by an able review of Anglo-Irish relations from the time of Henry II, from which he deduced that there was no justification for Union. It was true that Ireland was now dependent on the British militia;

[1] p. 75.
[2] p. 147.
[3] Beresford to Auckland, 23 Jan. 1799 (Add. MSS. 34455).
[4] p. 94.

but twenty years before, during the American war, Ireland
had denuded herself of troops and left her defence to the
amateur Volunteers, in order to support the British war
effort. It was argued by the unionists that any growth of
absenteeism among the landowners would be compensated
by the development of a middle class; but the same prophecy
had been made, and proved false, at the introduction of free
trade in 1779. As for Ireland's expected admission to equal
overseas trading rights with Great Britain, this had been
promised already by every Chief Secretary since Hobart, and
there was no need to barter national autonomy for this
privilege. The union of the crowns meant that Ireland
already acknowledged British leadership in the appointment
of the executive, in foreign policy, and in all matters concerning the army and militia; was this not adequate?[1]

Thereafter the arguments followed the pattern made fami-
liar on the previous night. The House was jaded: 'violence
subsided evidently in the progress of the second night', wrote
Castlereagh.[2] However, tempers were frayed: Castlereagh
and Isaac Corry attacked the Dublin Bar, and in return were
well slated by George Ponsonby and Arthur Moore.[3] The
Government seems to have persuaded more of its supporters
to voice their opinions; but it was not able to avert defeat.
The Opposition was reinforced by four votes, including one
member who crossed the floor.[4] The Government, on the
other hand, gained only the vote of Colonel F. N. Burton,
who had been absent the first night, and they were deprived
through illness of John Beresford, Thomas Conolly, Sir
Hercules Langrishe, and Charles Knox.[5] Parsons's motion
for the deletion of the 'Union paragraph' was carried by 109
votes to 104, exclusive of tellers. This was the first defeat
that the Government had sustained since the Regency crisis.

---

[1] *Parl. Reg.*, pp. 96–97.   [2] Castlereagh to Portland, 28 Jan. 1799 (H.O. 100/85).

[3] Castlereagh described the lawyers' opposition as 'pettyfogging' (p. 113) and
Corry said it emanated from 'the juvenile, warm, and inexperienced part of the
profession' (p. 135). In fact the Bar meeting of 9 Dec. was attended by many
respected practitioners, and was presided over by Ambrose Smith, Father of the
Bar. George Ponsonby said that, compared to the talents and abilities represented at
that meeting, Castlereagh was 'but a puny child' (p. 106).

[4] Colonel Robert Taylor, M.P. for Kells, brother to the earl of Bective.

[5] Beresford to Auckland, 24 and 25 Jan. 1799 (*Beresford Correspondence*, ii,
pp. 194–7).

George Ponsonby at once followed up his victory by proposing 'that this House will ever maintain the undoubted birthright of Irishmen, by preserving an independent Parliament of Lords and Commons resident within this kingdom, as settled and approved by His Majesty and the British Parliament in 1782'.[1] In this he found himself separating from some of his supporters. Two anti-unionist county members, Lord Cole and W. C. Fortescue, declared that, although strongly opposed to a legislative union at the present time, they did not wish to pledge themselves permanently on the issue; and they were backed by J. C. Beresford.[2] Unwilling at this stage to risk a rebuff, Ponsonby withdrew his motion and the House adjourned to the next day. In the House of Lords, the dominant personality of Clare had no difficulty in securing the passage of the address by a majority of 52 to 16.

On 26 January Castlereagh was put to a little further embarrassment, when he attempted to move that Isaac Corry should vacate his seat at Newry in virtue of his new office as Chancellor of the Exchequer, only to be informed by Sir John Parnell that he had not yet received formal notice of dismissal.[3] The main business of the day was a vote of thanks for the services of the British militia. This was moved by the anti-unionist Viscount Cole, seconded by several gentlemen on his side of the House, and passed almost unanimously.[4] It was a pretty compliment to pay to a body which, a day or two earlier, had been described as capable of enforcing the Union against the wishes of the Irish people. Two days later Castlereagh moved the adjournment of the House until 7 February. This was resisted by Parnell and Barrington, who felt that Parliament should await news of the attitude to be taken by the British ministry. Barrington, in his usual high-flown style, urged that 'the House ought vigorously to sit from day to day, to guard against every advance of this insidious measure'.[5] Plunket demanded that the King should remove Pitt and Castlereagh from his counsels, but nobody else took any notice of this suggestion. Cooler heads

---

[1] *Parl. Reg.*, 22–25 Jan. 1799, etc., p. 155.
[2] Beresford to Auckland, 25 Jan. 1799 (Add. MSS. 34455).
[3] *Parl. Reg.*, 22–25 Jan. 1799, etc., p. 156.
[4] pp. 156–8.   [5] pp. 160 et seq.

prevailed: Dobbs and Egan pointed out that, while Pitt's conduct required the closest scrutiny, there was no need to resist the adjournment. Colonel Maxwell Barry asked for a call of the House when sittings resumed, and Castlereagh agreed. Shocked by his miscalculation of strength, the Chief Secretary was awaiting the reaction of the British Cabinet; while the anti-unionists, although they had won the first round, required time to attempt to weld their heterogenous elements into an effective force.

Pitt and his ministers, however, stood firm by the proposal. Already on 22 January a message from the King had been laid before the British House of Commons, similar in content to that in which Cornwallis recommended the Irish legislature to strengthen the connexion between the two countries. When Dundas had moved a vote of thanks, promising to study the question, it had been opposed by Sheridan, who moved an amendment expressing surprise and regret that the 1782 settlement had not been found satisfactory, and imploring the King not to listen to the counsels of those who advocated Union.[1] The speeches which followed were, on both sides of the argument, generally of higher calibre than in the Irish House of Commons. Sheridan's statement of the case against Union marshalled its arguments fluently and ably. He considered the timing of the measure inauspicious, as it might provide a focus for insurrection by leading some of the Irish to suppose that they were being coerced in a moment of weakness. He quoted no less an authority than Clare on the ignorance of the British ministry and Parliament about Irish affairs. Their consequent lack of sympathetic insight into Irish problems, was one of the most forceful arguments against the Union. After expressing doubts about the ability of the United Parliament to force through a solution of the religious problem, Sheridan turned to the basic roots of Irish discontent: 'In Ireland, the British government has two formidable enemies, poverty and ignorance. . . . Remove the cause of that misery, and you best consult the prosperity of the empire.'[2]

The Government case was put by Canning and Pitt. The former confined himself largely to arguments of national

---

[1] *Parliamentary History*, xxxiv, pp. 209–24.   [2] p. 222.

security, and reminded the Opposition that Fox, as Home Secretary, had rebuffed schemes for parliamentary reform and Catholic emancipation when they had emanated from the Volunteers in 1782–3.[1] Pitt's speech, which some of his admirers thought one of his best, was a worthy match to Sheridan's eloquence. He began by arguing the competence of Parliament to pass the measure. After dealing with the eagerness evinced in recent years by the British Opposition to debate Irish affairs, Pitt went on to explain why he considered the grant of Catholic emancipation and parliamentary reform would be insufficient to pacify Ireland:

> But if men are in a state of poverty, in which it is impossible they can have any comfort—if the progress of civilization depends in a great measure upon the distribution of wealth—if the improvement of this wealth depends much upon the distribution of capital—if all the advantages to be derived from an increase of national wealth depend much upon the temper of the inhabitants—if those advantages, together with the still greater advantages of mental improvement, are all retarded by the distractions and divisions of party, by the blind zeal and phrenzy of religious prejudice, by old and furious family feuds—if all, I say, combine to make a country wretched, what is the remedy? An impartial legislature standing aloof from local party connexion, sufficiently removed from the influence of contending factions to be advocate or champion of neither—being so placed as to have no superstitious reverence for the names and prejudices of ancient families, who have so long enjoyed the exclusive monopolies of certain public patronages and property, which custom has sanctified and which modern necessity may justify—a legislature which will neither give way to the haughty pretensions of a few, nor open the door to popular inroads. . . .[2]

Despite the victory of the anti-unionists in Dublin, Pitt proceeded to introduce on 31 January nine resolutions stating the proposed outlines of the Act of Union, and these passed the British House of Commons by 149 votes to 24. The thinness of the House perhaps reflected the usual apathy shown by many members towards Irish and colonial affairs. There was no opposition from the country gentlemen about the enlargement of Parliament by 100 members. Sheffield had been so much concerned by the strength of the opposition (and by uncertainty about the rights of Irish peers to sit in the House of Commons) that he had looked like deserting at one stage, and was quickly brought to heel by Portland.[1] Otherwise only the usual Opposition declined to support the measure, and their objections were founded on considerations about the welfare of Ireland rather than on any ill effects feared for Great Britain.[2] It was therefore with the assurance of continued support from both Houses of his own legislature that Pitt announced his determination to press Union until it should be found acceptable by the Parliament and people of Ireland.[3]

This declaration tended to stiffen the resistance of the Irish anti-unionists, who had gone too far now to reconcile themselves with the Government. The old Irish Opposition aimed at cementing their alliance with the other anti-unionists, so as to form a majority against the Government on all issues.[4] Bowes Daly, the Ponsonbys' 'whip', was foremost in getting up a subscription among the Dublin bankers to pay off the debts of their new ally, the Speaker. This had first been proposed by John Ball, M.P. for the town of Drogheda, where the Speaker had considerable influence: the Ponsonbys' espousal of the fund drew comment from John Beresford: '. . . the Ponsonbys want to secure Foster to their party or faction, and then to fight Government in every way possible. Foster is too cunning for them, he will go just as far as his interest will urge him, but he will not tie himself down to those gentlemen. I am certain he will make use of them as far as he can, to drive Lord Cornwallis out of this country, but I imagine he will distinguish between him and Government, as far as he can.'[5] Indeed, for a few days there seemed some slight uncertainty whether Cornwallis might not go the way of Fitzwilliam. Under-Secretary Cooke wrote a long tirade to his influential friend Auckland, complaining of this Jonah: 'Lord Cornwallis is nobody—worse than nobody . . . his silly conduct, his total incapacity, and self

---

[1] Sheffield to Auckland, 19 and 21 Jan. 1799 (Add. MSS. 34455).

[2] *Parliamentary History*, xxxiv, p. 278 et seq.

[3] Ibid., p. 254

[4] Cooke to Auckland, 23 Jan. 1799: 'It will be difficult now to form a new administration, on new principles, without the Speaker and Parnell and the Ponsonbys' (Add. MSS. 34455). Cf. Johnson to Downshire, 5 Feb. 1799 (Downshire MSS.).

[5] Beresford to Auckland, 26 Jan. 1799 (Add. MSS. 34455).

conceit and mulishness have alone lost the question.'[1] The marquess of Buckingham pressed Pitt and Grenville for the dismissal of Cornwallis and Castlereagh, and was informed that only considerations of the effect on the British Government's prestige were likely to save Cornwallis.[2] Fox suspected that Pitt was hoping to provoke the Irish Parliament into demanding the recall of Cornwallis, a Lord Lieutenant appointed by the British ministry, so that the weakness of the 1782 constitution would be revealed by a conflict between the two kingdoms. The appointment of the King's representative had already emerged as a delicate issue during the Regency affair, and Fox thought Pitt 'would not be sorry to bring it in full view at a time when he thinks himself (and perhaps is) strong at home'.[3]

Cornwallis was indeed attempting to control the House of Commons with one hand tied. Several placemen had voted against the Union, yet further dismissals were inadvisable until the Government's position was stronger. Considering the importance of the issue, the House of Commons had not been particularly well attended during the Union debates. Only 218 members had voted out of 300; this was the largest division for some years, but it fell behind the 232 who had voted on the Bill to admit Catholics to Parliament in 1793, or the 250 who had chosen between Foster and William Ponsonby for Speaker at the outset of the 1790 Parliament. There were still 82 uncommitted members to count; as well as some of the Government's nominal supporters who chose this moment to extort some long-sought piece of patronage.[4] The most immediate cause for concern was the possibility that the anti-unionists might cut the ground from under the Government's feet by volunteering to support various measures held out by the Government as inducements to entering a Union. Cornwallis particularly feared that the

---

[1] Cooke to Auckland, 26 Jan. 1799 (Add. MSS. 34455).

[2] Grenville to Buckingham, 30 Jan. 1799 (Buckingham, *Courts and Cabinets of King George III*, ii, pp. 402–4).

[3] Fox to Grattan, 4 Feb. 1799 (Grattan, *Life*, iv, p. 435).

[4] e.g. Nesbitt to Castlereagh, 5 Feb. 1799. (Mt. Stewart MSS.), where Colonel Thomas Nesbitt, M.P. for Cavan borough since 1761 and a pensioner during pleasure, presses for a permanent annuity, which he had sought at least as far back as 1791.

Catholics, hitherto studiously neutral, might be enticed towards the Opposition by an offer of emancipation, and he again urged the British ministry to empower him to make some more positive declaration of goodwill.[1] Portland even now admitted only that the subject might, at some preferably distant time, be fitly considered by the United Parliament.[2] Fortunately for the Castle, the Catholic archbishop of Dublin, Dr. John Troy, continued to place his hopes in the Government, and discouraged negotiations with the anti-unionists. On this issue it was proving difficult for the old Opposition to reach agreement with such staunch conservative Protestants as Foster and Ogle. As John Beresford foresaw: '. . . if no violent steps are taken, the business of the session will go on smoothly and the S— and Mr. Ponsonby will not be able to form an efficient party, if on the contrary the House and the people are agitated, all will run into party and faction. . . . Leave the blessings of Union now impressed on the minds of the people to work as it may, and when it is again brought forward, it will come with more advantage.'[3]

When Parliament reassembled on 8 February, Castlereagh accordingly side-stepped any direct conflict. Two minor attempts were made to join issue with the Government. O'Donel moved a complaint against the *Sun*, a newspaper with Administration leanings, and Edgeworth proposed a vote of thanks to the Speaker for his discharge of his official duties; but these resolutions were suffered to pass unchallenged by the ministerialists. It was on 16 February that Parliament saw 'a grand exhibition of the troops on both sides'.[4] Lord Corry moved for a committee to inquire into the state of the nation; a useful device, since it saved the anti-unionists the necessity of agreeing on a substantive motion:

Lord Corry was called on to state the motion intended to be made in the Committee, should it be appointed. This was done by Ruxton, an Opposition member, and his Lordship stated it was an Address to the

---

[1] Cornwallis to Portland, 26 and 30 Jan. 1799 (H.O. 100/85).
[2] Portland to Cornwallis, 30 Jan. and 3 Feb. 1799 (ibid.).
[3] Beresford to Auckland, 25 Jan. 1799 (Add. MSS. 34455).
[4] Same to same, 16 Feb. 1799 (*Beresford Correspondence*, ii, p. 214).

Crown, expressing loyalty, &c., and requesting at this time no question concerning Union should be brought forward. But Barrington let the cat out of the bag by saying, if the Comm^ee. was appointed, they would follow up resolution upon resolution from day to day till they put an end to the measure completely.[1]

'In the course of the dullest debate I ever heard', wrote Beresford, 'much coarse and improper language was made use of. The Opposition were very much elevated and insolent and were making bets that they would carry the question.'[2] Once the House was in committee, Foster would be in a position to bring his eloquence to bear on the Union question, and his knowledge of commerce and of parliamentary procedure might be too much of a match for the game but inexperienced Castlereagh.[3] However, the division showed that the Government was gaining ground. Several of its supporters had arrived in Dublin, and Corry's motion was defeated by 123 votes to 103. The Opposition was reduced by the refusal of a few country gentlemen to enter into systematic opposition on any issue apart from the Union. 'This majority will, I think, settle the business of the session, as Opposition will not be able to keep their friends together when they see that they are not omnipotent, so that if Government are active to gain friends, they will be able soon to curb the exorbitant insolence of our great men.'[4]

Such was John Beresford's analysis: in fact the position was more one of stalemate. The Opposition made two more attempts during February to pit their strength against the Administration, both times with discouraging results. On 22 February, the former Prime Serjeant, James Fitzgerald, introduced a Bill 'to provide for the administration of the government of Ireland, whensoever and as often as it shall be administered by a Regent or Regency'.[5] This sought to

---

[1] Johnson to Downshire, 16 Feb. 1799 (Downshire MSS.).
[2] Beresford to Auckland, 16 Feb. 1799 (loc. cit.).
[3] Same to same, 14 Feb. 1799 (*Beresford Correspondence*, ii, p. 213).
[4] Cornwallis to Portland, 16 Feb. 1799 (H.O. 100/85). The earl of Kingston's brother, Col. Robert King, abstained, while his great-uncle, Henry King, voted with the Government. Lord Gosford's son, Arthur Acheson, abstained, as did George Knox, Henry Stewart, and W. T. Monsell, whose patrons (respectively Lords Abercorn, Longford, and Cremoren) were all unionists.
[5] *Commons Journal*, xviii, p. 24.

provide that the person appointed as regent in Great Britain should automatically assume the same office and powers in Ireland. By removing the ambiguities which had brought on the crisis of 1789, Fitzgerald hoped to rob the Administration of one of their main arguments for the Union, and at the same time to show the practicability of strengthening the Anglo-Irish connexion by methods short of that measure. Although the Government found several legalistic objections to the Bill, both Cornwallis and Castlereagh felt that 'it might have prejudicial consequences, if such an offer on the part of Parliament were to be negatived',[1] and the second reading was allowed to pass. At the same time, the business of Parliament was so organized that it was not until mid April that the Bill reached the committee stage.

Meanwhile, on 26 February, the Attorney-General had introduced a Bill 'for the more speedy suppression of the rebellion', authorizing the concurrent jurisdiction of courts martial and the normal civilian courts. It was expected that this Bill might bring the Government under fire from two quarters. The extreme Protestants, such as Ogle and Duigenan, would deplore the misguided lenity with which Cornwallis had departed from Camden's firm methods; while the Ponsonbys and their associates wanted 'to modify the power and localize the operations of the Bill'.[2] Dublin Castle believed that Foster, Parnell, and George Ponsonby would try to elevate the issue into 'a Union question': 'One principle privately urged was, that it gave a power to the ministry to force that question, and another, that it degraded Parliament, and tended to prove that it was incompetent to manage the country. . . .'[3] Few, in fact, of the country gentlemen wished to oppose a measure designed for their security, and a motion in committee that the Bill should be operative only in counties proclaimed under martial law was negatived by 121 votes to 18. Those in the majority included even the Speaker's

---

[1] Cornwallis to Portland, 23 Feb. 1799 (H.O. 100/85).

[2] Same to same, 28 Feb. 1799 (H.O. 100/85).

[3] Ibid., cf. Johnson to Downshire, 4 Mar. 1799 (Downshire MSS.). Johnson took the chair in the committee stage, to avoid commenting on a Bill about which he did not know the sentiments of his patron, Downshire. He himself thought the Bill was bad law, but approved of any move to give the Government arbitrary powers of suppression.

son, Colonel Thomas Foster.[1] On a question of this type, the minority against the Government could still be reduced to unimpressive proportions.

By now the Administration was recovering its confidence. Cornwallis wrote to Portland—and his diagnosis is confirmed elsewhere by such candid critics as Beresford and Cooke: 'The refusal of the country gentlemen to unite against this Bill proves that all attempts to form a party against Government, with a view to overturn this Administration has [sic] entirely failed, and that, however on some particular questions considerable opposition may appear, there is not any probability of its being successful in any measure which is necessary for the carrying on the King's Government.'[2] Yet it was with some relief that Castlereagh found himself quit of the responsibility of pressing the Union in so evenly divided a House: '. . . had we carried the parliamentary steps by a small majority, it would have been fought with sufficient obstinacy to pledge perhaps a formidable party both within and without irrevocably against it—Mr. Pitt's statement of the proceedings in England will enable us more extensively to prepare the public mind.'[3] So that, although 'the opposition has not been of that determin'd nature to make it *very* difficult for many who composed of it to find some good reason for a change of conduct',[4] the Chief Secretary soon decided that 'perhaps after the recent failure, it were best that the question was suffer'd entirely to sleep during the remainder of the session'.[5] Its subsequent agitation was almost completely due to the efforts of the Opposition, both from party opportunism, and from a genuine apprehension that the Government might gain strength from public apathy.[6] James Fitzgerald's Regency Bill went into committee in the House of Commons on 11 April. The debate was made the occasion

[1] 'A better soldier than a politician' (Cornwallis to Dundas, 1 July 1799 (*Cornwallis Correspondence*, iii, p. 111)).

[2] Cooke to Auckland, 30 Mar. 1799 (Add MSS. 34455); Cornwallis to Portland 20 Feb. 1799 (H.O. 100/85); Beresford to Auckland, 18 Feb. 1799 (*Beresford Correspondence*, ii, p. 217).

[3] Castlereagh to Camden, 4 Feb. 1799 (Mt. Stewart MSS.); cf. Johnson to Downshire, 14 Feb. 1799 (Downshire MSS.), where he is quoted to similar effect.

[4] Ibid.

[5] Castlereagh to Elliot, 28 Jan. 1799 (Mt. Stewart MSS.).

[6] Foster to Downshire, 23 Feb. 1799 (Downshire MSS.).

of John Foster's 'long threatened speech' about the Union:
in a powerful oration of some four and a quarter hours 'the
Regency Bill was not thought of'.[1] Indeed, Fitzgerald's
measure was subsequently allowed quietly to drop; but
Foster had been enabled to set out a substantial case against
the commercial consequences of the Union and to answer
criticism levelled against him in England. Castlereagh's first
impressions were optimistic: 'It was a speech of considerable
impression as such, but not calculated to produce an effect
to be apprehended, should he think fit to give it to the world.
. . . We have encountered our principal adversary, and his
arguments will be well understood and answered before the
subject comes again into decision.'[2] Two days later, his outlook was more sober: 'The clamour has certainly subsided,
and the measure has more open advocates who were before
silent; but I cannot perceive either in or out of Parliament
that impression which can lead me to form any opinion of
when the measure may be carried.'[3] This is not the language
of a man looking to secure a safe majority by the expenditure
of a little effortless corruption. Schooled by the reversals
which had met the ill-prepared attempt to introduce the
Union, the Chief Secretary perceived the necessity—in which
his more experienced opponents had anticipated him—of
mobilizing adequate support from public opinion. The country gentlemen were courted assiduously, and all Ireland was
canvassed to ascertain the views of the articulate public. Of
course, in most of Ireland, this public opinion was shaped
and guided by the local gentry, with their pliable tenantry
and command of patronage; but without their concurrence
overt official interference was difficult, and the Union discussions of 1799 were the most extensive and vigorous for
several years.

Most of the anti-unionists based their appeal to the nation
largely on the performance of the Irish Parliament in giving
expression to Irish nationalism. For all the exaggeration and

---

[1] Cooke to Auckland, 12 Apr. 1799 (misdated 1798) (Add. MSS. 34454); for
the text of Foster's oration, *A Report of the Important Debate in the House of Commons
of Ireland on Thursday, April 11, 1799 on the Regency Bill, including the admirable
speech of the Rt. Hon. John Foster (Speaker)*, Dublin, 1799.

[2] Castlereagh to Portland, 12 Apr. 1799 (H.O. 100/86).

[3] Same to same, 14 Apr. 1799 (ibid.).

brag of some of the lawyers, the anti-unionists were not insincere in their professions of patriotism. The objections to Union did not result solely from the commercial and parochial fears of a primary producing country, dependent on protective tariffs for the fostering of its infant industries, and for an appreciable part of its revenue. It might well be argued that, even in 1800, the cultural and religious differences between Ireland and Great Britain were no greater than those between Quebec and the remainder of the Canadian provinces. But the Irish could not cut loose from their history. The Anglo-Irish were unable to forget the neglect, apathy, and lack of consideration evinced towards them by Great Britain during the preceding century. Like other communities similarly placed, many of them, particularly those with no recent opportunity of exercising the responsibilities of office, preferred an inadequate and inefficient autonomy to the promise of good government from afar. The effectiveness of their resistance to the Union depended much on the support they could command outside Parliament. The precedents of the Volunteer period and the Regency crisis suggested that corruption alone could not save an administration, if the nation was aroused and hostile against it.

V

THE APPEAL TO THE COUNTRY

The idea of a Union engrosses the publick mind, and the
warmth with which argument is carried on becomes very
disagreeable . . . God grant we may learn wisdom ere it
be too late.

J. PATRICKSON TO LORD DOWNSHIRE, 1 January 1799.[1]

MUCH had been made by anti-unionist debaters in
January 1799 of the lack of spontaneous public
declarations in favour of the Union. County members who claimed to be bound by their constituents' wishes;
boroughmongers seeking a respectable pretext for neutrality;
nearly all who had declined to support the ministry, argued
that so momentous a proposal should be endorsed by a mandate from the people. Conscious that their victory in the
House of Commons might be narrow and temporary, the
anti-unionist leaders sought to rally respectable public
opinion to their side. Dublin was already theirs, and this
was a valuable centre for influencing national opinion; but
many of the provincial areas felt stirrings of rivalry towards
the capital, such as were expressed by Bishop Percy: 'Against
the Union are the local advantages of the city of Dublin. . . .
But the city of Dublin has long drained the public treasury
in jobs and schemes for its separate emolument, of no adequate use to the nation in general.'[2] Both sides needed to gain
the provinces. The day after the crucial House of Commons
vote, John Beresford commented: 'The country is yet un-
pledged against the measure and in many parts disposed in
favour of it. We have 82 members who have not yet voted . . .;
we have constituents perhaps to assist us with some of
those who have voted, and we have other chances to make
the House easy if we can gain ground in the country.'[3]

There were three customary means of ventilating public

---

[1] J. Patrickson to Lord Downshire, 1 Jan. 1799 (Downshire MSS.).
[2] Bishop of Dromore to his wife, 21 Jan. 1799 (Add. MSS. 32335).
[3] Beresford to Auckland, 26 Jan. 1799 (Add. MSS. 34455).

opinion for the guidance of local members and the Government. The sheriff of the county could be requested to convoke a meeting of the gentlemen and freeholders, at which resolutions indicative of the county's outlook might be submitted. Except where the forces for and against a question were nearly balanced, gentlemen representing a minority often stayed away from such meetings, rather than waste time and prestige in futile protest. If unsympathetic, the sheriff might refuse to convene a meeting when asked; but as he was usually nominated with the consent of the leading landowners in the county, and was often a young man just entering public life and keen to gain reputation and experience, a refusal seldom occurred. Petitioning was another vehicle of public opinion. Here the influence of an individual landlord often brought forward numerous signatures from his tenantry, and such petitions reflected the views of local magnates as often as any widespread popular viewpoint. Addresses and petitions were also framed by local corporations, usually faithfully reflecting the views of the patron. Where a difference arose this was sometimes more apparent than real. Thus in 1792, when the duke of Leinster felt that he had committed himself too far in favour of Catholic emancipation, he felt enabled to shift his ground honourably on the receipt of an address from the corporation of Athy beseeching its two members (both protégées of Leinster) to vote against any Catholic relief measures brought forward at that time. Since the reforms of 1793 Roman Catholics had been admissible to corporations, in theory, but as yet seldom in practice. The third, and to many the most respectable medium for sounding county opinion was the grand jury. This body met at assize times, and consisted of twenty-three of the most reputable freeholders in the county, varying little in composition from year to year. Apart from its judicial duties, a grand jury was charged with levying local taxation and directing expenditure on minor public works, such as road repairs, water supplies, and poor relief. Grand juries were also in the habit of expressing themselves on behalf of the community on important public issues. At the time when the Union question was first agitated, no assizes were on circuit and no grand juries assembled to pass resolutions.

The anti-unionists were first in the field with petitioning. By 5 February 1799 fourteen petitions about the Union lay on the table of the House of Commons, of which only one was in favour of the measure.[1] Charlemont, with his memories of the power of organized public opinion in the great years around 1782, was writing to an old friend:

> I now begin to perceive that our victory, though glorious, is not absolutely decisive, and that our arch enemy, enraged at a defeat to which he is wholly unaccustomed, may yet rally his discomfited mercenaries, and again attack us, and this he will most probably do, unless he shall find us armed with our only genuine defence. . . . The silence of the country is the only argument administration can bring forward against us, a silence principally occasioned by the torpor which their own measures, perhaps cunningly, have produced. I have been labouring in Armagh, and still hope for success, though thwarted by many obstacles. The freeholders, indeed, are willing, but many of the gentlemen are supine, and the sheriff is absent, I know not where. . . .[2]

At the spring assizes, several grand juries took the Union into consideration, although substantive resolutions were passed only by a few. Until the adjournment of Parliament at the beginning of June activity in the counties was relatively slight. Spontaneous demonstrations were neither expected nor encouraged by either side. Both the unionists and their opponents deemed it necessary for initiative to be taken by some 'leading interest' before a county could be expected to come forward and declare its sentiments.[3]

The anti-unionists were inactive during the recess. Perhaps they desired to maintain the peace of the country by avoiding agitation until it was definitely known that the ministry were proceeding with the scheme. The *Anti-Union* had ceased publication with the complacent reflection that the defeat of the measure had obviated, for the time being, the

---

[1] The anti-union petitions were from the cities of Dublin, Belfast, and Limerick and from the counties of Cavan, Dublin, Fermanagh, Galway, Limerick, Longford, Meath, Monaghan, Tipperary, and Wexford. The common council of Cork were in favour of the measure.

[2] Charlemont to Halliday, 2 Feb. 1799 (*H.M.C. Charlemont MSS.* ii, p. 345).

[3] The Revd. Edward Hudson, an anti-unionist of co. Antrim, wrote to Charlemont, 3 Feb. 1799, ibid.: 'A requisition for a meeting of Down has, I hear, been signed, but I fear there will not be one in this county, there being no person fit and willing to take the lead.' Cf. the unionist Altamont to Castlereagh, 7 Mar. 1799: 'King's County wants nothing but a leader to make a conspicuous figure among those fairly disposed' (Mt. Stewart MSS.).

need for its existence. But during the summer and autumn of 1799, the unionists busied themselves. Lord Cornwallis undertook two goodwill tours, one of the central and southern counties in July, the other around Ulster in October. Within the counties the Government preferred declarations from the gentlemen of property rather than popular demonstrations.[1] This was not altogether unrealistic, as having the weight of property on one's side indicated control of the tenantry whose votes might decide the next county election. But in some counties such as Galway and Tipperary, where it appeared that the members might be converted from anti-unionism if they received instructions from their constituents, Castlereagh was willing to risk a county meeting: 'as this very unconstitutional practice is but too prevalent in Ireland, it is fair to turn it to advantage if we can', he wrote to Portland.[2] Even then, the Government was selective about its supporters. Men of standing or property were preferred, and forty-shilling freeholders were deemed insufficiently respectable for an important county meeting.[3] This implied a possibility that the unionist petitions would be less numerously signed than those of their opponents. Of the 64 members representing 32 counties, 19 had voted in favour of union in 1799, 36 against, and 9 had abstained or not attended. In the main, the unionist members represented counties where there was an established, dominant religious majority. Twelve of them came from the Catholic south and west and five from Down, Antrim, and Londonderry where the Presbyterians were securely established.[4] The anti-unionists drew their strength from the counties close to Dublin[5] and from those 'border' counties of southern Ulster

[1] As the Lord Lieutenant wrote: 'I prefer, in general, resolutions of the men of property to county meetings, but when the members have voted against the Union, and are not *unwilling* to be converted, they are necessary' (Cornwallis to Ross, 4 Sept. 1799 (*Cornwallis Correspondence*, iii, p. 129)).

[2] Castlereagh to Portland, 23 July 1799 (H.O. 100/86). The county meeting was, in fact, a recognized and long-established means of sounding local opinion.

[3] Stanley to Castlereagh, 3 Sept. 1799 (Mt. Stewart MSS.).

[4] Two each from Clare, Cork, Galway, Kerry, and Mayo and one each from Limerick and Waterford. In Ulster, two members each from Antrim and Londonderry, and one from Down.

[5] Two each from Dublin, King's County, Louth, Westmeath, Wicklow, and— after a conversion—Carlow; one each from Kildare, Meath, and Queen's County.

where hostility prevailed between almost equal communities of Catholics and Protestants.[1] Of course, in most parts of Ireland, the resident gentry controlled local opinion as much as they reflected it, but this geographical division was not fortuitous. Although it is most improbable that the Union had as many supporters as opponents, an examination of the counties would indicate that genuine differences of opinion existed, which could not be attributed either to faction or corruption.

The metropolitan area

Dublin was the focal point of anti-unionism. It was feared that the removal of the seat of government from the capital would severely diminish commerce and land values. Foster prepared a paper in which he computed that the value of the 100,000 houses then in Dublin and its suburbs assessed at a total of £8,400,000, would be reduced by one-third.[2] Even greater loss might be expected in the value of the farmlands around the capital which supplied Dublin with produce. The Administration was constantly on the watch for support within the capital, and was as constantly disappointed. After the civic authorities of Dublin had led the opposition in January 1799—an opinion reinforced by the city mob, who celebrated the defeat of the measure by breaking every window not illuminated in honour of the event—there seemed little hope of making an impression. But in June Cornwallis wrote: 'The temper of Dublin remains strongly adverse, but not in the degree it did. Some of the commercial body have altered their sentiments. Dublin is not without materials for a counter-party, which I should have sanguine hope of collecting, if my endeavours to produce a schism in the Corporation should prove successful.'[3] The oligarchic corporation comprised a board of aldermen and a lower house of commons, and some of the former wanted to stand well with the Castle. An opportunity for assessing opinion on the Union came up in July, when the lower house voted a motion for presenting the lawyer, William Saurin, with the freedom

---

[1] Two each from Armagh, Cavan, Donegal, Fermanagh, Monaghan, Roscommon, and Tyrone, and one from Leitrim.

[2] Massereene and Ferrard MSS., P.R.O.N.I. (D.O.D. xl, 287.).

[3] Cornwallis to Portland, 22 June 1799 (H.O. 100/86).

of the city 'for his manly resistance to the legislative union'. Prompted by Alderman Alexander, the most reliable supporter of the Government, the board of aldermen by a majority of two votes deleted all reference to Saurin's anti-unionist activities, and confined themselves to a simple grant of the city freedom: but further than that Alexander did not care to venture. Several of his following withdrew from the meeting at that point, and the remainder of the board passed a declaration that they had not relinquished their former opinions.[1] In October the Common Council of Dublin passed a resolution affirming hostility to the Union, which was ratified by a majority of seven to two on the board of aldermen. The majority included Alderman James, formerly regarded as a spokesman for the measure there and in the Orange Lodges.[2] No further attempt was made on Dublin.

The counties surrounding Dublin were as staunch in opposition. Louth, the Speaker's county, was steadfastly anti-unionist, save only for the town of Dundalk where Cornwallis was presented with unionist addresses in October 1799, not only from the corporation, but also (unexpectedly and without solicitation) from the Catholic priest and congregation. As the local magnate, Lord Roden, was a strong Orangeman, his influence cannot have been responsible.[3] An attempt to secure a unionist declaration from Drogheda the same month met with failure. Ralph Smyth, who had run in vain for that seat with government encouragement in 1798 endeavoured to get up an address, but found so discouraging a response that when Lord Conyngham came to lend his aid, he was informed by Cornwallis that the prospect was not 'sufficiently promising . . . to persevere'.[4]

In the county of Meath there was more scope for manœuvre.[5] The leading landowners were the strongly

<hr />

[1] Castlereagh to Portland, 20 July 1799 (H.O. 100/86).

[2] Elliot to Castlereagh, 19 Oct. 1799 (*Castlereagh Correspondence*, ii, p. 431). Elliot thought that 'by a little exertion, a majority might be secured in the Court of Aldermen', but the experienced John Lees advised him against overt interference.

[3] His influence was not quite absolute. His uncle, Lord Clanbrassil, almost lost his hold in 1782 through the chicanery of his steward. Dundalk remained under the family's influence until 1812, when a 'Catholic' candidate, Thomas O'Callaghan, was returned.   [4] Cornwallis to Portland, 22 Oct. 1799 (H.O. 100/87).

[5] Castlereagh to Portland, 27 Mar. 1799 (H.O. 100/86); Castlereagh to Portland, 22 Oct. 1799 (H.O. 100/87).

anti-Catholic John Foster, the much milder earl of Bective, and the absentee Wellesley family, who were divided on the issue. Its grand jury was the first to carry a series of anti-union resolutions in March 1799: but it was not long before a counter-protest was drawn up by the energetic bishop of Meath and circulated by the earl of Bective and Colonel Thomas Burrowes. Presumably this unionist activity helped the Government to win the support of Clotworthy Rowley, the hitherto uncommitted member for the county, and John Preston, anti-unionist part-owner and M.P. for Navan, a borough with a very strong Catholic element. However, the middle classes in Meath were less amenable, and in October 1799, the Roman Catholic bishop of Meath wrote to Castlereagh:

> The Roman Catholics of Meath are too near Dublin, and too much accustomed to listen to the opinions of the Protestants of Meath, to be as yet willing to declare in favour of the Union. They are not strangers to the principal arguments used to oppose it, and many of them believe these arguments to be unanswerable. The clergy depend upon the people, and they say here they would act imprudently did they wound the feelings of their respective flocks by stepping beyond their own sphere, and abetting a system to which the people are not yet reconciled.[1]

Although as late as 6 January 1800 the earl of Bective was to write 'Meath goes on tolerably, considering the enormous mass of ignorance, prejudice and positiveness with which we have to contend',[2] the Catholic bishop proved closer in touch with public opinion.

Anti-unionist influences were almost as strong in the counties south of Dublin, Kildare, Carlow, Wicklow, and Wexford. All these counties had suffered considerably in the aftermath of the 1798 rising, and especially in Wexford both sides claimed that the tenantry could be bullied into petitioning whichever way their landlords demanded.[3] In Kildare

---

[1] Dr. C. J. Plunket to Castlereagh, 29 Oct. 1799 (*Castlereagh Correspondence*, iii, p. 437).   [2] Bective to Castlereagh, 6 Jan. 1800 (Mt. Stewart MSS.).

[3] A Protestant landowner wrote that the anti-unionist address was mainly signed by 'poor miserable Romanists . . . for fear of their landlord' (Gordon to Castlereagh, 31 Jan. 1800 (*Castlereagh Correspondence*, iii, p. 229)); but the anti-unionist petition from Wexford, headed by Sir Laurence Parsons, Sir John Freke, and R. S. Carew (all of whom lived in other counties), alleged unionist coercion. The anti-unionist

the declining influence of the duke of Leinster was buttressed by the rising family of Latouche. This banking house was also influential in Carlow, and hostile to the Union. In Wicklow the Ponsonbys were very influential. Although they owned no land, they advised two of the most important landowners, Fitzwilliam and William Tighe. Fitzwilliam's estates were so considerable that both members owed their return to his tenantry. At the beginning of 1799, one seat for the county was vacant, owing to the murder by rebels of William Hume.[1] This, the first county election since the Union controversy arose, was contested early in February. There were two rival candidates, William Hoare Hume, son of the late member, and Captain Hugh Howard, the earl of Wicklow's brother, who rather exceptionally had been granted permission to resign his seat for the borough of St. Johnstown (Donegal) in order to fight the county.[2] Few details survive about the election, which took place in a county still not entirely recovered from the rebellion of the previous year. After two days' polling, Hume led his rival by 55 votes, and not long afterwards Howard withdrew.[3] He was backed only by Lords Carysfort and Wicklow, and against him were ranged the interests of Fitzwilliam, Downshire, Tighe, and probably the earl of Aldborough. Howard attributed his defeat to his support of the Union, but this was an oversimplification.[4] The backing of the Fitzwilliam tenantry was essential for election to Wicklow, and Howard, a consistent ministerialist, lacked the sound whig principles sought by Fitzwilliam. The county had long been in the Ponsonby orbit, and an anti-unionist petition was duly sent up to Parliament.

Catholic, E. Hay, *History of the Insurrection*, p. xxxiii, claims that a unionist M.P. threatened him with immediate arrest if he organized an anti-union petition.

[1] William Hume (*c*. 1740–98), member for co. Wicklow 1790–8, was son-in-law of Sir Joseph Hoare; was not officially supported by Fitzwilliam, but was the sole 'outside' candidate authorized to canvass his tenantry, on the understanding that he would give up his seat to Fitzwilliam's candidate, Westby, if the latter were defeated. (Wainwright to Fitzwilliam, 21 Mar. 1790 (Wentworth Woodhouse MSS., F. 93)).

[2] At the time of the Wicklow by-election the Government was generally refusing borough members permission to take the escheatorship in order to contest a county seat. (Saunders to Downshire, 16 Oct. 1798 (Downshire MSS.).)

[3] *Cork Advertiser*, 7 Feb. 1799: Carysfort to Grenville, 17 Jan. 1801 (*H.M.C. Dropmore MSS.* vi, p. 344).

[4] Hartigan to Downshire, 18 Oct. 1798; Hume to Downshire, 20 Oct. 1798 (Downshire MSS.); Howard to Abbot, 30 Jan. 1802 (Add. MSS. 35711).

Four midland counties

Connected to Dublin by road and canal were the agricultural inland counties of Leinster—Longford, Westmeath, King's County, and Queen's County. In each of these opinion was divided, often reflecting traditional feuds and rivalries. The situation was most ambiguous in Longford, where most of the proprietors were absentees, and in the words of R. L. Edgeworth: 'During the war, and in consequence of what were called the war-prices, graziers, land-jobbers and middlemen had risen into comparative wealth; and, instead of turning, in due season, according to the natural order of things, into Buckeens and Squireens, they had been metamorphosed into justices of the peace and committee men.'[1] One group of freeholders had declared against the Union, even before the measure came to Parliament, and another had decided to stay uncommitted until detailed information about the terms was available. In February 1799 the earl of Longford declined to circulate a protest against the antiunionist declaration, for fear of provoking a decisively antiunionist full-scale county meeting. It was not until September that the Roman Catholics of the county sent up a declaration in favour of the Union and it took three months longer for the uncommitted member for the county, Sir Thomas Fetherstone, to join his colleague, Newcomen, in supporting the measure.[2]

Both King's County and Westmeath sent up addresses for and against the Union. Although both members for the former county were staunch against the measure, the unionists were first to obtain declarations.[3] In Westmeath, on the other hand, the influence of an anti-unionist sheriff was alleged to have delayed for twelve months the circulation of resolutions approving the measure.[4] In Queen's County,

---

[1] R. L. Edgeworth, *Memoirs*, London, 1820, ii, pp. 176–8.

[2] Cooke to Castlereagh, 18 Sept. 1799 (*Castlereagh Correspondence*, ii, p. 403). Cooke to Beresford, 11 Dec. 1799 (*Beresford Correspondence*, ii, p. 234).

[3] Burke to Castlereagh, 8 Mar. 1799 (Mt. Stewart MSS.); Cornwallis to Portland, 22 June 1799 (H.O. 100/86).

[4] Buckingham to Castlereagh, 26 Dec. 1799 (*Castlereagh Correspondence*, iii, p. 34). The petition is included among the Mt. Stewart MSS., as is another, dated 23 Apr. 1800, from 128 unionist residents of the neighbourhood of Moate. I have no

union was supported by C. H. Coote, whose family had long contested Maryborough with the anti-unionist Sir John Parnell.[1] Coote was backed by the marquess of Drogheda and Lord Mountrath: Parnell by Sir Robert Staples and Thomas Pitt. These interests were so nicely balanced that neither side could claim Queen's County. In July 1799 Parnell and Pitt expressed their strong disapproval of Union to the grand jury, but declined disturbing the county with any resolutions there or at any subsequent meeting. This argued a lack of confidence in their strength; but the unionists were no more venturesome.[2]

Ulster: Antrim, Down, and Londonderry

Bound by cultural and religious ties to Scotland, settled by a dominant Protestant majority, Antrim, Down, and Londonderry in many respects bore a different character to the rest of Ulster. It was here that the radical ideas of the United Irishmen had gained their greatest hold. Of the 183 Presbyterian clergy of Ulster, eighteen were known to have sympathized with the 1798 rebellion, all of them resident in these three counties.[3] But the last years of the century saw increasing prosperity for the *bourgeoisie*, inclining them to place stability before reform. When Castlereagh and his father, Londonderry, moved away from their early Whig Club ideas, they reflected the shift of the Presbyterians towards conservatism. As late as 1805 Castlereagh was still lampooned as the candidate of politically minded dominies, and his neighbours the Wards and Blackwoods benefited at elections because the growing Presbyterian interest preferred them to the powerful marquess of Downshire.[4]

details about the organization of anti-unionist petitions in King's County and Westmeath.

[1] His enemies alleged he had been brought over by a colonelcy of militia (*Parl. Reg.* 22–23 Jan. 1799, pp. 18, 82; *The Anti-Union*, 28 Jan. 1799). In fact, he was only offered the situation after another unionist, Major John Warburton had refused it (Cornwallis to Castlereagh, 16 Jan. 1799).

[2] Castlereagh to Portland, 20 July 1799 (H.O. 100/86).

[3] Cf. A. T. Q. Stewart, 'The Transformation of Presbyterian Radicalism in Northern Ireland, 1792–1825' (M.A. thesis, the Queen's University, Belfast).

[4] In the collection of anonymous broadsheets, *County of Down Election, 1805*, it is suggested that Castlereagh sought to build up a power in Ulster like that of Dundas in Scotland, by granting cadetships in India to the sons of Presbyterian clergy, 'who

It was at Newry, in the south of Down, that two elections were contested in February 1799: and even in a borough considered 'open' by contemporaries, the traditional interests maintained their hold unaffected by the Union issue. Isaac Corry, who since 1776 had held one seat through his own interest, had to seek re-election on appointment as Chancellor of the Exchequer. The other interests in Newry were that of Colonel Robert Ross, backed by Downshire, and an 'independent' minority, who had attempted without success to put up a candidate in 1790. Downshire, although disinclined to the Union, and suspicious that Corry planned to jockey him out of the borough by securing the creation of additional freeholdings,[1] offered no opposition to his re-election: but the independents talked of putting up an anti-unionist, the pamphleteer Charles Ball. The Catholic archbishop of Dublin, Dr. John Troy, wrote to the priest at Newry, Dr. Lennan, requesting him to mobilize the Catholic vote in favour of Corry, whose religious views were known to be liberal. On 7 February Lennan replied:

I have the pleasure to inform your Lordship that your friend Mr. Corry was this day re-elected for the town of Newry. Mr. Ball, with his partisans, after canvassing the town for eight days, declined the poll, and surrendered yesterday. The Catholics stuck together like the Macedonian phalanx, and with ease were able to turn the scale in favour of the Chancellor of the Exchequer. He is very sensible of the efficacy of your interference, and their steadiness.[2]

In the same month Downshire's member, Ross, died. His patron's advisers were worried lest Corry should be emboldened by his victory to put up his brother, or some stronger candidate, who might squeeze out a Downshire

had bartered the confidence of a virtuous and enlightened people, for his favor, and a little paltry pelf'. Cf. The Revd. William Bruce to Castlereagh, 9 Apr. 1800: 'we naturally look to your Lordship, as a native of Ireland and of Ulster, interested in the welfare and ambitious of the approbation of this part of the Kingdom, and descended from a father and grandfather who have been distinguished by singular constancy in their adherence to our principles and communion' (*Castlereagh Correspondence*, iii, p. 269); and J. Gamble, *View of Society and Manners in Northern Ireland*, 1812, p. 34: 'Much of the landed property of this part of the country has passed from the extravagant children of idleness to the sons of the thrifty merchants of Newry and Belfast.'

[1] Ross to Downshire, 3 July 1798; Johnson to Downshire, 20 Oct. 1798 (Downshire MSS.).

[2] Lennan to Troy, 7 Feb. 1799 (*Castlereagh Correspondence*, ii, p. 168).

nominee: especially since it was known that Ball intended to offer himself again.[1] Within a week after Ross died, Downshire had seized upon the first promising aspirant, John Moore of Drumbanagher, formerly M.P. for Lisburn.[2] As he wrote to his man of electoral affairs, John Reilly: 'I know him not. I can at this distance only say that I think I owe it to Ross's memory, I owe it to myself to keep Mr. Corry out of Newry, if I can, and to do that I will spend, if necessary, £1,000 or £1,200. . . . If I am to act in Newry, it will be with the hope of strengthening myself in Downshire.'[3] Corry, faced with this intervention, did not offer fight: but Ball forced a poll, and on the first day registered 32 votes to 33 for his opponent. Moore then went away to an easy lead, and on the third evening, Ball gave up the contest, with the tally at 112 votes to 50.[4] Subsequently Newry was divided over the Union. The Catholics, whose support had been so useful for Corry, came out in favour of the scheme; and it was reported that 'many of the Downshire friends privately favour the measure, but will go with his party in the case of a town meeting or other resolutions',[5] so that the anti-unionists also managed to secure a petition addressed from the merchants and gentlemen of Newry.

Within the county much depended on the tenantry of the marquess of Downshire, who was gradually manœuvring into opposition. In July 1799 Castlereagh had found it expedient to visit his native county at assize time, in order to confront any move on the grand jury: 'My object in attending the assizes being purely defensive, of course nothing was undertaken in favour of the measure. Had anything been brought forward against an Union by Lord Downshire's friends, the numbers would have been against us, but our minority would have been numerous, and composed of the most considerable gentlemen in the county. . . .'[6] A pact to

---

[1] Sir George Anderson to Downshire, 10 and 12 Feb. 1799 (Downshire MSS.).

[2] Lord Drogheda had nominated him to a seat in the marquess of Hertford's borough of Lisburn, 1790–7; but by now he was unconnected. Cf. Moore to Downshire, 26 Feb. 1799 (Downshire MSS.).

[3] Downshire to Reilly, 28 Feb. 1799 (Downshire MSS.).

[4] *Belfast Newsletter*, 8 Mar. 1799.

[5] Acheson Thompson to Castlereagh, 3 Jan. 1800 (Mt. Stewart MSS.).

[6] Castlereagh to Portland, 5 Aug. 1799 (H.O. 100/86). The High Sheriff was a Downshire nominee (Matthew Corry to Downshire, 27 Feb. 1799 (Downshire MSS.)).

refrain from canvassing the question was made between Downshire and Castlereagh, and although the Castle was sanguine about Down, the only move before the end of 1799 came from the bishop of Dromore, a petty diocese within the county, who presented the Lord Lieutenant in October with a unionist petition signed by all but five of his clergy.[1]

The city of Belfast, on the border of Down and Antrim, once a centre of disaffection, was now anxious to keep out of politics. The corporation was controlled by the marquess of Donegall, who moved from indecision to unionist views only in September 1799. A month later, the corporation gave Cornwallis a formal dinner, which was intended as a unionist demonstration. About 150 merchants and citizens attended, and the banquet was accounted a success, particularly since prominent anti-unionists such as the bishop of Down and Charlemont's friend, Halliday, were politely advised against attending a function which might embarrass them. But no unionist address was secured from the city, and Dublin Castle had to be content with assurances that the two or three groups of merchants who sent anti-unionist petitions to Parliament were in a minority.[2]

Somewhat unexpectedly, Antrim and Londonderry were whole-heartedly for Union. The tenantry of Antrim were notably independent-minded, and at first such landlords as John Staples and the marquess of Hertford were reported to find difficulty in obtaining the support of their tenantry for the measure.[3] Even after Castlereagh reported every appearance of the most general concurrence in its support, a local canvasser was still bemoaning the slow rate of progress at the beginning of September.[4] However, within the next month the member for the county, E. A. McNaghten, secured for publication 1,600 unionist signatures[5] and the anti-unionists in Antrim failed to muster any counter-petitions. Similarly,

---

[1] Bishop of Dromore's petition, 9 Oct. 1799 (C.S.O. 513/73/5).

[2] Robert Bradshaw to Castlereagh, 13 Jan. 1800 (Mt. Stewart MSS.).

[3] The Revd. Edward Hudson to Charlemont, 9 Mar. and 1 May 1799 (*H.M.C. Charlemont MSS.* ii, pp. 347, 351).

[4] Castlereagh to Portland, 5 Aug. 1799 (H.O. 100/86); Hon. Chichester Skeffington to Castlereagh, 3 Sept. 1799 (Mt. Stewart MSS.).

[5] Marsden to Castlereagh, 28 Sept. 1799 (*Castlereagh Correspondence*, ii, p. 406); McNaghten to Marsden, 16 Oct. 1799 (C.S.O. 513/73/8). The petition was published in the *Belfast Newsletter*, 11 Oct. 1799.

in Londonderry the Union at first failed to commend itself
to those of tender Protestant susceptibilities.[1] But as early as
2 January 1799, Cornwallis could report that 'most of the
respectable merchants are in favour', and the combined
influence of the Beresfords, Conolly, and Lords Caledon and
Londonderry left no opening for the opposition.[2] In March
the grand jury divided 18 to 5 in support of Union, counter-
ing hostile declarations at the Meath and Cavan assizes.[3]
During the summer unionist resolutions were passed unanimously in both city and county and in October the corporations of Londonderry and Coleraine presented addresses to
the Viceroy in favour of the measure.[4] By the end of the year,
according to John Beresford, there were not more than
twelve gentlemen in the entire county who opposed it.[5]

The other Ulster counties

   This success story was not repeated in the rest of Ulster.
Donegal was divided. Both county members were anti-
unionists, claiming local support for their attitude, and
although the Government continually toyed with the notion of
calling a county meeting to convert them, no action was taken
despite 'fast and numerous' signatures to the unionist petition.[6]
Stronger resistance to the Union was met in 'the frontier
of the plantation'—the counties of Tyrone, Fermanagh,
Armagh, Cavan, and Monaghan, where the nationalism
of the Protestant Ascendancy had thriven on religious
animosity ever since 1641. These counties had been foremost
in the Volunteer movement, had remained loyalist during
the stresses of Camden's administration, and had provided
many of the yeomanry.[7] With a highly developed national

   [1] Sir George Hill to Castlereagh, 9 Dec. 1798 (Mt. Stewart MSS.).
   [2] Cornwallis to Portland, 2 Jan. 1799 (H.O. 100/85); Downshire to Reilly, 13
Oct. 1799 (Downshire MSS.).
   [3] Henry Alexander to Castlereagh, 28 Mar. 1799 (*Castlereagh Correspondence*,
ii, p. 243).
   [4] Littlehales to Castlereagh, 18 Oct. 1799 (Mt. Stewart MSS.).
   [5] Beresford to Castlereagh, 14 Apr. 1800 (*Castlereagh Correspondence*, iii, p. 140).
   [6] Marsden to Castlereagh, 28 Sept. and 29 Oct. 1799 (ibid. ii, pp. 406, 435);
Cornwallis to Ross, 24 Oct. 1799 (*Cornwallis Correspondence*, iii, p. 141); Castlereagh
to Beresford, 11 Apr. 1800 (*Beresford Correspondence*, ii, p. 246).
   [7] Sir Richard Musgrave (*History of the Rebellion* [1801], p. 194) says that Tyrone,
Fermanagh, Cavan, and Armagh produced 14,000 Protestant yeomen, many of
them Presbyterians. But Gamble (op. cit., p. 285) states that many of the Protestants

self-consciousness and a mistrust of English 'softness' towards the Catholics, this area became a centre of Orange anti-unionist sentiment. Plunket was an Enniskillen man, Francis Hardy came from Cavan: whilst the noblemen of the region, Charlemont, Enniskillen, and Farnham, were all more or less anti-Catholic as well as anti-unionists. This was an area of such determined temper that Cornwallis avoided it during his tour in October 1799.[1]

Tyrone was perhaps the least strongly anti-unionist area. Here the influence of the absentee marquess of Abercorn was exerted in favour of the Government, especially in the country near Strabane. It was claimed that the Union was supported in this county by property worth £75,100 a year, with £44,900 opposing. However, the county was among the first to send up anti-unionist resolutions, and with both M.P.s hostile, Tyrone could be written off.[2] Fermanagh, dominated by the anti-unionists Enniskillen and Mervyn Archdall, seemed to Castlereagh 'hopeless'.[3] As for Cavan, its grand jury spoke out against Union both at the March and August assizes.[4] Later in the year government observers thought they discerned signs of a change, and by January 1800 Cooke was sanguine of winning over both county members.[5] But no opposition was offered at the end of that month to a county meeting condemning the measure, and the members were unconverted.[6] The western part of Monaghan was also strongly opposed to the measure, but around the borough of Monaghan the influence of the earl of Clermont's family turned the scale more favourably towards the Government. The anti-unionist county resolutions of February 1799 met with a dissentient protest from the majority of resident gentry, and later in the year an address favouring the

of Fermanagh and Cavan—two notable centres of Orange activity—were not Presbyterians but Episcopalians.

[1] Cornwallis to Portland, 24 Oct. 1799 (H.O. 100/87).
[2] Memorandum by Edward Cooke, 16 Oct. 1799 (Mt. Stewart MSS.).
[3] Castlereagh to King, 1 May 1800 (H.O. 100/93).
[4] Castlereagh to Portland, 27 Mar. and 5 Aug. 1799 (H.O. 100/86). But the grand jury passed no resolutions in April 1800 (Colonel Nesbitt to Littlehales, 6 Apr. 1800 (H.O. 100/93)).
[5] Cooke to Beresford, 14 Jan. 1800 (*Beresford Correspondence*, ii. p. 237). Cf. James Dawson to Castlereagh, 28 Aug. 1799 (Mt. Stewart MSS.).
[6] Cornwallis to Portland, 27 Jan. 1800 (H.O. 100/93).

measure was received from the corporation and inhabitants of the borough.[1]

Only two years before the introduction of the Union proposals, the county of Armagh had been one of the most disturbed counties in Ireland. Large portions had been proclaimed under the Insurrection Act at the end of 1796, and there was no county in Ireland where Protestants and Catholics feuded more bitterly.[2] Yet both sides of the Union question were canvassed extensively throughout 1799, and the part taken by individuals deviated from traditional alliances. In January 1799 a county meeting had been called by Charlemont's anti-unionist friends: his son Lord Caulfield, M.P. for the county; William Brownlow and William Richardson, two of his predecessors; Sir Capel Molyneux and William Todd Jones.[3] Postponed until after the parliamentary debate, the meeting was held at Armagh on 19 February, when a series of moderately phrased anti-unionist resolutions was passed unanimously.[4] Surprise was expressed that viscount Gosford, a government supporter who had supplanted Charlemont as governor of the county, had offered no opposition: but his son, Archibald Acheson, and son-in-law Robert Sparrow, had sided with the anti-unionists.

Until October the solidarity of the anti-unionist front was unbroken. Upon Caulfield's elevation to the Lords at his father's death, however, two candidates came forward at the by-election: Sir Capel Molyneux, garrulous and bombastic heir to a name honoured in the history of Irish nationalism, and Colonel Robert Cope, a staunch Protestant landowner, and an enthusiastic hunter of Catholics suspected of being United Irishmen.[5] Both were anti-union men, but Gosford

[1] Castlereagh to Portland, 9 Feb. 1799 (H.O. 100/85); Elliot to Castlereagh, 19 Oct. 1799 (*Castlereagh Correspondence*, ii, p. 432).

[2] 'The county of Armagh Presbyterians are the very Spadassins of Protestantism', wrote Gamble in 1812 (op. cit., p. 37); and his views are borne out by Plowden, *History of Ireland from 1801 to 1810* (i, pp. 66–67). But the radical Dr. Drennan wrote in June 1801 to his sister, Mrs. McTier: 'The savagery of the lower Catholics was even greater than the rule of retaliation could account for' (Drennan MSS., P.R.O.N.I.).

[3] The Revd. Nathaniel Alexander to Alexander Knox, 17 Jan. 1799 (*Castlereagh Correspondence*, ii, p. 123).

[4] Robert Boyd to Charlemont, 20 Feb. 1799 (*H.M.C. Charlemont MSS*. ii, p. 346).

[5] Plowden, op. cit. i, pp. 68–69.

and the unionists swung their support behind Cope, and this was probably decisive in ensuring his victory by 1,810 votes to 1,282.[1] Two months later, James Verner, one of the few Orange leaders to espouse the Union cause, and hence a suitable person for the negotiation, succeeded in attaching Cope to the unionist ranks before Parliament met in January 1800. However, even with this support, the unionists found it slow going to get up 'a respectable petition'; by mid-January they had acquired 987 signatories, including the Primate and six peers.[2] Here, then, was a situation in which the Protestant archbishop of Armagh, Gosford, and Cope found themselves siding against equally staunch anti-Catholics in Brownlow, Richardson, and Gosford's son and heir, Acheson. Nothing is known of the views of the Armagh Catholics.

The Catholic west and south

This area, comprising the western part of Munster and all of Connaught, was a source of support for the union. The city of Cork had produced the first declarations in favour of it, and the hope of greater prosperity kept it constant throughout the ensuing campaign.[3] The Catholic vote, looking for more liberal conditions under the United Parliament, was also significant in this region. Thus the county of Kerry, which under the inspiration of Sir Thomas Mullins and the Catholic viscount Kenmare came forward with a unanimous address in favour of the Union from 'the entire property of the county',[4] was the home of a large Catholic population. Limerick provided another example of their influence. Here the corporation of the county town was closely controlled by John Prendergast Smyth, under whose persuasion it sent up

[1] Blacker to Cooke, 12 Oct. 1799 (C.S.O. 513/73/6); Littlehales to Castlereagh, 31 Oct. 1799 (Mt. Stewart MSS.); *Belfast Newsletter*, 29 Oct. 1799.

[2] Ibid., 14 Jan. 1800.

[3] W. O'Sullivan, *Economic History of Cork City to 1800*, Cork, 1937. Cf. Donoughmore to Isaac Corry, 6 July 1799, conveying a plan for a store and customs house at Cork: 'In providing storage for the port of Cork, its probable situation after the Union as a great place of depot and export of West India produce is to be considered, and therefore nothing but what will be very extensive could be adequate' (Mt. Stewart MSS.).

[4] Mullins to Castlereagh, 31 May 1799; Altamont to Castlereagh, 'Sunday morning' (undated; somewhere about the same time) (Mt. Stewart MSS.).

an anti-unionist address: this body was entirely free from Catholic influence. The Castle's information about feeling in the county was at first conflicting. Lord Clare, whose estates were in that part of the country, alleged that orders had been sent to the Roman Catholics of Limerick to oppose the measure, but John Lees was more hopeful.[1] In July, a local landowner, Lord Glentworth, went to drum up support for the Union, but found his opponents had got the start of him in canvassing. He countered by requesting the Catholic archbishop of Dublin, Dr. Troy, to send him a letter expressing support for the measure, after which a petition was received from the Catholics of Limerick. Within a month Cornwallis wrote: '. . . the Chancellor and Lord Glentworth have perfectly succeeded in attaching to the measure every person not of the Corporation, and the property of the county through his Lordship's exertions, will be brought forward not less decidedly in its support'.[2] There could be little doubt that the Catholic interests in Limerick, enlisted by a nobleman of more conciliatory temperament than the ultra-Protestant Clare, was useful in producing a unionist response in the county.

But in Mayo, where there was also a strong concentration of Catholics, they had less to do with the success of the unionists. Early in June the earl of Altamont, who was foremost in promoting the measure in that area, reported the Catholics unwilling to commit themselves; however, the landowners of the county were almost unanimously for the measure.[3] On 6 July Castlereagh forwarded a copy of their resolutions to Portland, with the comment that they were endorsed by 'the entire property' of the county; but it was not until a week later that the Catholic archbishop of Tuarn, Dr. Edward Dillon, and a leading landowner of that communion, Thomas Dillon, authorized their names to appear on the published copies of this declaration. In the county

---

[1] Castlereagh to Portland, 7 Jan. 1799 (H.O. 100/85); cf. Lees to Castlereagh, 11 Dec. 1798 (Mt. Stewart MSS.).

[2] Cornwallis to Portland, 14 Aug. 1799 (H.O. 100/86); but *Dublin Evening Post*, 28 Jan. 1800, reports that the Limerick Catholics repudiated the petition.

[3] Altamont to —— [probably Cooke or Marsden], 5 June 1799 (Mt. Stewart MSS.). There was 'nobody worth £100 a year against it' except his hereditary rivals, the O'Donels, who later got up two anti-unionist petitions.

of Leitrim after the Catholics had taken a lead by sending up their own unionist petition, a set of resolutions in favour of the measure was endorsed by 1,836 signatures.[1]

I now pass to four of the most hotly contested counties, all of them in Connaught or Munster: Galway, Roscommon, Tipperary, and Waterford.

Galway

Both in the city and the county, the anti-unionists were first to declare themselves. The corporation of Galway was divided between unionist and opposition branches of the Daly family: but in January 1799 it passed resolutions against the measure. Early in February, a county meeting was convened, which, despite the strictures of the earl of Clanricarde, the largest landowner in the district, sent an anti-unionist address to the House of Commons.[2] The members for the county were divided. Richard Trench was an anti-unionist, while Joseph Blake, although he obediently transmitted to the House of Commons petitions against the measure, voted for it. The prospects of canvassing the county were doubtful. During the winter of 1798–9 there had been an outbreak of agrarian crime. Exaggerated reports about the losses incurred through cattle-houghing circulated Dublin. Unaware that such activities were almost entirely due to local economic grievances, the authorities in Dublin saw in this development evidence of new plots for rebellion.[3]

When St. George Daly came to Galway in February, to seek re-election after taking office, he found the climate of opinion 'less unfavourable than expected'.[4] Much, it was

---

[1] Troy to Marshall, 13 July 1799 (*Castlereagh Correspondence*, ii, p. 349). Plowden, op. cit. ii, pp. 322–3.

[2] Clanricarde to Castlereagh, 14 Jan. 1799 (Mt. Stewart MSS.) and M. Burke to Castlereagh, 16 Apr. 1799 (*Castlereagh Correspondence*, ii, p. 277): 'The friends of Union, considering that reason and moderation would not be listened to, from their knowledge of some of those who attended it, and who were the orators at it . . . did not attend.'

[3] Cornwallis to Portland, 14 and 23 Feb. 1799 (H.O. 100/85): cf. Robert Johnson to Downshire, 14 Feb. 1799 (Downshire MSS.): 'Galway is completely organized by the rebels . . . the principle of the attack is neither vague nor local, but systematic and imperial.' Martial law was declared on 20 Feb. But Burke informed Castlereagh on 31 Mar. 1799 that the destruction had been exaggerated. Claims for losses did not exceed £15,000 (Mt. Stewart MSS.).

[4] St. George Daly to Castlereagh, 11 Feb. 1799 (Mt. Stewart MSS.).

apparent, would depend on the Catholics. There were more men of property of that description in Galway than in any other county of Ireland.[1] Close connexion with them was maintained by two Members of Parliament, Joseph Blake, whose father was still a practising Catholic, and Richard Martin, M.P. for Lanesborough.[2] Another loquacious but hard-working contact man between Government and Catholics was Michael Burke of Loughrea, who busied himself by assisting the earl of Clanricarde to collect signatures for a protest contradicting the anti-unionist meeting, 'containing property to four times the amount of all those who attended it, and a majority of those as yet committed on the question'.[3] His sanguine hopes of gaining the Catholics were damped by a letter from Blake's father, previously a unionist, who had been beset by qualms that Westminster would be less sympathetic than a local parliament to the repeal of Catholic disabilities—an argument recently advanced by the Speaker during the discussions on the Regency Bill.[4] On the other hand, Richard Trench was reported to have second thoughts about his opposition, and his father, Lord Kilconnel, wrote complaining that he had been passed over for promotion in the peerage, although his family had backed every government measure save the Union and had 'taken no part whatever to bias the publick mind on the measure'.[5]

To influence the county members it was determined to convene a formal meeting of the county—a medium of public opinion which some administration supporters disliked as allowing too much scope for opposition oratory. But 'the Sheriff had zeal and his heart was with us',[6] while Blake and Martin were indefatigable in preparation. The county

[1] Burke to Castlereagh, 8 Mar. 1799. Elsewhere (same to same, 14 Apr. 1799) Burke assessed the value of property in Galway owned by Catholics at nearly £20,000 per annum (Mt. Stewart MSS.).

[2] Martin succeeded Blake as M.P. for co. Galway 1800–6, 1818–27. In 1827 his return was disallowed by the House of Commons because of irregular practices. One of the charges brought against him was intimidation of the returning officers by bringing into Galway mobs of his Catholic tenantry, inflamed with liquor and anti-Protestant slogans (*Report of the Select Committee of Enquiry into the Election for County Galway* (H. of C. Accounts & Papers, 1826–7, iv, p. 953)).

[3] Burke to Castlereagh, 16 Apr. 1799 (*Castlereagh Correspondence*, ii, p. 277).

[4] Ibid.: cf. Blake to Burke, 12 Apr. 1799 (Mt. Stewart MSS.).

[5] Kilconnel to Castlereagh, 1 June 1799 (ibid.).

[6] Martin to Castlereagh, 2 Sept. 1799; cf. same to same, 26 and 27 July 1799 (ibid.).

meeting was held at Loughrea on 30 August, and seemed a genuine trial of strength. Daly, the Prime Serjeant, and Stanley, the Third Serjeant, two of the Government's leading orators, attended the meeting: but the anti-unionist Bowes Daly brought along a number of his forty-shilling free-holders, described by Martin as 'a mob disposed to riot and to break the windows of the hall in which we sat'.[1] The Catholic vote, however, was with the unionists,[2] as was the majority of that respectable class, the £20 freeholders, con-voked by the exertions of the earl of Clanricarde. It was estimated that there was £83,300 of Galway property in favour of the measure, and no more than £31,700 against.[3] Meanwhile the borough of Galway rescinded its former opinions, and the corporation now put their names to a unionist petition.[4] If further evidence was required, it would come in April 1800 when the grand jury of Galway resolved for Union by 18 votes to 5.[5] But already both county members had distinguished themselves by their advocacy of the cause. The Government's concern about Galway was to be reflected about profuse distribution of titles to those who had taken part in the unionist campaign there.[6] Nevertheless, the uncertainty surrounding the outcome of the county meeting, and the endorsement of its verdict by the grand jury in the following year would suggest a reasonably accurate reflection of public opinion had been given—always remembering the limited number of those who were in any position to shape public opinion.

Roscommon

The importance of Catholic goodwill was revealed by the unionist reverses, Roscommon and Tipperary. Bordering

---

[1] Martin to Castlereagh, 26 and 27 July 1799. Martin was confident, however, that given warning the union magnates could match their rivals in forty-shilling freeholders: '. . . the better way would have been to have kept a hall open from day to day, and in two days I could have from my own estate, independent of any con-nexion, have brought a force of eleven to twelve hundred freeholders.'

[2] Dr. Dillon, archbishop of Tuam, to Dr. Troy, archbishop of Dublin, 1 Sept. 1799 (*Castlereagh Correspondence*, ii. p. 387).

[3] Stanley to Castlereagh, 3 Sept. 1799 (Mt. Stewart MSS.).

[4] Cornwallis to Portland, 13 Aug. 1799 (H.O. 100/86). The petition is repro-duced in Hardiman, op. cit., p. 191.

[5] Martin to Castlereagh, 15 Apr. 1800 (Mt. Stewart MSS.).

[6] One earldom, one viscountcy, and three baronies came to Galway.

Connaught, each of these counties contained a substantial Catholic population, who, unlike those in Galway, had suffered considerable persecution during the last three or four years from local squireens wielding the power of a government commission. Even Camden commented on the illiberality of the Roscommon landlords.[1] Prominent among them was Viscount Kingsborough (who succeeded his father as 3rd earl of Kingston in April 1799). His militia regiment was notorious for their maltreatment of 'Papists'.[2] His colleague as member for the county, Arthur French, was said to be returned principally on Lord Kingston's interest,[3] but had hereditary claims of his own to represent the county. Both these members voted against the Union in January 1799. The ministry expected to work up substantial opposition to them among the Catholics of the county: 'If you will give me the *least assistance*', wrote the earl of Altamont, 'I will shake Roscommon.'[4]

Unionist confidence perhaps grew from the belief that the earl of Kingston's interest would be weakened by the recent sale of most of the family's Roscommon estates:[5] and although, on Kingsborough's succession to the earldom, his brother Robert King resigned his seat for Boyle in order to contest the by-election, he soon stood down in favour of Colonel Thomas Mahon, of an ancient and widely connected local family who had previously supplied the county with several members.[6] But at the end of March an observer with Catholic contacts had reported the Papists of Roscommon as inclined against the measure. Lord Altamont was also pessimistic, but his brother, Denis Browne, reported in July to Cornwallis: 'The great proportion of all classes are Catholicks, if it be possible they shall know their true interests. French is with you in his opinions, he will not be very angry to have it in his power to talk over this matter with your

[1] Camden to Pitt, 21 May 1795 (P.R.O. 30/8/326).
[2] Plowden, op. cit. i, p. 104.
[3] Thomas Knox (ed. Johnston), op. cit., p. 34.
[4] Altamont to Castlereagh, 7 Mar. 1799 (Mt. Stewart MSS.).
[5] Michael Burke to Castlereagh, 8 Mar. 1799 (ibid.).
[6] His grandfather, Thomas Mahon, was M.P. for Roscommon borough 1739–63, and for the county 1763–82, owing his success to 'all his relations residing in the county and marrying through one another'.

Excellency. Mahon is not ill disposed to the measure. . . .'¹
But the assizes revealed a less satisfactory state of affairs.
Edmond Stanley stated in a post-mortem that, possibly
because the Sheriff of the county had been a nominee of
French, only eleven out of the twenty-three members of the
grand jury had supported a unionist address prepared by
Henry Moore Sandford, owner of Roscommon borough and
a prospective peer:

. . . some respectable men were on it, certainly, many Catholics, and
some men I never saw on any Grand Jury in this county before—
under these circumstances, we thought it would be highly imprudent
to agitate the question or bring it forward—our plan to procure signatures to a declaration was frustrated by a requisition to the Sheriff to
call a county meeting, which was brought forward at the assizes, and
acceded to by Mr. Lyster the Sheriff, to be held 2nd November next.²

The only prospective convert to the unionists was Colonel
Mahon: 'tho' from election policy his family are alledged to
yield to the current of things—yet I don't think their private
opinion averse', Stanley wrote. However, the freeholders, on
whose opinions French had said he would base his stand,
looked very hostile, not least the Catholics. Undeterred,
Cooke determined to attempt the promotion of a Catholic
declaration, and throughout the autumn unionist agents
canvassed Roscommon pertinaciously.³ But the tenantry
were reluctant to come forward in support of the Union
without the prior consent of their landlord, and this was
seldom proffered: so that Under-Secretary Marsden had to
admit: 'We are not getting forward in Roscommon',⁴ just
before the county meeting, which produced a series of anti-
unionist resolutions.

Tipperary

The largest county in Ireland, Tipperary had been described by Camden in 1798 as 'the scene of most outrage

---

¹ Browne to Cornwallis, 20 July 1799 (Mt. Stewart MSS.).
² Stanley to Cooke, no date (C.S.O. 525/163/2).
³ Cooke to Castlereagh, 18 Sept. 1799 (*Castlereagh Correspondence*, ii, p. 403).
⁴ Marsden to Castlereagh, 29 Oct. 1799 (ibid., p. 435).

and the most marked acts of rebellion'.[1] It had also figured as the scene of some of the most brutal reprisals. One of the county members, Colonel John Bagwell, is asserted to have given his militia regiment *carte blanche* in dealing with the rebels, so long as he had no official cognizance of their activities. Among those whom he upheld was the High Sheriff of Tipperary for 1798, Thomas Judkin Fitzgerald, a brutal ruffian whose zeal for flogging suspects without trial was, even by contemporary standards, excessive.[2] Despite all this, by the next year conditions in Tipperary were sufficiently normal to allow of a closely fought political campaign.

The most prominent figures in this county were the earl of Donoughmore; the earl of Landaff—himself a unionist, although his sons opposed; Lord Lismore, one of the Ponsonby connexion; John Toler the Attorney-General; and the Prittie and Bagwell families. At the assizes of March 1799, Lords Lismore and Mathew, with forty-eight other anti-unionists, requested a county meeting to signify disapproval of the measure. Donoughmore thereupon got up a unionist counter-requisition, to which were affixed 'two hundred respectable signatures', including nearly all the leading Roman Catholics, whose support the anti-unionists had tended to spurn. Some of his signatories, commented Donoughmore, were not great enthusiasts for union, but wished to display their hostility to the anti-unionists, in particular to Colonel Bagwell.[3] Accordingly, the High Sheriff, Donoughmore's brother John Hely-Hutchinson, was called upon to convene a county meeting in the first week of August.[4] This was 'most numerously and respectably attended' and strong unionist resolutions were passed unanimously. Lord Lismore

---

[1] Camden to Portland, 23 Apr. 1798 (H.O. 100/76).

[2] In *Wright* v. *Fitzgerald*, at the Clonmel assizes, Mar. 1799, the sheriff was mulcted of £500 damages for administering 500 lashes to a teacher of French, whose only crime was the possession of a note in a language which Fitzgerald could not read. However, Toler and Castlereagh arranged for his immediate compensation out of the secret service money (C.S.O. 513/64/10) and he was made a baronet in 1801. According to F. Plowden, op. cit. ii, p. 954, Bagwell supported, and his colleague for Tipperary, Lord Mathew, opposed, Fitzgerald's indemnification; yet both were half-hearted anti-unionists.

[3] Donoughmore to Castlereagh, 25 Mar. 1799 (Mt. Stewart MSS.).

[4] *Cork Advertiser*, 27 Aug. 1799. As published, the requisition for the meeting bears 183 signatures, including seven peers.

and some of his allies, finding themselves outnumbered, withdrew from the meeting before the motion was put. The two county members promised to model their conduct on their constituents' instructions; it was also hoped to gain Mathew's brother and Bagwell's two sons, in all an accession of five members to the unionist side. The Catholics of the county produced a separate petition, and Cornwallis seemed justified in stating: 'The accession of Tipperary to those counties before declared, gives us the entire province of Munster; and its weight will be the more authoritative, as it is an inland county, and not decided merely by commercial prospects.'[1]

Waterford

The Union campaign in Waterford was a straightforward contest along the lines of traditional local political rivalries. As an outport hoping for increased participation in the American and colonial trade, Waterford was expected to support the union. But the corporation had for long been resisting the encroachments of the local magnate, the marquess of Waterford, and in reaction against him the city members had at least a thirty-year-old tradition of opposition to the Government. It was not until June that canvassing began to find signatories for a unionist petition, and then the brunt of the work was borne by the dean of Waterford, Charles Butson. It was thought desirable that Lord Waterford should keep out of city politics, and the bishop, Marlay, was Grattan's uncle and one of the two anti-unionists on the Irish Bench. Butson's account of his labours[2] showed that disagreements on the Union issue cut right across family ties. The city members, Henry Alcock and R. S. Carew, were opposed to the measure; the mayor, Boyse—Carew's brother-in-law, and reputed an intimate friend of the Ponsonbys—was 'not unfavourable to a union, but would not sign any public document'; while the most influential families on the corporation, the Alcocks and Newports, were completely

---

[1] Cornwallis to Portland, 14 Aug. 1799 (H.O. 100/86). The Catholic petition, with ninety signatures, was published in the *Cork Advertiser*, 24 Aug. 1799.

[2] Butson to Cooke, 25 June 1799 (C.S.O. 513/73/3); and same to same, 4 July 1799 (Mt. Stewart MSS.).

divided. 'Almost all the consequence, magistracy, and property of the place are with us', claimed Butson, 'We do not
descend below decent shop and house-keepers.' The city
petition was published with 350 signatures.[1] The other
religious denominations had given a mixed response. The
Methodists were mainly unionists, but the Quakers steadfastly refused to take sides. As for the Roman Catholics,
'a wealthy and estated body here', their Dean would not
encourage a move until advice had been received from the
Government through the local Catholic bishop, Dr. Hussey.
Forty Catholics authorized their names for publication early
in July, and eventually a separate unionist petition appeared
bearing the names of 209 Waterford residents of this faith.[2]
The corporation still refused to be responsible for presenting these resolutions, which were ultimately sent up to the
Government, together with a county resolution bearing 363
signatures, by the marquess of Waterford.[3]

'Twenty-eight out of thirty-two counties, and thirty-eight
out of sixty-four county members have declared against an
union', wrote R. L. Edgeworth to his friend Dr. Erasmus
Darwin.[4] Other anti-unionists besides took this as evidence
of the unpopularity of the Government's measure. On the
other hand, at one stage in 1799 Cooke estimated that
£370,700 of the property represented in the House of Lords
was in favour of Union, £132,000 against, and £91,000
undeclared: and this entailed the influencing of a good many
tenant farmers throughout Ireland. Of course, each side tried
to impugn the validity of the addresses secured by the others.
J. M. O'Donel accused the Administration of coercing
signatures from the very prisoners in the gaols.[5] 'For the
whole summer', said J. C. Beresford in January 1800,[6]
'. . . every village has been ransacked for signatures and
means been used which the Noble Lord [Castlereagh] would
be ashamed of were he acquainted with them.' On the other
hand, unionist landlords complained that emissaries from the

---

[1] *Cork Advertiser*, 3 Aug. 1799.   [2] Ibid.
[3] Waterford to Castlereagh, 9 Sept. 1799 (*Castlereagh Correspondence*, ii, p. 394).
[4] Edgeworth to Darwin, 31 Mar. 1800 (Edgeworth, op. cit. ii, p. 252).
[5] *Debates*, 15–16 Jan. 1800, p. 67.   [6] Ibid., p. 186.

Opposition were misrepresenting them in order to cozen signatures from their tenantry, and in Wexford, a county suffering the aftermath of a violent rebellion, coercion was used by landlords on both sides.[1]

Nevertheless, the enfranchisement of Roman Catholic forty-shilling freeholders in 1793 had increased the political weight of that group. Much of the unionist success in the west and south of Ireland was due to the assiduity of the landlords in that area in soliciting their votes. The influence of the Catholics should not be over-estimated. In regions such as the environs of Dublin, it has been noted above that Catholics followed their Protestant neighbours in opposing the measure, and the best for which the Government could hope was neutrality.[2] Where, however, the Protestant element was negligible, Catholic goodwill was often serviceable to the unionists. This was not due to any especial rapport between the landlords of Munster and Connaught and their tenantry. Often the local Catholics at first evinced no great enthusiasm for Union, and before they would declare themselves required prompting from their priests and gentry, themselves inclined to await a lead from the bishops. As for the Ascendancy landlords, the earl of Altamont put their attitude well enough:

If the Roman Catholics stand forward, it will be unwillingly; they are keeping back decidedly, but many will be influenced, and some few who connected themselves with the Protestants during the disturbances will be zealously forward on the present occasion. The priests have all offered to sign; and, though I am not proud of many of them as associates, I will take their signatures, to prevent the possibility of a counter-demonstration . . . I may be mistaken, but in my judgment, the wish of most of them would be to stand neuter; or, perhaps, if they had any countenance, to oppose it—that is the fact. Several will sign from influence, some from fear; but the majority, I believe, will pretend that they have given opinions already, and can't decently retract them. . . . Every man applied to, of all persuasions, wants to make it personal compliment.[3]

[1] See footnote 3, p. 132 this chapter; also William Rogers to Castlereagh, 19 Feb. 1800 (*Castlereagh Correspondence*, iii, p. 242).

[2] The parish priest of Tullamore (King's Co.), the Revd. Hugh Dowling, writing to Castlereagh, 17 Jan. 1800, drew a distinction between the political conduct of Dublin and country Catholics (ibid., p. 226).

[3] Altamont to ——, 5 June 1799 (ibid. ii, p. 328).

But the western gentry needed Catholic support. The enfranchisement of that sect enhanced their potential political consequence. Hitherto Dublin and the surrounding counties of Leinster had been the political centre of gravity of Ireland. Many of the magnates of eighteenth-century politics—Leinster, the Ponsonbys, Ely, Foster, Parnell—and nearly all the orators, such as Grattan, Forbes, Curran, Saurin, and Flood—came from this area.[1] The westerners were, by contrast, regarded a little in the light of backwoodsmen. 'Denis Browne with his voters from Croagh-Patrick'[2] somehow did not cut so impressive a figure as a Ponsonby from Kilkenny. During the 'nineties, however, there had been a decrease in the number of voters in some parts of Leinster. The number of registered voters in Kildare was reported as decreasing between 1790 and 1797 from 1,500 to no more than 300, including the clergy.[3] The ravages of the 1798 rebellion were thought to have lessened the number of freeholders in county Wicklow.[4] In the western counties, untouched by similar losses, the enfranchisement of Catholics had created in 1793 a new block of voters whose weight had never been evoked before 1799, for want of an important issue dividing the Parliament of Ireland—the reformers being in too hopeless a minority to appeal to the country. The Union, however, aroused a controversy in which both sides attached importance to the appearance of popular support. Here was a situation in which the landlords of Connaught and Munster could deliver the goods, and obtain as a reward more public patronage than had hitherto come their way. Of the eighteen new peerages attributable to services in the Union controversy, at least eleven went the way of gentry from the western counties—Cork, Galway, Kerry, Longford, Roscommon, and Tipperary. The changes on the Board of Revenue in 1799 were no less suggestive. Four commissioners from the neighbourhood of Dublin, one deceased and three dismissed for anti-unionist sympathies, were replaced by members from Clare, Cork, and Kerry, of known unionist beliefs.

---

[1] One of the exceptions was the earl of Clare.
[2] Francis Hardy to Charlemont, 6 Nov. 1798 (*H.M.C. Charlemont MSS.* ii, p. 338).
[3] *Belfast Newsletter*, 31 July 1797.
[4] Carysfort to Grenville, 17 Jan. 1801 (*H.M.C. Dropmore MSS.* vi, p. 427).

The Catholics were far from becoming politically asser-
tive; but some inkling was given of their possible efficacy as
a political pressure-group. Where, as in Kerry, they gave
their backing whole-heartedly, it provided the Castle with
a much-needed model of a county solidly behind the Union.
Where, as in Roscommon, their reaction was more tardy or
divided, the unionists failed to make their expected gains. It
was a long way yet to 1828, and the organized Catholic vote
which swept Daniel O'Connell into the seat for county
Clare: but in several parts of Ireland, the Union was the
first occasion when Catholic clergy and middle-class laity
were given the slightest political consequence. Of course, no
such development was envisaged by the Administration.
Strict instructions from that solid Protestant, Portland, provided that no positive incentives were to be held out to the
Catholics. The most for which they could hope was that the
United Parliament might view their claims more objectively
than the Ascendancy's legislature at Dublin. 'I should hope',
wrote Portland, when informed of the Opposition's plans to
introduce measures for the relief of Catholic disabilities,

. . . that it will not be found impossible to satisfy every reasonable
Roman Catholic and every man of property of that persuasion that
such an attempt could not be made in the present circumstances without the most imminent danger to their properties and persons; . . . and
that a Union is as indispensably necessary for the purpose of affording
them a reasonable probability of being admitted to a full participation
of rights in common with the Protestants, as it is to remove and quiet
those apprehensions which are at present entertained of them on account of the superiority of their numbers, and to render them no longer
objects of terror or jealousy.[1]

This hardly encouraged the Catholics to enthusiastic exertion; and until June 1799, all observers vouched for their
general neutrality. Nor were the Catholic bishops either confident or eager in exercising whatever secular guidance they
possessed over their flocks. Still recovering from the strains
and tensions created among their communion by the '98
risings, they were reluctant to commit themselves to overt
partisanship on either side. As the Catholic archbishop of
Cashel wrote to his superior, Dr. Troy:

[1] Portland to Cornwallis, 3 Feb. 1799 (H.O. 100/85).

I need not observe to you, who know so well the dispositions of our respectable Catholics, what little influence we have over them in political matters, and with what reserve and secrecy we should interfere on the present occasion, in order to ensure any degree of success to it, and to avoid censure.

If we act in any ostensible capacity in the business of Union, either by a personal signature to an address in favour of it, or otherwise, in my humble opinion, instead of serving the cause, we may injure it.[1]

Subsequently, towards the end of 1799, the balance of Catholic opinion veered towards the Union question. Organized Protestant opinion was much more hostile. Although the exertions of James Verner and J. C. Beresford, respectively Grand Master and General Secretary of the United Orange Lodges, committed that body officially to a policy of neutrality, many of the lodges in the North made no secret of their opposition. Except for one Belfast lodge, all who published their views were anti-unionists.[2]

It would, however, be misleading to attempt the assessment of the response to the Union proposals in terms of nation-wide pressure-groups. Most of the declarations of opinion about the Union were evoked by the leadership of local landowners, with the intention of influencing their friends and neighbours in Parliament. The county was still the important unit in the expression of public opinion, even though it can be accepted that most tenantry voted as they were told and that free opinions were probably expressed only by a few of the more wealthy and literate members of the community. To a considerable extent, one can disregard the charges flung about by both sides, accusing the other of intimidation of tenantry, faking of signatures, and other malpractices.[3] That such activities were known in Ireland was amply testified by the election committees of the United Parliament in the next generation; but petitions intended to

---

[1] Dr. Bray, archbishop of Cashel to Dr. Troy, archbishop of Dublin, 1 July 1799 (*Castlereagh Correspondence*, ii, p. 344).

[2] Verner and Beresford (who took opposite sides on the issue) published an appeal for neutrality in 1799 and repeated it in 1800 (*Belfast Newsletter*, 22 Jan. 1799; 4 Feb. 1800). But in Mar. 1800, thirty-two north-of-Ireland Orange Lodges inserted a notice in the newspapers, repudiating the policy of neutrality, and reprobating the Belfast Lodge which had declared for the Union (ibid. 4 Mar. 1800).

[3] 'These mutual charges and recriminations were unfortunately but too well founded' (F. Plowden, op. cit. ii, p. 977).

influence the conduct of members resident in the county could not deviate too wildly from the consensus of local opinion, otherwise their effect would be wasted. There was clearly some correlation between the views of county members and their constituencies. There were four counties, Antrim, Kerry, Waterford, and Londonderry, in which no anti-unionist petition could be got up: seven of the eight members for these counties were anti-unionists. Of the 26 unionist county members, 23 came from the 19 counties in which petitions were obtained favouring the measure. Of the 38 anti-unionists, 23 represented counties in which no unionist petition was organized. It seems reasonable to assume that a minority of articulate public opinion favoured the Union, a rather larger group, perhaps half as many again, opposed the measure, and the rest were apathetic.[1] Had the Dublin legislature been able to arouse the nationalist spirit of 1782, of which it claimed to be the repository, the anti-unionist resistance must have been brilliant and successful. Their failure can be explained by the absence of a vigorous public opposition to the measure outside Dublin, as well as to the Government's advantage in parliamentary manœuvre and the operation of patronage.

[1] A comparison is difficult, because the unionists concentrated on winning over the weight of property, whereas the anti-unionists relied more on numbers. I arrive at this proportion after considering that 26 county members supported and 38 opposed the Union: 19 petitions were received from the counties in favour of the measure, and 28 against. There can be no serious doubt that the unionists were outnumbered, but, because of the publicity accorded to the Opposition in Dublin, I believe that the strength of anti-unionist feeling in the country at large has sometimes been over-estimated.

VI

THE WINNING OF A MAJORITY
1799–1800

> My occupation is now of the most unpleasant nature,
> negotiating and jobbing with the most corrupt people
> under heaven. I despise and hate myself every hour for
> engaging in such dirty work, and am supported only by
> the reflection that without an Union the British Empire
> must be dissolved.
>
> CORNWALLIS to ROSS, 8 June 1799.[1]

T HE Union divisions of January 1799 admitted of few
easy generalizations about the motives guiding members in their choice of sides. Few common characteris-
tics may be discerned between the four major interests
supporting the Union—the Beresfords, prepared to support
any administration that assured them of good places, but
rendering serviceable assistance to the machinery of government in return; Lord Shannon, the veteran trimmer, equally
at home in opposition or in office; his Cork rival, Lord
Longueville, a parvenu frankly on the make; and Lord
Abercorn, whose parliamentary interest was a means of
feeding his sense of personal consequence. Nor did the less
prominent borough patrons conform to any type. Some, such
as the earls of Wicklow and Roden, had been consistent
supporters of the Government for decades, earning their
decent share of county patronage in their own corner of
Ireland, and seldom if ever needing to resort to the bluster
of their hungrier brethren. One or two, such as the marquesses of Hertford and Wellesley, were absentee landlords who supported Pitt in England, and naturally backed
his Irish ministers.[2] Others had proven their capacity for

---

[1] *Cornwallis Correspondence*, iii, p. 102.

[2] Cf. the letter from William Wellesley Pole to his brother, Mornington, 16 Dec.
1798 (B.M. Add. MSS. 37308), where Pole states that, although himself an anti-
unionist, he will instruct the two members for the family borough of Trim to vote
for the measure, as he knows Mornington is a supporter of Pitt.

disinterest. Lord Donoughmore was eclipsed from favour as recently as 1795 for pressing the Catholic cause too hard and unseasonably,[1] while Thomas Conolly was the pattern independent country gentleman, even to his occasional inconsistencies. Among the other unionist supporters were the interests of two recently deceased politicians who had almost always been in Opposition, Henry Bruen and the great liberal Lord O'Neill.[2] The cousins, Lords Bective and Longford, inherited a family tradition of frequent oppositions to the Castle: indeed, their followings were so divided on the issue that each of them had to remove one member for anti-unionist sentiments.[3] Several families, too, were to cover themselves both ways, by giving the support of the head of the family in the House of Lords, while the eldest son opposed it in the Commons.[4] Thus the earl of Leitrim supported, but the two members for his borough of Carrick-on-Shannon, and his son, Viscount Clements, voted against Union in January 1799. Lord Landaff supported, and his two sons opposed: while Richard Dawson, M.P. for co. Monaghan, and a prominent anti-unionist, was heir to the courtier, Lord Cremorne.[5]

The anti-unionists were drawn from two numerically equal but very diverse groups. One was the regular 'whig' Opposition centred around the Ponsonby cousinhood. The

[1] Camden to Portland, 8 July 1797 (H.O. 100/70).

[2] Bruen's executors, Henry King and Robert French, were anti-unionists. Three of his four members for the boroughs of Duleek and Taghmon had sat since before his death in 1795; the newcomer was his widow's brother. Although without an adult patron, this group continued to act as a team, uninfluenced by Bruen's executors. On the other hand O'Neill's estate was administered by two strongly unionist M.P.s, James McClelland and Isaac Corry.

[3] Bective and Longford were grandsons of Hercules Langford Rowley, M.P. for co. Meath 1761–92, and almost always in opposition. The Longford interest was originally attached to the duke of Leinster.

[4] One explanation of such conduct is given by Bishop Percy of Dromore. Writing to his wife, 30 Jan.1800, he comments: '... what is singular is that although Ld. Gosford *supports*, his son, the member for the county, is a convinc'd opponent. I suspect Lady G., who rules the roost in that family. . . .' (B.M. Add. MSS. 32335.)

[5] 'Lord Cremorne was at cards with the Royal family at Windsor when the despatches came in, which contained the proceedings of the Irish parliament on this grand question, and the names of the members who voted on it. Lord Cremorne was so much shocked at seeing his nephew's name on the obnoxious list, that he fainted' (Gamble, op. cit., pp. 180–1).

other wing of the anti-unionists was headed by those office-holding magnates, usually of anti-Catholic tendencies, who had hitherto approved of Dublin Castle for its strong measures, but could not trust an absentee British Government to keep the country pacified by time-honoured methods. Into this group fell Foster, Parnell, Enniskillen, Farnham, Kingston, and their associates: also two prominent members of the Beresford connexion, Edward Lee and John Claudius Beresford. Foster, Parnell, and J. C. Beresford were all men of commercial experience, anti-unionists partly because they believed the existing system offered the best hopes of protecting some of Ireland's infant industries. They had little sympathy with the reform schemes of the eloquent liberals with whom they found themselves allied. It was not easy to coalesce two such groups, approximately equal in number, but very different in origin and outlook. The Orange group was believed to resent George Ponsonby's alacrity in taking on himself the organization of anti-union strategy.[1] Throughout the Union contest, Castlereagh, in hopes of creating a split in the ranks, systematically treated the 'right wing' anti-unionists more amicably than the old Opposition.[2] This strategy was unsuccessful: but on the other hand, the anti-unionists found it impossible to agree on any constructive alternative to the Government's policies.

It seems too facile a generalization to suggest that the difference between unionists and anti-unionists merely lay between those who succumbed to the lure of government patronage and those who stood fast. How was it that the duke of Leinster opposed the Union, his brothers Lord Charles and Lord Robert Fitzgerald supported it,[3] while the famous Lord Edward had but lately met his death planning a rebellion in disgust and exasperation at the practices of the Irish Parliament? Why did the banker John Latouche, with his two sons, oppose the measure when his brother David Latouche—equally rich, respected, and independent, and also the recent purchaser of a pocket borough—made a

---

[1] Richard Griffith to Pelham, 25 Jan. 1799 (Add. MSS. 33106).
[2] Castlereagh to Portland, 28 Jan. 1800 (H.O. 100/93).
[3] Lord Robert Fitzgerald to Lord Grenville, 13 Dec. 1799 (*H.M.C. Dropmore MSS.* vi, p. 402).

considerable impression by his advocacy of the scheme?[1]
What difference in economic status or background could be
drawn between the two brothers of Lord Massereene who sat
for his borough of Antrim, Henry and William Skeffington?
Both were veterans who sat in the Commons from 1768,
both were retired army officers of modest means, back-
benchers, each holding a sinecure valued at £365 per annum.
Yet Henry Skeffington supported, and William opposed the
Union.

The absence of effective 'party discipline' among the
groups in the Irish House of Commons was clearly revealed
during the Union debates. Hardly any great faction on either
side of the question got through 1799–1800 without suffering defections. However strong the habits of parliamentary
co-operation had been within the factions, this issue managed
to divide them. This was partly because genuine differences
of opinion were aroused by this new proposal, and partly
because it appeared that the Union crisis would be the last
chance for many members to win a share of ministerial
patronage, and better bargains might be made by individuals
than by those regarded merely as one of a pack. It would be
unduly cynical to belittle the first of these factors: the pressures which shaped members' decisions were often mixed.

To say that most of those who voted with the ministry
were placemen was tautologous. Office was regarded as the
proper and natural consequence of supporting Dublin Castle,
and few were so rich or so disinterested as to eschew this
return for their services. But it was not yet accepted universally that a placeholder who went into opposition would be
dismissed. J. C. Beresford was thought scrupulously con-
siderate when he resigned his offices on voting against the
Union.[2] It was true that rebellious placemen had been ousted
by Townshend in his struggle with the Undertakers, by
Portland during the reform administration of 1782, and by
Buckingham at the Regency crisis: while Fitzwilliam had
been prepared to dismiss John Beresford and Clare on the
less well-founded grounds of unpopularity and ill repute,
without waiting for proof of their defects or disloyalty to the

---

[1] Henry Alexander to Pelham, 15 Jan. 1800 (H.M. Add. MSS. 33106).
[2] Beresford to Auckland, 25 Jan. 1799 (*Beresford Correspondence*, ii, p. 198).

Administration. Yet, as McDowell has pointed out, in 1781 Sir Frederick Flood denounced an Administration 'which would take away gentlemen's employment because they voted according to the dictates of their conscience'.[1] And as late as 1794 the future duke of Wellington took it for granted that the Government would not dismiss a veteran office-holder whose patron went into opposition.[2] The anti-unionists were in all probability sincere when they condemned the dismissals of Parnell and Fitzgerald, and subsequently of anti-unionist commissioners of revenue and accounts, as an attempt to carry the Union by coercion; but the doctrine on this point was not yet well clarified.[3]

While there was some controversy about the inalienability of office, nearly all M.P.s regarded the purchase of a seat for a parliamentary borough as a cash investment. Almost Castlereagh's first reaction to the defeat of January 1799 had been a systematic computation of the private interests affected by the measure.[4] This took the form of a realistic appraisal of the business conventions of Irish politics, as affected by the abolition of the local parliament. Thus Castlereagh considered that the opposition of the county members would be mollified if the original plan of returning one member only from each Irish shire to the United Parliament could be replaced by the normal British principle of two members. This would give existing county interests security of tenure. Conflicts would be obviated in such counties as Castlereagh's own constituency of Down, where two rival interests maintained a truce by each returning one member. Similarly, Castlereagh sought and obtained permission to introduce the principle of compensation for borough proprietors, on which point the draft articles of Union had been silent. Here he followed a practice

[1] R. B. McDowell, *Irish Public Opinion, 1750–1800*, p. 29. quoting *Parl. Reg.* i, p. 41.

[2] Clermont, *A History of the Family of Fortescue in all its Branches*, pp. 204–5 (1880 ed.), quoting Arthur Wellesley to Sir Chichester Fortescue, 20 Dec. 1794: '. . . even should Mornington desire you to go into opposition with him, your office was given to you long ago, long before you became a Member of Prlt., and if one may judge of the future conduct of Irish ministers by the former, your opposition will not deprive you of it'.

[3] *Parl. Reg.*, 22–23 Jan. 1799, pp. 40, 59, 120 *et al.*

[4] Memorandum sent to the duke of Portland, 1 Feb. 1799 (H.O. 100/85).

suggested in Pitt's early reform bills: and it was not un-
reasonable to expect compensation for what was virtually
the nationalization of a form of private property.[1] Portland,
with a not unusual lack of grasp of Irish politics, suggested
that the borough proprietors could best be compensated by
a dissolution of Parliament, which would afford them the
opportunity of one last *coup* on a sellers' market. The embarrassment and difficulty to his Irish colleagues of fighting
a general election does not seem to have occurred to him.[2]

The assumption that a borough was a saleable piece of
property has given rise to many of the stories of corruption
which surround the Union transactions. At that time it was
expressly denounced by several members. John Foster described the Government's proposals to abolish a number of
boroughs and to compensate the owners with £15,000 each,
as 'a monstrous and unconstitutional offer': 'Do you publicly
avow that borough representation is a private property, and
do you confirm that avowal by the Government becoming
the purchasers?'[3] Similar expressions fell during the debates
of 1800 from Parsons, Dobbs, and most eloquently from
Plunket: 'I state it as a fact, that you cannot dare to deny,
that £15,000 a piece is to be given to certain individuals as
the price for their surrendering—What? their property?
No; but the rights of the representation of the people of
Ireland; and you will then proceed in this, or in an imperial
parliament, to lay taxes on the wretched natives of this land
to pay the purchase of their own slavery.'[4] Were then the
methods employed by the Government unusually corrupt
and repugnant to the better class of Irish politician? Con-
clusive proof emerged in the reports of the commissioners
appointed to assess claims and distribute compensation for
losses under the Act of Union.[5] Without exception, every
patron of a borough deprived of its franchise, applied for

---

[1] Or, as Castlereagh himself described the task, 'to buy out and secure to the Crown
for ever the fee-simple of Irish corruption' (Castlereagh to Cooke, 21 June 1800
(*Castlereagh Correspondence*, iii, p. 333)).

[2] Portland to Cornwallis, 8 Mar. 1799 (ibid. ii, pp. 201–6).

[3] *Report of the Speech of the Rt. Hon. John Foster, Speaker of the House of
Commons . . . 17 Feb. 1800* (Moore, 1800), p. 21.

[4] *Parl. Reg.*, 15–16 Jan. 1800, p. 101.

[5] *H. of C. Accounts and Papers*, 1805, viii, p. 527 et seq.

the £15,000 compensation. Foster was compensated for his half share in Dunleer. Plunket's own patron, Charlemont, accepted £15,000 for the representative rights of his borough; William Ponsonby received the same sum for Banagher. The duke of Leinster, the marquess of Downshire, William Tighe, and other anti-unionists received compensation for several seats.

These transactions indicated that everyone in Irish politics at that time accepted the convention that a borough was a marketable piece of property, and might in consequence be viewed as an investment providing a means either to lucrative office or to the gratification of figuring in Parliament. To such an extent were the boroughs regarded as a sort of property that in many instances the commissioners directed that the compensation money was not to be handed over to the borough-owner in person, but to the trustees of his marriage settlement or his predecessor's will, with the injunction that the money should be used for paying off encumbrances on the estate, and any remainder invested in the purchase of new lands.[1] Such a borough proprietor was regarded as the trustee of his property, able if he wished to enjoy the fruits of patronage and honour entailed in its possession, but limited in his rights of disposal. It was not surprising that both Government and Opposition should seek a majority on the assumption that the rights of property must be satisfied.

Of the 111 members who voted against the Union on 25 January 1799, 32 had been independent of any connexion,[2] 26 belonged to connexions who habitually voted in opposition with the Ponsonbys, and as many as 53 were associated with groups customarily supporting the Administration before the arrival of Cornwallis. The 109 members who had supported the measure included 18 independent members,

---

[1] *Report of the Commissioners of Compensation, supra.* Payment was made to the trustees of the marriage settlements of the duke of Leinster, Lords Aldborough, Clanmorris, Clifden, Glandore, Headfort, Midleton, and Mount Sandford, and five commoners, the part-owners of boroughs. Compensation for fifteen boroughs was awarded to the executors of deceased proprietors, sometimes (as at Athboy and Granard) under wills proved over thirty years previously.

[2] Of these, 14 were county members, 5 were borough owners, 5 represented open boroughs, and 8 had become borough members by purchase.

some of whom had often voted in opposition hitherto, 82 members of connexions, and 9 who were either returned for government boroughs or were law officers of the Crown. The 80 members who had not yet voted on the issue consisted of 19 from connexions that had sided with the ministry, 19 from anti-unionist connexions, 19 independents (including 13 county members) and 23 from neutral or divided connexions. In order to build up its majority the Administration could look to four main sources. Rebellious or abstaining members from supporting groups could be won over. Direct converts might be made from the anti-unionist ranks. The neutrals, some of whom had seen in the Government's moment of weakness the opportunity to strike a good patronage bargain, could be recruited to the ministerialist side. Alternately, neutral or hostile borough members might be persuaded to sell their seats, perhaps at a profit, to a friend of the Government.

It had only recently become possible to secure the resignations of members during the life of a Parliament, with the provision that M.P.s could relinquish their seats by accepting nominal sinecures such as the escheatorships of Munster and Ulster. The bestowal and refusal of escheatorships was vested in that hard-worked supervisor of patronage, the Chief Secretary. During the period 1793 to 1798, applications were never refused.[1] But the Castle reserved the right of refusal, and viewed the grant of this office as a favour, not as an automatic right. In 1798 restrictions were imposed. Only one application was granted, that of Lord Lyttleton for the two members for his borough of Granard. Of these one, his son George Lyttleton, was in a state of ill health bordering on imbecility. The other, Captain William Fulke Greville, was a naval officer absent for long periods, whose seat was required for a revenue official. Even then the escheatorships were granted only as a personal favour by Pelham on the understanding that 'no pecuniary consideration whatever, directly or indirectly, will be received from his successor'.[2]

---

[1] The records concerning escheatorships are preserved in the Dublin Public Record Office, series C.S.O. 507/15.

[2] *Cornwallis Correspondence*, iii, p. 100, editorial note from correspondence then in the Irish State Paper Office (no reference given), but now apparently lost.

All other applications, from government and opposition supporters alike, were refused. The grounds seem to have been a desire to stop members vacating their seats for cash, rather than to avoid electioneering during the rebellion, although the latter consideration probably also counted.[1]

In any event, the need to secure a majority soon caused a reversal of government policy. Six escheatorships were granted at the opening of Parliament in January 1799, and others soon followed. Among those conferred in January was one for Charles Kendal Bushe, an able young lawyer whose patron, Lord Callan, replaced him by a nephew of unionist sentiments. Further instances of quarrels between patron and member emerged over the Union. For voting against the Union, Robert Taylor, M.P. for Kells, was obliged by his brother Lord Bective to step down in favour of a more amenable cousin, Thomas Pepper. Lord Longford, under similar circumstances, replaced Henry Stewart by his brother, Edward Pakenham. Lord Clermont, whose family were divided on the issue, found that his member for Monaghan borough, William Fortescue, had abstained on the Union divisions for January 1799. On Lord Corry's motion in February, Fortescue was sent to Dublin 'under orders to support', but pleaded incapacitation from gout.[2] He was replaced by his more compliant son, Faithful Fortescue.

A parliamentary storm was nearly precipitated when the anti-unionists were refused escheatorships. The earl of Enniskillen's second son, Galbraith Lowry Cole, an army officer, was transferred to Malta. He desired to vacate his seat for Enniskillen in favour of his brother-in-law, Blayney Balfour, whose strong anti-unionist resolutions had been carried in the Louth county meeting of January. Simultaneously Tighe renewed his application about Wicklow borough, intending to sell to an anti-unionist. Castlereagh refused both applications and professed great surprise when attacked for this in the House of Commons on 15 May. A motion from John Claudius Beresford, that Lowry Cole should be granted a Crown pension in order that his seat might be vacated, was

[1] Tighe to Castlereagh, 4 May 1798, and minute (C.S.O. 511/49/7).
[2] Clermont to Castlereagh, 24 Feb. 1799 (Mt. Stewart MSS.).

defeated in a thin House by 47 votes to 32. The Administration took the lofty stand that the Crown's prerogative to grant or withhold favours of this nature should not be impugned. Cornwallis then sought the advice of Portland, who replied that, although the British ministry would if necessary uphold the decision of the Irish authorities, there seemed to be no constitutional precedent for denying such applications, at any rate within recent practice. For this reason, and from the pointlessness of a policy which could not increase the number of government supporters in the House, the Administration granted without demur all future applications for escheatorships from any source.[1]

Several M.P.s, hitherto neutral or even hostile to the Union, took money from the Government or from a borough-owner expecting some mark of favour from the Government so as to vacate their seats for replacement by a unionist. Although in eighteenth-century politics the representation of boroughs was a marketable commodity, with a cash price varying with demand, the anti-unionists considered this practice bribery. It is possible that the entry of the Government into this traffic, which involved the expenditure of public money—most of which came from London in response to appeals from Castlereagh—was considered irregular. But many previous Governments had been in the business; and the anti-unionists had no objection in principle to the purchase of borough seats. Henry Grattan paid a sum variously stated at £1,200 and £2,400 for the vacancy at Wicklow borough, whose owner was a follower of the Ponsonbys and, like Grattan, a firm anti-unionist.[2] In February 1800 the Opposition paid a deserting unionist £4,000 'to reimburse his electoral expenses' for a close borough.[3] Cornwallis deplored the direct payment of cash to a member changing sides. 'If we had the means', he wrote to his brother, '. . . and were disposed to make such vile use of

---

[1] Cornwallis to Portland, 16 and 19 May 1799; Portland to Cornwallis, 25 May 1799 (H.O. 100/86).

[2] Grattan's *Life* (v, p. 76) states the figure as £1,200; Castlereagh to Portland, 7 Jan. 1800 (H.O. 100/93) says £2,400.

[3] Castlereagh to Portland, 7 Feb. 1800 (H.O. 100/93); T. Whaley, *Memoirs*, ed. Sullivan, p. xxlx.

them, we dare not trust the credit of Government in the hands of such rascals.'[1] Apparently a nice distinction was drawn between this practice and the Government's habit of rewarding converts with office. At any rate, Dublin Castle was aggrieved when the anti-unionist owners of Enniscorthy and Kilbeggan boroughs filled with their own sympathizers vacancies created by the resignation of a member intending to make room for a government supporter.[2]

The Government sometimes acted as intermediary in transactions between borough owners and intending unionist members. Two brothers, Silver and Charles Oliver, who sat for their family borough of Kilmallock, had abstained from voting in January 1799. They were not enthusiastic politicians, and had only entered the House when the previous purchasers of their seats had found more convenient access to Parliament elsewhere.[3] It was known, however, that Lord Camden had been in touch with a neighbouring baronet, Sir Richard Quin, who was hankering for a peerage and, with that end in view, had already contemplated the purchase of a seat for Lord Longueville's borough of Mallow.[4] Quin's father had been member for Kilmallock (1769–76), and it was no difficult matter to persuade Sir Richard to buy both seats for that borough during the remainder of the 1797 Parliament, thus allowing the grateful Olivers to retire in March for a good purchase price.[5] Quin, for returning himself and a friend to support the Union, received the peerage of Adare in July 1800.

The case of Sir Thomas Mullins was more involved. Created a baronet at the recommendation of Lord Glandore in 1797,[6] Mullins, although worth £14,000 a year, was relatively a parvenu among the closely knit families of Kerry:

---

[1] Cornwallis to bishop of Lichfield and Coventry, 8 Feb. 1800 (*Cornwallis Correspondence*, iii, p. 184). 'A great deal appears to have happened after that date', comments Lecky, but he gives not the slightest evidence for this assertion, and indeed hardly anyone changed sides after 8 Feb.

[2] Castlereagh to King, 25 Jan. 1800 (H.O. 100/93).

[3] C. W. Bury had purchased Carlow borough, and was created baron Tullamore in 1797; Peter Holmes had chosen to sit for Doneraile, which belonged to his kinsman.

[4] Camden to Castlereagh, 16 Oct. 1798 (Mt. Stewart MSS.)

[5] Quin to Castlereagh, 3 Mar. 1799 (ibid.).

[6] Camden to Portland, 8 July 1797 (H.O. 100/69).

and he was the only important landowner of that county to profess anti-union principles when the measure was first proposed. But by the beginning of May he had confided a change of heart to the earl of Altamont, and volunteered to bring his two sons as unionists into the House of Commons. Expecting all the aid which Government can properly give him in procuring seats for them at his own cost,[1] he requested in return an Irish peerage when others similarly circumstanced go up.[2] Altamont pressed his friend's claim assiduously, and the offer was apparently accepted: but by 31 May Sir Thomas was writing directly to Castlereagh, stating that he had worked hard to obtain a unanimous address in favour of Union from Kerry and wanted his peerage without further exertions. This was expecting his honours a little too cheaply, and eventually on 10 February 1800 his elder son, William Townsend Mullins was returned for the purchased seat of Dingle-icouch. The seller was William Monsell, a lawyer who had quitted the anti-unionists at the time of Lord Corry's motion. It would seem that Monsell, through the mediation of Under-Secretary Marsden, accepted £1,500 from the earl of Altamont for his seat in October 1799 and that Altamont later resold it to Mullins for £2,000. However, Mullins was created baron Ventry in 1800, and in the following year was still allocating his electoral interest under Altamont's guidance, so presumably he was satisfied with his bargain.[3]

Several of the other Union peerages were granted in this way, not for individual votes, but for the outlay involved in purchasing the seat for the return of a unionist. Some of these transactions occurred only during the progress of the 1800 session. Thus when Thomas Mahon, M.P. for co. Roscommon, withdrew from the House in order to avoid offending his constituents by supporting the measure, his father brought in a second son, Stephen Mahon, by purchasing his

---

[1] Altamont to Castlereagh, 1 May 1799 (Mt. Stewart MSS.).

[2] Same to same, 'Sunday morning' (ibid.).

[3] Marsden to Altamont, 2 Oct. 1799 (C.S.O. 513/66/7); Marsden to —— 29 Apr. 1801 (C.S.O. 518/116/1). The Knight of Kerry to Marsden, 3 Dec. 1801 (C.S.O. 518/108/7). His eldest son was not so satisfied; he complained that the title of Ventry sounded too much like 'a coarse French expression' to be of any use in making an impression on his foreign travels.

seat at Knocktopher from the ailing Sir Hercules Langrishe,[1] and was later created Lord Hartland. Frederick Trench, later first baron Ashtown, was member by purchase for Portarlington; in February 1800 he brought in a brother for the neighbouring borough of Ballinakill, resigned by Montague Matthew, anti-unionist son of the earl of Landaff.[2] Henry Prittie, M.P. for Carlow borough, had abstained from voting in 1799, and was believed to be an anti-unionist;[3] but in July 1799 a unionist nobleman wrote to Castlereagh: 'I have reason to think that something might be done with young Mr. Prittie.'[4] Something was done. Young Mr. Prittie was offered a peerage for his family in return for his own support and the purchase of another seat for his brother. Although a visit to his native county of Tipperary nearly changed his mind for him once more, Prittie was kept to his bargain by his ambitious father, and a death in the family of his kinsman Lord Doneraile created a vacancy at Doneraile borough, for which Francis Prittie was duly returned.[5] In all these instances, the Government augmented its vote by complimenting with a peerage a man of property who had purchased one or two seats in order to support the Administration. Such transactions were not out of harmony with the code of ethics prevalent in eighteenth-century Irish politics. None of these accessions of strength to the Government entailed any loss of numbers to the Opposition.

Indeed, the number of converts from the anti-unionist side was so small as to be almost insignificant in a House of 300 members. I can find no more than twelve who voted against the measure in 1799 and for it in 1800:[6] against

---

[1] This seat was filled for an intervening month by Thomas Staples, son of the M.P. for co. Antrim. He seems to have been merely a caretaker.

[2] Barrington (op. cit., pp. 297–9) claims that this peerage was given because Trench changed sides during the debate of 22–23 Jan. 1799. It is true that Trench altered his mind during the debate; but where Barrington says he was bribed in a conversation with Edward Cooke, *The Anti-Union* attributes his conversion to Richard Archdall, and nowhere mentions the peerage (no. 16, 31 Jan. 1799). Trench was not promoted with the main body of Union peers, and Cornwallis went out of his way to call him 'honourable and disinterested' (Cornwallis to Portland, 15 Nov. 1800 (H.O. 100/94)).

[3] Donoughmore to Castlereagh, 25 Mar. 1799 (Mt. Stewart MSS.).

[4] Glentworth to Castlereagh, 2 July 1799 (ibid.).

[5] Henry Prittie to Castlereagh, 18 Oct. 1799 (ibid.).

[6] Abel Ram (co. Wexford) and Richard Trench (co. Galway); also Arthur

them, we can offset three who crossed to the anti-unionists from the Government benches.[1] Several of those who came over to the Government side were individuals who had broken loose from the line of their patrons, and were later induced to come to heel. William Gore was reclaimed from the anti-unionists by the earl of Leitrim, for whose borough he was a representative. On 24 June Leitrim wrote to Castlereagh, promising to vouch for Gore's vote if an office was found for him: and within two days Gore was a commissioner of the Barrack Board, with a salary of £400 per annum.[2] Less promptitude was shown in rewarding Captain James Cane, who in 1798 had been returned for Ratoath by his friend Gorges Lowther. A man of small estate, usually resident in England, Lowther had inherited the borough from his father and treated it mainly as an investment. Cane was not under strict control, and when in December 1799 John Beresford sounded Lowther about his friend's anti-unionist vote, the explanation was ingenuous in the extreme:

> I know my friend Capt. Cane is favourable to the Union, but as I returned him for Ratoath unconditionally, I never scarcely touched upon the subject, but I heard him say that he supposed Ld. Castlereagh was indifferent about how people voted, as he had never even mentioned the subject of Union to him. If you should think it necessary to have any conversation with Capt. Cane, I will venture to affirm that you will find him as safe as he is honest and upright and steadily attached to your interest, which he has always considered as my own, from the honor I derive of being connected with you.[3]

Accordingly Cane was entered among the supporters of the Administration and voted unionist throughout 1800. In return for these services he demanded a position worth £400 a year; and in 1803 this undertaking was still unsettled, through his refusal to accept any situation which entailed

Browne (Dublin University), James Cane (Ratoath), Abraham and John Creighton (Lifford), William Gore (Carrick-on-Shannon), William Handcock (Athlone), Richard Neville (Wexford town), John Preston (Navan), Benjamin Stratford (Baltinglass), and Thomas Stannus (Portarlington). I do not include members believed hostile but abstaining in January 1799.

[1] William Blakeney (Athenry), James Butler (co. Kilkenny), and Thomas Whaley (Enniscorthy). I do not count six members who abstained in 1799, voted unionist on 16 Jan. 1800, and later turned anti-unionist.

[2] Leitrim to Castlereagh, 24 June 1799 (Mt. Stewart MSS.).

[3] Lowther to Beresford, 12 Dec. 1799 (C.S.O. 513/73/9).

residence in Ireland.[1] Minor office may also have influenced
Abraham and John Creighton, respectively brother and son
to the 1st earl of Erne. Members of a family who had been
in opposition between 1767 and 1782, but had since supported, the Creightons took no part in the Union debates,
and except for their change of vote I can find no record of
them.[2] Abraham Creighton was Register of Forfeitures in
the Revenue Department, a situation worth £300 a year, and
his nephew held a sinecure worth 10s. a day. More direct
pressure was exerted on the banker Richard Neville, who
was removed from his seat on the Board of Accounts after
voting against the Union in 1799, and restored in 1800 after
a change of heart.[3] Thomas Stannus, who retired from the
House of Commons in February 1800, soon afterwards received a pension of £100 a year. There is evidence to suggest
that Stannus, an inexperienced and elderly back-bencher,
was at first intended to retire before the opening of the 1800
session; but his patron, Lady Portarlington, could not find
a unionist prepared to pay her price for the vacancy, so that
Stannus had to remain (and vote unionist) until his successor
was found. The pension would have been as compensation
for vacating his seat, rather than his unionist vote; the distinction was a very fine one, but the Government must have
considered it valid. Two converts of rather greater importance than Stannus, Abel Ram and William Handcock,
received no emolument at all for changing sides.[4]

Peerages and promotions within the peerage were not
given to reward members who changed sides. There are only
two apparent exceptions. As earlier described, Richard
Trench, M.P. for county Galway, was converted to Union
by a county meeting, and later brought in a relative for a
purchased seat. His father was promoted from baron to

[1] Memorandum in Hardwicke MSS. (B.M. Add. MSS. 35784).

[2] They are not included in Castlereagh's memorandum of likely supporters in
Oct. 1799 (Mt. Stewart MSS.).

[3] But he afterwards resisted considerable pressure from the anti-unionists to
reverse his decision: Castlereagh to Portland, 7 Feb. 1800 (H.O. 100/93).

[4] Barrington (op. cit., p. 299 [1834 ed.]) claims that Handcock was created
baron Castlemaine as a reward for changing sides. In fact the peerage was not
granted until 1812, and then for accommodating the Government with his borough
of Athlone.

viscount; but it was fairly evident from seniority and weight in the county that the family would soon have been due for promotion in any event. John Preston, M.P. for Navan borough, is the one example of a turncoat who wangled himself a peerage without giving the unionists any vote except his own. But even he was a borough-owner, controlling one seat at Navan, and believed capable of influencing his uncle and colleague of vacating the other in favour of a unionist; a hope in which the Government was deceived. The most interesting of the converts was the member for Dublin University, Dr. Arthur Browne. Since his first return in 1783 he had consistently voted for liberal reform measures, and in 1799 had subscribed to the doctrine that the effect of the Union would be the abolition of the constitution, and hence the subversion of good order. In January 1800 he voted for hearing the Union propositions, arguing that the Dublin legislature had lost the confidence of the people which it claimed to represent:

Had I seen, after the rejection of the union last year, any measures brought forward to conciliate the people, to heal the distractions of the country, had I seen any reminiscence of that spirit, which produced the constitution of 1782, coming forward to preserve it, I should not have listened to proposals of union, nor would you have again heard them now. But for gentlemen to suppose that if Parliament does not support itself it can be supported; to suppose that, without domestic virtues, the nation will trouble itself about its existence, is absurd. The truth is, apathy has gone through the nation upon the subject; the thing is evident—in 1782 the idea of a union could not have been brought forward; in 1785, it could not have been brought forward; why can it now? Because then the Parliament had the warm affection of the nation, now it has not.[1]

As instances of the illiberality of the 1799 Parliament, he cited Toler's Rebellion Bill regularizing the coexistence of martial and civil law, and the indemnification of the High Sheriff of Tipperary for excesses committed in the questioning of suspects. Such arguments did not commend themselves to many Members of Parliament, and Plunket, who aspired to represent Dublin University in Browne's stead, reminded his hearers that Browne, having been born in

[1] *Debates*, 15–16 Jan. 1800, p. 134.

America, was no true Irishman. Moreover, Browne's conversion was followed by his appointment to the Board of Accounts, from which he rose to be Prime Serjeant in 1802. Nevertheless his criticisms of the Dublin legislature were not easy to refute, and he should be allowed the merit, rare in contemporary politics, of having put up a tenable case to support a shift in opinion.

All these converts belonged to the smaller, more insignificant parliamentary groups, but lately sprung into prominence. Several of them were members of a tightly knit family group. Richard Trench was brother-in-law to William Handcock, patron of Thomas Stannus and kinsman of Frederick Trench (who changed sides during the debate of 22-23 January). Frederick Trench, as well as being one of the few burgesses for Athlone borough not a member of the dominant Handcock family, was cousin to Henry and Francis Prittie, who were also connected with the Bagwells of Tipperary, a family who changed sides during the recess of 1799 but later reverted to the anti-unionists. Although it may have been expected that these rising new families, ambitious to gain honours quickly before the Union restricted the field of enterprise, offered the best prospects of converts, the Government's gain by direct secessions from the Opposition was not great. Castlereagh had hoped to take twenty-two members from the anti-unionists of 1799;[1] a gain of twelve, from which three desertions had to be deducted, was not a decisive element in the balance of forces. The majorities required for the passing of the Act of Union were won from among those who had stood neutral.

Of the groups abstaining in January 1799, the most important magnates were Lords Ely, Donegall, Darnley, Downshire, and de Clifford. Of these the latter two eventually threw in their lot with the anti-unionists, strengthening them by twelve members, so that the gaining of the other three interests barely balanced the scale in favour of the Government.

Lord Ely

'Lord Ely's conduct', wrote the duke of Portland, after his defection in January 1799, 'is deserving of any punish-

[1] Castlereagh to Portland, 28 Jan. 1799 (H.O. 100/85).

ment that can be inflicted.'[1] But once it was apparent that
Cornwallis was to be backed by the Home Government, Ely
had no further hesitation in rallying to his side. This was not
immediately helpful, for, of the ten members associated with
his faction, three had already voted as unionists, one (Major-
General William Loftus) was absent in England, and at least
three of the others betrayed strong anti-unionist inclinations.[2]
The recalcitrants were accordingly made to give up their
seats, but by some curious mischance it unfortunately happened that two of Ely's new members also turned out to be
anti-unionists, and it was the end of March before Castlereagh thought it safe to announce Ely's conversion to the
Home Government.[3] Even then, it was not until after the
end of the 1799 sitting that Ely got around to evicting his
two new anti-unionists. Meanwhile, in cajoling the Government for a better situation for his cousin Ponsonby Tottenham, he found it useful to remind them that 'he is not in
principle much attached to the Union'.[4] There is not much
record of his services to the Government during the rest of the
year, apart from a unionist petition from the Roman Catholics of New Ross.[5] Possibly he had some hand in the conversion of two prominent local anti-unionists, Richard Neville
and Abel Ram.[6] But he was not conspicuous by his activity.

Having filled all his seats with nonentities who would vote
unionist, Ely dunned for his marquessate until Castlereagh
obtained for him a letter from Pitt, which, without making
definite commitments, led Ely to be 'satisfied to leave himself
in the hands of Government—a mark of confidence which

---

[1] Portland to Cornwallis, 26 Jan. 1799 (H.O. 100/85).

[2] The three anti-unionists were Henry Alcock (who had been independent M.P.
for Waterford city 1783–97), Ephraim Carroll, and James Boyd. Cf. Ely to Castlereagh, 16 Feb. 1799 (Mt. Stewart MSS.): 'I have asked Alcock and Carroll to support on Corry's motion. Alcock is entangled by his Waterford interest not to vote
for any measure leading to an Union, and Carroll, who is a mule, and having been
called to the Bar, thinks he is bound to vote likewise. Neither of them will appear
against us. I shall get rid of each of them as soon as possible. My other friends in
Town will attend you. . . .'

[3] Castlereagh to Portland, 26 Mar. 1799 (H.O. 100/85).

[4] Ely to Castlereagh, 12 June 1799 (Mt. Stewart MSS.). In fact Ponsonby
Tottenham was one of the three Ely members to cast a vote for Union in Jan. 1799.

[5] Ely to Castlereagh, 19 Oct. 1799 (Mt. Stewart MSS.).

[6] Ely owned one seat at Wexford town, where Neville owned and sat for the other.
His son, Lord Loftus, was Ram's colleague for the county.

relieves us from much embarrassment and augurs well for his Lordship's determination to give the measure a fair support'.[1] This, however, 'Lord Ely, who never willingly relinquished anything',[2] later construed into a promise for higher rank. In June 1800, when the British Government were proving reluctant to approve all the Union peerages, they showed surprising kindness to Ely. Not only did Portland believe that Ely should be the only Irishman admitted to the British peerage, but also that if any marquessates were created 'that it may be confined to Lord Ely, whose influence is so extensive, and has of late been so usefully employed as to make it less objectionable in his, than in . . . other cases'.[3] He gained both honours. These concessions to a shifty and reluctant parliamentary huckster cannot have been an inspiring example to the Administration's more consistent supporters.

Lord Donegall

Lord Donegall's members had voted against the Government in January 1799, just after the death of the first marquess. His successor's views were uncertain; but he was at odds with his stepmother, whose opposition views had influenced her husband, and he was thought worth sounding by that indefatigable contact man for the Government, Henry Alexander. Protesting that he did not 'understand the question', the second marquess was indecisive. Alexander wrote: 'Perhaps some favor to Lady Donegall's father, who is in the Fleet prison, or a commission or some such thing to her brother, young May, tho' it might not illuminate his understanding, might convince him.'[4] It is a little surprising that Donegall's father-in-law, Edward May,[5] should have been so embarrassed by debt: for the marquess had the largest rent-roll of any peer in Ireland, including much estate in Belfast, and it was for this reason as well as his House of Commons influence that the Government courted him.[6] Little progress

[1] Castlereagh to Portland, 11 Dec. 1799 (H.O. 100/87).
[2] Cornwallis to Portland, 17 June 1800 (H.O. 100/94).
[3] Portland to Cornwallis, 13 June 1800 (ibid.).
[4] Alexander to Castlereagh, 26 Feb. 1799 (Mt. Stewart MSS.).
[5] Son and heir of Sir James May (1724–1811), M.P. for co. Waterford 1761–97.
[6] Cooke (in a memorandum among the Mt. Stewart MSS.) estimated his

was made until July, when Alexander reported Donegall 'a Unionist, but determined from a variety of grievances to oppose Administration', adding that his lordship would be gratified above all else for permission to raise his own yeomanry corps of cavalry.[1]

The wish was fulfilled, and Donegall gradually swung into support of the Administration. In September 1799 he backed the unionist address from Antrim; next month his father-in-law, at large amid the respectable merchants of Belfast, was 'a most active and zealous agent'[2] in promoting the corporation dinner for Cornwallis when that city gave its most convincing display of unionist sympathies. It remained to deal with Donegall's two members in the House of Commons. One of them, Alexander Hamilton, had apparently already been conducting his own negotiations with the Government; but he was compelled to retire in January 1800, although consoled with the government interest at the next elections for county Dublin.[3] He was succeeded by Edward May. His colleague, George Crookshank, was replaced by John Congreve, a Belfast merchant who never took his seat in the House of Commons. Donegall's successor in the pot-walloping borough of Carrickfergus, Noah Dalway, although an anti-unionist, had too secure an interest of his own to be disturbed.

The earl of Darnley

An absentee, normally resident in England, the earl of Darnley returned two relatives for the manor borough of Athboy. Both were absent from the divisions of 1799, and the earl's attitude remained uncertain until he visited Dublin in December. Assuming 'the inconvenient character of a doubtful, hesitating friend', Darnley pressed Cornwallis, in his capacity of British Master-General of the Ordnance, to grant the vacancy of storekeeper at Chatham to one of his clients. As this applicant had been particularly abusive to Cornwallis when previously refused, the Viceroy at first

rentroll at £32,000. Another source, cited by the *Complete Peerage* (iii, p. 581), gives £22,000.

[1] Alexander to Castlereagh, — July 1799 (Mt. Stewart MSS.).
[2] Cornwallis to Portland, 22 Oct. 1799 (H.O. 100/86).
[3] Marsden to Hardwicke, 8 July 1802 (B.M. Add. MSS. 35723).

declined: 'whether this will make Lord D. an Anti-Unionist is a doubtful question', he reflected; 'it is a sad thing to be forced to manage knaves, but it is ten times worse to deal with fools.'[1] A month later, when the competition for supporters had increased, Cornwallis laconically advised his deputy in the Ordnance: 'Lord Darnley's members are on the road, and as he is very friendly, I should wish to make his friend Clerk of Survey at Chatham.'[2] This piece of patronage was completely without effect. Darnley's members failed to appear at the Union debates, and the earl himself, objecting to the provision made for the representation of Irish peers in the United Parliament, also refused to vote when the measure came before the British House of Lords.

Lord de Clifford

Inheritor of the ancient English barony of de Clifford, the absentee Edward Southwell returned his uncle and three cousins of the Rowley family, for the potwalloping boroughs of Downpatrick and Kinsale. From 1789 to 1794, de Clifford and his members went into opposition, as his father-in-law the archbishop of Tuam was a leading Portland whig. The death of the archbishop coincided with the Pitt–Portland coalition, and from then until 1799, de Clifford's members supported. Although in favour of Cornwallis's policy of clemency, he stood neutral in the first Union divisions. Sounded about the issue in July, de Clifford expressed strong doubts about the timing of the question, and said that he would be guided by the consensus of opinion among the country gentlemen:

If, by forcing a Union upon the country, you disgust one half of these gentlemen and convert the other half into absentees, you will leave the country a prey to the machinations of the disaffected, and the consequences I fear would be fatal. By bringing forward the question at a time that the rebellion is but half suppressed, and the popular clamour against it, you give every disaffected rascal in the kingdom an opportunity of calling himself in the defence of the independence of Ireland and in support of its Parliament.[3]

[1] Cornwallis to Ross, 28 Dec. 1799 (*Cornwallis Correspondence*, iii, p. 153).
[2] Same to same, 21 Jan. 1800 (ibid. iii, pp. 167–8).
[3] de Clifford to Townshend, 23 July 1799 (*Castlereagh Correspondence*, ii, p. 355).

After these sentiments, he went on to inquire about the compensation likely to be granted him for his boroughs: because these were nominally open, he feared he 'should immediately lose upon such a measure being carried into execution'. So much was de Clifford concerned about this question that he left his normal residence in England for a six weeks' visit of his Irish estates. Despite the offer of 'a mark of Government favour', de Clifford informed Castlereagh of his intention of opposing the Administration on the Union question alone.[1]

Lord Downshire

To his old friend General Ross, Cornwallis wrote:

Lord Downshire, holds at best a very unsatisfactory language, and a man who has for many years exacted and enjoyed the exclusive patronage of the Crown in the north must be a formidable enemy. To court a proud, ill-tempered, violent fellow raised to any importance by the weakness of former Governments, and who, if he had the power, would in a week drive this wretched country again into rebellion, is a pill almost too bitter for me to swallow. If Lord D. declares against us, many of our recruits will insist on higher bounty.[2]

But a man believed to control eight seats in the House of Commons had to be courted, and in the early months of 1799 his neighbour Castlereagh was most attentive to the undecided Downshire. Two days after the defeat of January 1799 Castlereagh was attending to Downshire's patronage requests, and assuring him that the Union was 'for the present laid asleep'.[3] In March the Chief Secretary was particularly anxious that Downshire 'should early be appraised of the scheme of representation at present in the contemplation of Ministers. It may tend to reconcile him.'[4] But Downshire,

---

[1] de Clifford to Castlereagh, 10 Jan. 1800 (*Castlereagh Correspondence*, iii, pp. 223-4): 'I feel truly sensible of the very delicate and flattering manner in which your Lordship has been pleased to communicate Lord Cornwallis's kind intentions towarde me; but I must take the liberty of observing that your Lordship does me but justice in supposing that my conduct upon this important question would not be influenced by any such considerations.'

[2] Cornwallis to Ross, 19 June 1799 (*Cornwallis Correspondence*, iii, p. 104).

[3] Castlereagh to Downshire, 27 Jan. 1799 (Mt. Stewart MSS.).

[4] Castlereagh to Portland, 27 March 1799.

although still officially neutral, was already tending towards the Opposition. He was in very guarded contact with the Speaker in February 1799, and that same month wrote to Pitt magnanimously suggesting that he himself should be appointed Lord Lieutenant in place of Cornwallis. It irked him that the letter went unanswered.[1]

Ostensible civility prevailed between the Castle and Downshire when he visited Ireland during the summer of 1799. At the end of June Downshire wrote to Castlereagh, thanking him for some favours in county patronage, and denying that personal rivalry between them could make him an anti-unionist:[2] but shortly afterwards, Downshire reported a personal visit from Castlereagh to his man of affairs, John Reilly, in terms of obvious relish: '... he has no reason to be satisfyed with me on the subject of U——, but he talks big but is damnably frightened about it, it is plainly to be discovered by the conversation of the family.'[3] Nor could the Lord Lieutenant make any impression on him: 'Union is the only thing talked of, thought of, or wished about in the Castle. I have had some conversation with Lord Cos: which had no effect on either side, but he assured me that the subject was gaining popularity in the minds of all descriptions, that it would pass in Parliament by a great majority. I was sorry that terror or corruption could take such hold of men's minds. I staid with him above two hours—and was tired.'[4] During the rest of the year, while Downshire was in England, the struggle for his support was carried on with diminishing optimism on the part of the Castle. In November Pitt intervened personally: but Castlereagh was well advised to comment: 'I earnestly hope that the effect of Mr. Pitt's conversation with my Lord Downshire may be what we all wish it, but I have my fears that his Lordship has already gone too far with Opposition to lend us any active assistance. As matters stand, I shall be well pleased to compound with neutrality.'[5]

Two of Downshire's following, Richard Annesley and

1 Downshire to Mornington, 20 Mar. 1799 (Add. MSS. 37308).
2 Downshire to Castlereagh, 27 June 1799 (Mt. Stewart MSS.).
3 Downshire to Reilly, — July 1799 (Downshire MSS.).
4 Same to same, 23 Aug. 1799 (ibid.).
5 Castlereagh to Portland, 27 Nov. 1799 (H.O. 100/86).

Robert Johnson, had compromised themselves by supporting the measure in January 1799. Annesley, one of the more
active of the commissioners of revenue, and an advocate of
union since before the official consideration of the scheme,
was undoubtedly a conscientious supporter of the measure,
and his apologia for his conduct, while tailored to humour
Downshire's susceptibilities, was plain: '. . . if there was a
Union on fair terms (and no other I think Great Britain out
of policy should grant, tho' she thought only of self), I am
satisfyed that the wealth of the country wd. increase, and
that *Dublin* from local situation wd. reap great benefit, but
tho' I have said so much in favour of a Union, do not think
I approve of the time it is brought forward, or the manner of
management. . . .'[1] Robert Johnson, an adventurer who
thought scurrilously of almost everyone in politics except
himself, excused his vote on the grounds that the defeat of
even so misguided and incompetent an administration as that
of Cornwallis and Castlereagh should be avoided, if only to
keep out the Ponsonbys.[2] Neither he nor Annesley could
reconcile Downshire to their stand. Correspondence between the two members and their patron, formerly frequent,
came to an end, and by December Downshire was contem-
plating their removal from his boroughs.[3] Another rebel in
Downshire's ranks was less easy to shift. Richard Magennis,
M.P. for Carlingford, had paid the marquess £1,000 for his
seat, but was accustomed to act under his directions in Parliament, as he owed to his intercession one or two substantial
favours in the way of government patronage.[4] But in December, having been promised 'some good preferment' for a son
in the clergy, Magennis pledged his vote for the Union.
Downshire at once offered to return him his £1,000—which
under the conventions of borough management would have
placed Magennis in the role of a dependent, instead of
the lessee of a seat in the House—but this was refused.[5]

[1] Annesley to Downshire, 30 Jan. 1799 (Downshire MSS.).
[2] Johnson to Downshire, 8 Feb. [1799] (ibid.).
[3] Downshire to Reilly, 24 Dec. 1799. The Downshire MSS. include no letters
from Annesley of later date than Mar., or from Johnson later than Sept. 1799.
[4] Hobart to Hillsborough, 3 Apr. 1790; Camden to Downshire, 29 Mar. 1797
(Downshire MSS.).
[5] Bishop Percy of Dromore to his wife, 10 and 18 Dec. 1799 (Add. MSS. 32335).

Downshire's other members all stayed faithful to him, and by the end of 1799 his determination to oppose the Union was established.[1]

To what extent had the Government secured its majority by the allurements of place? A return of members holding offices compiled at the request of the House in April 1800 gave the names of fifty-two members holding places during pleasure.[2] These situations ranged from the veriest sinecures to important and responsible under-secretaryships. The official pension list provided the names of twelve unionist members of the House of Commons who drew sums ranging from £100 to £600—in the case of Sir John Blaquiere, £1,200 per annum, but this was in commutation of an abolished office.[3] Several anti-unionists were also in receipt of pensions, including George Ogle, William Blakeney, and the wife of W. B. Ponsonby.[4] During Cornwallis's régime, the total increase of the pension list was very small, compared with the prodigality of Westmoreland and Camden. The increase was £3,945 per annum, nearly half of it to indigent peers and their relatives—as Namier pointed out, a customary 'dole' without political significance. No pensions were granted to members of the House of Commons or their wives.[5] Nor were members supplied from Secret Service money. This fund had been set up in 1793, and its disbursements were applied to rewarding informers, police, and others whose services had aided the suppression of disturbances since 1795.[6] There was no secrecy about the operations of

---

[1] Downshire to Reilly, 13 Oct. 1799 (Downshire MSS.).

[2] *Commons Journals*, 1800, ii, p. dccclxxvii.

[3] Members receiving pensions were Sir John Blaquiere, £1,200; Denham Jephson, £600; William Montgomery, £600; Thomas Nesbitt, £500; John Monck Mason, £300; Ponsonby Tottenham, £300; W. A. Crosbie, £250; the Hon. James Cavendish, £150; Faithful Fortescue, £100; and the wives of Sir Hercules Langrishe, Sir Boyle Roche, and Luke Fox, respectively £300, £200, and £100.

[4] Blakeney (who changed sides after voting unionist in 1799) had received his pension at the solicitation of the duke of Northumberland. Mrs. Ponsonby's pension had been increased from £70 to £200, at a time when Ponsonby was firmly in opposition, and was in no financial straits.

[5] But £100 was granted to Thomas Stannus, M.P. for Portarlington 1797–1800, some months after his retirement.

[6] The accounts for secret service money, 1795–1804, are preserved in the Royal Irish Academy, Dublin, and have been printed in Dr. John Gilbert's *Documents Relating to Ireland*, 1795–1804, pp. 3 et seq.

place and pension: the public money financed the Government's expenditure, and account was given to the House of Commons.

Undoubtedly many of the unionists were alive to the attractions of office. The efforts of Cornwallis and his successor Hardwicke to provide satisfaction for 'Union engagements' have been commented on often enough.[1] To men who had entered the Irish Parliament with the hope of ultimately securing office, the Union seriously curtailed their prospects. The Government in fairness had to ensure that they would be no losers by their support of the measure. Lecky has pointed out that of the twenty-three practising barristers who voted for the Union in 1800, six were on the Bench by 1803, and eight others had received high legal appointments.[2] But it was hardly any time before the most prominent anti-unionist lawyers were figuring in important offices, many of them as colleagues of Pitt and Castlereagh, whom they had so heartily denounced.[3] Opposition had never been a permanent impediment to a successful professional career in Ireland. The most notable feature about the patronage arrangements of 1799–1800 was the ousting from office of oppositionists to make way for government supporters, on perhaps the largest scale hitherto known; but the development of the theory that office-holders should support the Government with their votes hardly deserved contemporary accusations of corruption.

It could be argued that some of the most determined opponents of the Union were those borough-owning magnates who had thriven under the constitution of 1782, who had newly enlarged their spheres of influence by the purchase of constituencies, and who were unwilling to see the closing of the theatre in which they had hoped to cut a great figure. Such considerations might be held to apply to rising noblemen such as Kingston, Belmore, and Enniskillen, as well as to longer established magnates such as Leinster, Downshire, and the Speaker. It is noteworthy that this second group, as

[1] e.g. by M. McDonagh, *The Viceroy's Post-Bag* (London, 1904).

[2] Lecky, op. cit., v, p. 303.

[3] Plunket was Solicitor-General in 1803 and Attorney-General in 1805; Bushe was Solicitor-General 1805–22; Saurin was Attorney-General 1807–22; Curran was Master of the Rolls 1806–14.

several other anti-unionists, were landowners in financial difficulties, dependent on the continued control of the Irish patronage machine for part of their prosperity and consequence. The duke of Leinster was eventually given £28,800 compensation for his boroughs of Athy and Kildare, but this money was tied to the clearance of debts on his property.[1] Despite an annual income of £22,000, the marquess of Downshire was also in difficulties;[2] while in January 1799 the regular Opposition had celebrated their coalition with Foster by opening a subscription list for a fund to pay his debts.[3] Probably the disruption of the national economy by the 1798 rebellion temporarily increased the embarrassments of some; Leinster's property and part of Downshire's lay in the seriously disturbed areas of Kildare and Wicklow. But many encumbrances were of longer standing. The anti-unionist Lord Clanwilliam wrote: 'My parental inheritance is involved, and liable to more debts and charges than it is worth, and not of my creating.'[4] The earl of Ormonde, whose members voted for Union in 1799 and against it in 1800, was stated by John Beresford to have been under a very direct form of pressure. After the divisions of January 1799 the Dublin merchants foreclosed on all the bills which Ormonde had outstanding with them.[5] I can find no evidence that the voting of any parliamentary interest was influenced by the bankers to whom they were indebted, and am inclined to believe that such direct forms of pressure were unusual.[6] Lacking detailed studies by the economic historians, it

[1] Cf. the remarks of Lady Louisa Conolly to the duke of Richmond, 18 June 1798: 'The county of Kildare, where his whole estate is, is in a manner laid waste—and no chance that I can foresee of his getting in his half-year's rents: he is worse off in that particular than any of us, and I do not know what he can do' (Bunbury MSS.).

[2] George Stephenson to Downshire, 2 Sept. and 12 Dec. 1798 (Downshire MSS.); bishop of Dromore to Mrs. Percy, 17 Feb. 1799 (Add. MSS. 32335).

[3] Beresford to Auckland, 26 Jan. 1799 (*Beresford Correspondence*, ii, pp. 199–200); Cornwallis to Ross, 13 Feb. 1799 (*Cornwallis Correspondence*, iii, p. 60). Political gossip put his debts at £30,000 (J. Farington, *Diary*, ed. J. Grieg (1922), i, p. 250). In July 1797 Foster borrowed £1,000 at 6 per cent. from Francis Saunderson, anti-unionist M.P. for co. Cavan. (Receipt for interest, 3 July 1798 (Massereene and Ferrard MSS., lxxviii).)

[4] Clanwilliam to Hardwicke, 13 Sept. 1801 (B.M. Add. MSS. 35783).

[5] Beresford to Auckland, 26 Jan. 1799 (B.M. Add. MSS. 34455).

[6] Several banking houses, such as Latouche's and Beresford's, were divided on the issue. Other bankers in Parliament, such as Cotter, Lighton, and Neville, tended to follow the lead of their aristocratic patrons.

would be quite unsafe to explain the anti-unionist vote by a 'decline of the gentry', despite the examples cited in the last paragraph. Several leading anti-unionist groups—Enniskillen, Belmore, the Latouches, the Bagwells—were prosperous enough to have purchased boroughs in the decade before the Union. The unionist magnates were likewise divided between those such as Longueville and Ely, whose prestige was largely based on office, and noblemen like Abercorn and Waterford, whose means were unembarrassed. A series of regional studies will be necessary before the economic implications of the Union can accurately be gauged; but it is feasible to suppose that those who voted unionist in Connaught looked to an increased pastoral trade with Great Britain, in Cork hoped for its advancement as an entrepôt port, in Ireland generally were attracted by prophecies of a greatly stimulated inflow of English capital.[1] These considerations, as much as the allurements of place, surely had their part in determining votes; just as the anti-unionists in Dublin and Leinster feared that their infant textile industries would be withered by British competition. It is a superficial and exaggerated view to assume that corruption was the main factor which carried the Union. When due allowance has been made for contemporary conventions in Irish politics, respecting borough transactions and the giving of honours for parliamentary services, it may be suggested that much which the nineteenth century condemned as 'corruption' was accepted practice both to Government and anti-unionists. The pressures affecting members' votes were many and varied, and would continue to influence the shaping of the Union for some time after the Government had secured its majority.

[1] *Cork Advertiser*, 7 Mar. 1799, provides an example of this sort of propaganda.

VII

THE UNION PASSES, 1800–1801

> I yesterday gave the Royal Assent to the Act of Union,
> when there was not a murmur heard in the street, nor I
> believe an expression of ill-humour throughout the whole
> city of Dublin; had anyone prophesied this, when the
> measure was first proposed, he would not have met with
> more credit than my friend Mr. Dobbs did respecting the
> appearance of the Messiah at Armagh.
>
> CORNWALLIS TO ROSS, 2 August 1800.[1]

IN this chapter I do not propose to report in detail the
debates which occupied the Irish House of Commons
between January and June 1800. These have been frequently described by historians. In particular Lecky's summary, with its copious extracts and summaries of the principal
speeches, has well contrasted the moving eloquence of the
leading anti-unionists with the bulldog tenacity of Castlereagh, and stands in little need of correction or repetition.[2]
But these speeches provide no adequate reflection of the
passage of events. Despite the return to Parliament as anti-
unionist borough members of some of the finest orators of
the day—Grattan, Saurin, Curran—it must be admitted that
very few fresh arguments were advanced on either side.
Instead, there was an increasing inclination to descend to
invective and repetition. The Government law officers, Toler
and Daly, set a bad example which the Opposition were not
slow to imitate. Evidence of this deterioration may be found
in the anti-unionist publication for 1800, the *Olio*. It is much
less effective propaganda than its predecessor, the *Anti-Union*,
because much of its material consists of personalities about
the unionist members, but little space is given to refuting
their arguments.

Argument no longer swayed votes as it had in January 1799.
Both Government and Opposition laid a tighter discipline

---

[1] *Cornwallis Correspondence*, iii, p. 285.
[2] Lecky, *History*, v, pp. 344–418.

on their members. What could be opposed to the Administration's resources of place and favour? The experience of the past suggested several expedients. The Irish House of Commons owed its very autonomy to the pressure of organized public opinion, as evinced through the Volunteer Movement. The commercial propositions of 1785 had been killed by the lobbying of mercantile interests in combination with a vociferous Opposition. In both instances the Lord Lieutenant of the day had commanded resources of patronage at least equal to those available to Cornwallis and Castlereagh, yet these had proved useless. Might the same outcome be produced in 1800? Much would depend on the skill with which the Opposition chose points of pressure on the Government. If the measure could not be defeated completely, their influence might at least be expected to modify its provisions substantially.

At first the Irish authorities had intended to convene a short session of Parliament for less controversial matters in November 1799: but this scheme was abandoned, and the adjournment lasted until 15 January 1800. Also abandoned was the proposal to settle the details of Union by a meeting of commissioners, 'which is an awkward moment of suspense and cabal'.[1] Instead a parliamentary strategy different from that of 1799 was designed. No reference would be made to Union in the Speech from the Throne, but the measure would be introduced separately after an adjournment of three weeks, during which escheatorships could be granted and seats refilled in many of the boroughs. If the Union was then approved in principle, the articles would be discussed, and if necessary modified in committee by the Irish Parliament. The scheme, with as few alterations as possible, would then be submitted to the British legislature. Once a satisfactory formula acceptable to both parliaments had been devised, the articles of Union would be cast into the form of a Bill, and put simultaneously through each legislature.

Accordingly Parliament was opened on 15 January without any reference to Union. A trial of strength nevertheless must have been expected, for the House of Commons was better attended than at any time during the previous year.

---

[1] Cornwallis to Portland, 22 June 1799 (H.O. 100/86).

There were 239 members present, twenty-two absent, and thirty-nine vacancies where a change of borough members was taking place. Anticipating that many of these vacancies would be filled by unionists, Sir Laurence Parsons moved an amendment to the Address, expressing the loyalty of the House to the Crown, the British connexion, and the 1782 constitution and pledging itself to the maintenance of an independent resident parliament.[1] A debate of eighteen hours ensued, marked by the dramatic intervention of Henry Grattan as newly elected member for Wicklow borough; his speech was a powerful exposition of the nationalist argument against Union. But at 10 a.m. the House divided, and Parsons's amendment was rejected by 138 votes to 96.[2] Of the Government's majority, eight had voted against the Union in 1799, ninety-seven had supported the measure, and the rest were either former neutrals or newcomers to the House.

This action spurred the Opposition to mobilize anti-unionist opinion outside Parliament. After a meeting of members at Lord Charlemont's house on 20 January 1800, a circular was sent out under the names of Downshire, Charlemont, and W. B. Ponsonby to stimulate a wave of petitions from the counties.[3] This move, and the formation of a 'fighting fund' alleged to command promises for £100,000 for the purchase of borough seats in the anti-unionist interest, produced some disparaging comment from the Government, who under-rated its effect.[4] Instead of the off-season canvassing which had secured support for the unionists, public opinion was arrested by a concentrated barrage of anti-unionist appeals to Parliament at the very moment when the question was to be considered. This campaign was particularly successful in counties where the balance of forces was fairly evenly divided—that is, precisely in those counties where the unionists had taken such pains during the recess. Now they were repudiated in several districts. The Roman Catholics at Dundalk and in county Limerick abandoned their

[1] *A Report of the Debate in the House of Commons in Ireland on Wednesday and Thursday the 15th and 16th of Jan. 1800* . . . (J. Moore, Dublin, 1800).

[2] These, and all other voting figures in this chapter, are exclusive of tellers.

[3] Composed by Sir John Parnell, a copy of the petition is included in Castlereagh to King, 25 Jan. 1800 (H.O. 100/93).

[4] Castlereagh to King, 25 Jan. 1800 (ibid.).

support of Union and those in county Longford produced
between 2,000 and 4,000 signatures to an anti-unionist petition. The freeholders of Monaghan produced 4,440 signatures for an anti-unionist petition, and thirty-six Orange
Lodges in Monaghan and Armagh, representing a member-
ship of 2,400, declared themselves similarly.[1]

The campaign produced one or two lively incidents in the
counties. In Down a county meeting was convened at a
week's notice at the behest of Downshire, whose 'unlimited
exercise of all the powers and patronage of Government
for many years, has enabled him to establish a dangerous
authority'.[2] Lord Londonderry and the bishop of Dromore
went to combat the marquess, but his tenantry got possession
of the meeting house at Downpatrick and excluded all opposition.[3] The Castle was not disheartened: '. . . it does not
appear that Lord Downshire has much reason to plume himself upon the success of his meeting in the county of Down;
where, although he was supported by the rabble, he met with
little countenance from the gentlemen and respectable freeholders, most of whom signed a protest in favour of Union.'[4]
On the other side, it was alleged that a meeting of King's
County freeholders convened on 2 February in the court-
house at Birr was dispersed by the High Sheriff,[5] who summoned a detachment of British artillery 'to burn the court-
house about the ears of the freeholders'. Brought before the
Bar of the House on the motion of Sir Laurence Parsons,
M.P. for the county, the sheriff was acquitted of the charge
after careful interrogation. By an almost unanimous vote, the
House resolved, on the motion of the anti-unionist Plunket
'that the conduct of the High Sheriff and Major Rogers

---

[1] *Dublin Evening Post*, 28 Jan., 1 and 4 Feb., 20 Mar. 1800.
[2] Cornwallis to Ross, 21 Jan. 1800 (*Cornwallis Correspondence*, iii, p. 167).
[3] Bishop of Dromore to his wife, 30 Jan. 1800 (Add. MSS. 32335).
[4] Cornwallis to Portland, 3 Feb. 1800 (H.O. 100/93). It was stated by Charles
Grey in the British House of Commons (*Parl. Hist.* xxxiv, p. 424) that 7,000
signed the petition against the Union, and only 415 in favour. But the unionist
petition printed in the *Belfast Newsletter* on 4 Feb. 1800 (well before Grey's speech)
bore 505 names, and it was asserted that others had been omitted through considerations of space. The total of 7,000 anti-unionist freeholders seems a little surprising
when it is remembered that it took a two months' poll to turn out 6,000 voters at the
hotly contested election of 1790—of whom over 3,000 had supported Castlereagh.
[5] Verney Lovett Darby, in April 1800 returned as M.P. for Gowran.

was not calculated to prevent the exercise of the right of petition'.[1]

Cornwallis, influenced by his memories of America, was worried about the yeomanry. 'Inflammatory handbills', he reported on 21 January, 'asked of them, whether 60,000 Irishmen with arms in their hands will tamely stand by and see the constitution of their country destroyed?';[2] and although he himself had little fear of a rising, he calmed the misgivings of timid unionists by posting a unit of British troops in Dublin. By 31 January the Lord Lieutenant had come to expect 'every degree of violence'.[3] Parliament was to reassemble on 3 February, but the meeting was postponed for two days because of Castlereagh's indisposition. On the 4th, it was learnt that the Downshire militia, stationed at Carlow, had appended numerous signatures to an anti-unionist petition sent them by their colonel, the marquess of Downshire. On the hustings of Maryborough the perenially indiscreet Jonah Barrington asserted that the Downshire regiment 'were determined not to volunteer for service but to remain within the kingdom to resist the measure'. Lecky tends to discount the possibility of a demonstration by the yeomanry, and to point to the size of the British forces then in Ireland—45,419 in all.[4] Most of them, however, were Irish militia, and Cornwallis, who was not the man to lose his head in an emergency, saw them as a potentially formidable pressure-group, especially in co-operation with the Orange organization. To Portland he wrote:

The yeomanry and militia were in some instances successfully tampered with, and a general impression effected that the native force of the country was prepared in conjunction with the mass of the people to overcome if not to resist the decision of the legislature on this question . . . and to these impressions may be attributed in a considerable degree . . . the feelings of alarm and despondency which had affected our friends.[5]

---

[1] *Commons Journals*, 12 Feb. 1800; Cornwallis to Portland, 13 Feb. 1800 (H.O. 100/93).

[2] Cornwallis to Ross, 21 Jan. 1800 (*Cornwallis Correspondence*, iii, p. 167).

[3] Same to same, 31 Jan. 1800 (ibid.).

[4] Lecky, *History*, v, pp. 344 and 358. The number is taken from Cornwallis to Dundas, 19 July 1799 (*Cornwallis Correspondence*, iii, p. 118).

[5] Cornwallis to Portland, 14 Feb. 1800 (H.O. 100/93).

Alarm and despondency certainly affected the House of Commons. On 5 February, in what was probably the best attended House hitherto known, 278 members heard a message from the Lord Lieutenant conveying a strong recommendation from the King in favour of a legislative union. Castlereagh delineated the proposed articles of union, and another lengthy debate ensued. At the division 158 members voted for considering the Union and 115 against. The Government's majority of forty-three exceeded by one that of 16 January, but was about twenty less than Castlereagh had predicted.[1] The Opposition's increase was made up of six new members, two borough members displaced by a unionist patron and now returned for other seats, five who had not voted in the division of January 1800, and six who had been unionists three weeks previously. The latter class included three county members—Sir Richard Butler, M.P. for co. Carlow, the area affected by the Downshire militia's declaration; Thomas Mahon, M.P. for co. Roscommon, and John Bagwell, M.P. for co. Tipperary. In the last two counties government complacency had underrated the effect of the last-minute petitioning campaign by the anti-unionists. In Roscommon, between November and January, a unionist canvasser named Myles Keon had obtained over 1,500 Roman Catholic signatures for the measure. Even then the influence of the landlords was a serious drawback. The names appended to Keon's address were not published, 'that the common freeholders and landowners may not be exposed to the resentment of their landlords by having acted contrary to their advice. Very few would have signed if this had not been promised to them.'[2] This petition justified Thomas Mahon's support of the Union in January; but in the ensuing three weeks he was subjected to concerted pressure from the anti-unionists in his county, and having voted against the measure on 6 February, obtained leave of absence

---

[1] Castlereagh to King, 25 Jan. 1800 (H.O. 100/93) predicted a unionist majority of 175 votes to 111. Between 16 Jan. and 5 Feb. the unionists attracted the votes of nineteen new members, as well as eight who had voted with them in Jan. 1799 but were not present at the division of Jan. 1800; but they lost six members to the Opposition, and one county M.P. (The Knight of Kerry) was absent seeking re-election after accepting office.

[2] Keon to Castlereagh, 8 Jan. 1800 (*Castlereagh Correspondence*, iii, p. 222).

for the remainder of the parliamentary session.[1] In Tipperary, Lord Landaff, although shaken by the decision of his son Lord Mathew to remain an anti-unionist, had advised Castlereagh to ignore renewed activity by the Opposition in that county.[2] Such confidence was misplaced. 'Stating that the principal part of the respectable freeholders of the county of Tipperary have signed resolutions against the Union',[3] John Bagwell, the other county M.P., reverted into opposition with his sons.[4] In Longford, county pressure swung its M.P. Sir Thomas Fetherstone from benevolent neutrality to opposition to the Union. The unionist member for Kildare, Maurice Keatings, withdrew to England and refused to take part in any further divisions on the Union unless given notice so ample as to be impracticable.[5] These defections dismayed the Government considerably. Cooke foresaw another defeat, while Cornwallis exclaimed: 'How it will end God only knows! I think there are not more than four or five of our people that can be either bought off or intimidated, but there is no answering for the courage or integrity of our Senators . . . .'[6] At any rate, the House of Lords gave no trouble. Dominated by the earl of Clare, they resolved in favour of Union by 75 votes to 26.

Meanwhile Cornwallis acted promptly to ensure that the Downshire militia's venture into politics was not imitated. Lord Downshire was summoned to Dublin, while Major-General Sir Charles Ross went to Carlow to assess the local situation. Although Downshire protested that only officers and freeholders had been invited to sign the anti-unionist resolutions, and that no compulsion of any sort had been employed, Ross reported that many of the signatories had been under age, and that the number of names subscribed

---

[1] Cornwallis to Portland, 7 Feb. 1800 (H.O. 100/93); *Commons Journals*, 10 Mar. 1800. Mahon retired in 1802.

[2] Landaff to Castlereagh, 15 Jan., 25 Jan. 1800 (Mt. Stewart MSS.).

[3] Cornwallis to Portland, 5 Feb. 1800 (H.O. 100/93).

[4] Richard Bagwell, whose unionist speech on 15 Jan. had signified the family's conversion, abstained. He soon afterwards left politics and went into the Church. I do not think there was much co-operation between the Bagwells and Lord Mathew; they were rivals at the county elections of 1790 and 1818.

[5] Keatinge to Castlereagh, 2 and 12 Feb. 1800 (Mt. Stewart MSS.).

[6] Cornwallis to the bishop of Lichfield and Coventry, 8 Feb. 1800 (*Cornwallis Correspondence*, iii, pp. 183–4).

equalled, if indeed it did not exceed the number of the regiment then Carlow. These practices were certainly no more corrupt than those of many other petition organizers on both sides of the question; but Cornwallis was determined that military excursions into politics should be discouraged. As it was necessary to make an example, no better scapegoat could be found than 'that proud leviathan, Lord Downshire'. The King agreed, and on 12 February the marquess was dismissed from his offices as colonel, privy councillor, and governor of county Down.[1]

Cornwallis was in no doubt that he had delivered a timely stroke: 'Whether the measure may appear strong in England, I cannot say, but it is perfectly suited to the genius of Ireland. The turn which it has given to the public mind is astonishing, and all our friends say that by this act of vigour I have saved the country and carried the Union.'[2] Whether or not Cornwallis had over-estimated the risk from intervention by the militia, in an Ireland recovering from the tensions of '98, a British Lord Lieutenant could not afford to relinquish control to the magnates of the Protestant Ascendancy. After Downshire's dismissal, there was no further deterioration in the Government's parliamentary situation. Two motions for the adjournment, put forward on 15 February as a trial of strength by George Ponsonby, were defeated by margins of 123–98 and 157–110. Three days later, a similar motion in committee by the Speaker was lost by 161 votes to 115, the biggest division of the entire session.[3] Castlereagh had hoped that after the principle of Union had been approved, some of the Opposition would secede. In this hope he was disappointed. On 25 February Cooke wrote: 'The opposition seems combined and more and more assuming the shape and consistency of party. This is a little alarming. Bowes Daly, who is whipper-in of Opposition laid me

---

[1] The latter office was given to his old rival, Castlereagh's father, the earl of Londonderry. Portland to Cornwallis, 9 Feb. 1800; Cornwallis to Portland, 14 and 15 Feb. 1800 (H.O. 100/93).

[2] Cornwallis to Ross, 13 Feb. 1800 (*Cornwallis Correspondence*, iii, p. 189).

[3] Of those abstaining or not voting, fourteen were considered potential unionists, seven anti-unionists, and the Chairman of Committees (Henry Alexander) was a unionist; so that of the 300 members, 177 supported and 123 opposed the Union at this stage.

ten guineas the Union would not be passed by the first of August.'[1] That night the House divided 150–108 against an Opposition adjournment motion. But the committee stage still presented the Government with difficulties in particular the two sections of the Union resolutions dealing with representation in the United Parliament and with the future commercial arrangements.

Lobbying by commercial interests in the late eighteenth century seems to have been less highly developed in Ireland than in England. The commercial propositions of 1785 do not seem to have evoked in Ireland anything comparable to the storm among the manufacturers of Lancashire and Staffordshire. Even the free trade agitation of Lord North's time may have had more use as a political weapon than as a means to commercial concessions, for the merchants of Ireland seem to have developed a considerable contraband trade. Moreover industrialization was less advanced than in Great Britain. It had been the aim of the autonomous Irish Parliament to foster local industries. Bounties had promoted the rise of the linen trade, especially in Ulster;[2] and it was proposed under the Act of Union that these bounties would be kept up by the British Government, as would the 33 per cent. tariff on the import of foreign linens, giving preference to the Irish product. Owing to injudicious attempts to introduce large-scale methods in a peasant society, the linen industry had not thriven in the south of Ireland, and during the twenty years after 1780 attempts had been made to establish cotton manufacturing in its stead.[3] It was now proposed to reduce the protective tariffs of between 30 and 50 per cent. under which the industry had flourished free of the competition of Lancashire, to a flat 10 per cent. The same rate would apply to a number of other products hitherto protected by the Irish Parliament, of which the most important were glass, pottery, lace, haberdashery, and wrought iron.

Towards the end of 1799, as it became apparent that plans for the Union would not be abandoned, loss of confidence in the business world caused a marked commercial recession in

[1] Cooke to King, 25 Feb. 1800 (H.O. 100/93).
[2] C. Gill, *The Rise of the Irish Linen Industry* (O.U.P. 1925), pp. 64 and 203.
[3] Ibid., pp. 227–34.

Dublin.[1] Considerable unemployment followed; Alderman Darley, a building contractor, employed in March 1800 only three-quarters the number of hands required twelve months previously.[2] Several cotton manufacturers who each claimed to have invested between £30,000 and £40,000 in the industry, and normally to give employment to up to 4,000 hands, attested that trade became so slack over the winter of 1799–1800 that they were obliged to dismiss many and to keep others on only for charitable reasons. The anti-unionist petitions sent to the House of Commons early in February 1800 included several from cotton manufacturers in Dublin and Belfast. Some factory owners stated their grievances by writing directly to Castlereagh; others preferred to present their case before the Bar of the House of Commons. Evidence was heard mainly from representatives of the cotton and calico industries, with more cursory surveys of the silk, glass, sugar, and iron trades. At a single hearing which lasted late into the night, many expressed their fears that the removal of high tariffs would lead to 'dumping' by British manufacturers in hard times, fatally undercutting the local industry. Although Jacob Geoghegan thought that a 25 per cent. tariff would give sufficient protection, most spokesmen for the industry urged the retention of all existing duties, and like John Orr, distrusted a Westminster legislature in the belief 'that a Parliament will always be influenced by the opinion of the manufacturers of the country wherein it resides'.[3] Nor were they much impressed by arguments that free trade would benefit the consumer.

The Irish Opposition failed signally to make full use of this commercial disquiet. The whigs, with Plunket as their spokesman, declined on 25 February to enter into any detailed consideration of the Union proposals, lest by trying to improve the measure they should seem to give it tacit approval.[4] This may have been high-minded, but it was not sound politics. The main burden of arguing in detail the commercial provisions accordingly fell on Foster's wing of

---

[1] *Report of Evidence taken before the Irish House of Commons on the Legislative Union* (U.K. *House of Commons Papers*, 1833 (517), vol. 35, pp. 541 et seq.).

[2] *Dublin Evening Post*, 18 Mar. 1800.

[3] U.K. *House of Commons Papers*, 1833, xxxv, p. 541 et seq.

[4] Cooke to King, 25 Feb. 1800 (H.O. 100/93).

the anti-unionists, particularly on his nephew Maxwell Barry and on J. C. Beresford. Beresford had proposed that the Irish share of responsibility for future expenditure should be reduced from two-fifteenths to one-ninth; but, deprived of the whigs' backing, his amendment was easily defeated on 25 February. Maxwell Barry was the chief critic of the commercial proposals, and it was on his initiative that the arrangements were made for representatives of Irish manufacturing interests to give evidence before the Bar of the House. It was admitted by Castlereagh that 'the Opposition have . . . adopted a conduct which cannot fairly be imputed to the mere object of delay', and that there was substantial support for their criticisms.[1]

Through the mediation of John Beresford, at whose house he met representatives of the cotton industry, Castlereagh had already been induced to seek permission of the Home Government for a more gradual reduction of duties. On 20 February he wrote proposing that the tariff on cotton yarn, calico, and muslins should stand unchanged to 1808, then to be progressively reduced until yarn stood at zero and the other items at 10 per cent. in 1816, and entirely abolished in 1821. In England, Lord Liverpool was inclined 'to think that such a concession would hurt the principle of the whole commercial arrangement',[2] but Pitt and Auckland had no wish to jeopardize the success of Union over a single detail, and the settlement of the point was left to Castlereagh's discretion.[3]

After further conferences at John Beresford's house, Castlereagh eventually offered representatives of the cotton trade the full concessions authorized by Pitt—the extension of the period of full duties on cottons and calicoes from five years to seven, with subsequent progressive reductions. 'By manœuvre of the anti-Unionists', as Castlereagh believed, the Dublin cotton men rejected these terms. But on 21 March Sir James Blackwood and the Hon. Robert Ward, two borough members from county Down who acted as spokesmen for the cotton industry of the Belfast district, pressed

---

[1] Castlereagh to King, 7 Mar. 1800 (H.O. 100/93).

[2] Auckland to Castlereagh, 6 Mar. 1800 (*Castlereagh Correspondence*, iii, p. 248).

[3] Portland to Castlereagh, 6 Mar. 1800; Pitt to Castlereagh, 7 Mar. 1800 (ibid., pp. 248 and 250).

Castlereagh to provide for the proffered concessions by an amendment to the commercial schedules of the Bill. The Ulster manufacturers would not give up solid concessions for the sake of playing politics. Ward and Blackwood, although unionists, were independent of their neighbour Castlereagh, and carried some weight with him. The Chief Secretary consented to the adjustment, but did not refrain from warning the House 'of the danger of furnishing arguments to the British manufacturers for insisting upon similar protection to their fabrics against Ireland'.[1]

Representation was the next issue to be tackled. Throughout 1799 the problem of selecting the constituencies to return members from Ireland to the United Parliament had exercised the ingenuity of statesmen on both sides of the Irish Sea. Portland was still adamant that the Irish should have no more than 100 members, and Castlereagh's principle that two members each should be returned from the counties, and from the cities of Cork and Dublin, accounted for sixty-eight of them. Giving one member to Dublin University, the problem remained of reducing 114 Irish boroughs to thirty-one United Kingdom constituencies. The least complicated procedure would have been the abolition of eighty-four close boroughs, granting pecuniary compensation to the owners, much on the lines of Pitt's Reform Bill 1785. This would have reduced the number of Irish members in the United Parliament to ninety-eight in all; but the Government was 'unwilling to make any admission which might found an argument for Parliamentary Reform'.[2] Another plan provided that the franchise should be removed from boroughs created later than the Parliament of 1559: but Grenville and Buckingham. who spent much time mulling over this question, objected that 'to extinguish these on the plea of their being created so late as the reign of James I, or by inquiring why they were created, would be very dangerous in principle'.[3]

---

[1] Cornwallis to Portland, 22 Mar. 1800 (H.O. 100/87).

[2] *Project for the Representation of Ireland in the Imperial Parliament*, an unsigned memorandum in the Mt. Stewart MSS., reproduced in *Castlereagh Correspondence*, iii, p. 56.

[3] Grenville to Castlereagh, 8 Oct. 1799 (ibid., pp. 58-61).

Their own recommendations were rather more complicated. In their scheme all the boroughs would be grouped in
threes, open and close alike, on the pattern of the Scottish
burghs in 1707. Borough owners should receive compensation to the value of two-thirds of their interest. After deduct-
ing the bishops' boroughs, this would bring the number of
amalgamated constituencies to 105, which could be reduced
to 100 by further purchase. This plan supposed a laborious
amount of negotiation; moreover, it probably made an anti-
unionist of Lord de Clifford, whose influence lay in two
nominally open boroughs, for which no compensation would
be awarded. Eventually Castlereagh had to leave the point
unsettled in the debates of February 1800. It was not until
April that it was decided to select the surviving boroughs on
a population basis. In the absence of a reliable census, population would be estimated from the returns of taxation,
particularly hearth money.

Cornwallis anticipated an Opposition attack on the proposal to give monetary compensation to disfranchised borough
owners: 'Their object is to fix upon the most unpopular
points of the measure, and to endeavour to inflame the people.
The subject of giving compensation to boroughs is obviously
the most exceptionable in the present arrangement, and they
will of course endeavour to make an impression by debating
the principle.'[1] Notice was accordingly given by George
Ponsonby of a motion to take the sense of the House on this
subject, and 13 March was appointed for the debate. Ponsonby failed to show up on that day, and the Administration
were probably right in assuming that the borough owners
on his side had refused to support him. Instead Sir John
Parnell filled the breach by moving for the dissolution of
Parliament. After yet another lengthy debate this was negatived by 150 votes to 104.[2]

Greater difficulty awaited the Government in an unexpected quarter. The House of Lords, usually docile, objected in
strong terms to the proposed retention by the Crown of the
power to create Irish peerages. It was an old grievance of
the Irish nobility that their peerage was often used by the

[1] Cornwallis to Portland, 11 Mar. 1800 (H.O. 100/87).
[2] Same to same, 14 Mar. 1800 (ibid.).

British Government to compensate minor worthies deemed unworthy of the British House of Lords.[1] Under the Union proposals the King was to be authorized to keep up the Irish peerage to its number in 1800, and as late as 7 February Portland expressed the hope that the Irish lords would not insist on limiting the Crown's rights in this respect.[2] For several weeks in February and March the Dublin Government tried to devise some formula satisfactory to the peers. Lord Carysfort, a Wicklow nobleman related to the Grenvilles, made the suggestion that the Crown should retain the power of creating new peers 'to the amount of two-thirds of the actual vacancies at any period', the total number of peers at no time to decrease below 100. At length a modification of this idea was accepted, the Crown retaining the right of creating one peerage to every three extinctions.[3] This gave the distinction enough rarity to be worth coveting, and assured the existing Irish peers that they would not be outnumbered by outsiders in the election of representatives to the British House of Lords. It also explains why so many country gentlemen with influence in the Irish House of Commons were anxiously bargaining for their peerages in 1800. Previously they could afford to play a waiting game; but after 1800 many would be deprived both of their parliamentary influence and of any early opportunity to improve their status.

Assured that the Irish peerage would not be cheapened beyond its present equivocal value, the House of Lords made no more demands. Few objected to the provision that twenty-eight temporal and four spiritual peers should be elected to the British House of Lords, the spiritual peers in rotation and the lay for life. Peers not chosen as representatives would be eligible to contest seats for the House of Commons, outside of Ireland. They had always enjoyed this right, and were not to be put on the same invidious footing as the

---

[1] Pelham to Portland, 1 Aug. 1797 (B.M. Add. MSS. 33113). Objections had been especially strong after the ennoblement of the Jewish financier, Sir Sampson Gideon (Orde to Rutland, 12 Aug. 1786 (*H.M.C. Rutland MSS.*, iii, p. 333)). Cf. the remarks of Hardy to Charlemont, 6 Nov. 1798 (*H.M.C. Charlemont MSS.*, ii, p. 338).

[2] Portland to Cornwallis, 7 Feb. 1800 (H.O. 100/87).

[3] Carysfort to Castlereagh, 25 Feb. 1800 (*Castlereagh Correspondence*, iii, p. 244). Cornwallis to Portland, 24 Mar. 1800 (H.O. 100/87).

Scots peers after 1707. This proviso was later assailed in the British House of Lords by an Irish peer, the earl of Mulgrave, who saw an affront to the dignity of great Irish noblemen if, as members of a future House of Commons, they were obliged to yield precedence to a much junior peer who happened to be one of the twenty-eight representatives. This was the sort of issue which interested many legislators of the time far more than abstract questions of nationalism; but he found no support, Lord Chancellor Loughborough observing that if the Commons was a sufficiently dignified forum for the eldest sons of the greatest British peers, it was surely good enough for the Irish.[1]

The adjustments over commerce and representation showed that the Government was neither able nor willing to bulldoze the Union regulations unaltered through the Irish legislature. Modifications of the original scheme could be secured by well-organized pressure-groups representing influential sections of contemporary public opinion. The Administration were prepared to grant concessions rather than risk antagonizing supporters. Several of these concessions (such as the restriction of future peerages, the selection of Irish members principally from the counties rather than the close boroughs, the maintenance of special protective tariffs on the cotton industry) answered criticisms which had been voiced by the anti-unionists in 1799. By refusing to enter into detailed discussions of the measure, but instead spending themselves on attacking the general principle of Union, the anti-unionists unnecessarily restricted their own influence on the shaping of the Act.

The defeat of Parnell's motion for a dissolution was followed by a meeting of Opposition members on 21 March at Charlemont's house, where it was decided to force no more divisions before the resolutions went to the House of Lords. It was by way of nuisance tactics rather than in hope of seriously embarrassing the progress of the Union that the question of tithe of agistment was raised in the House of Commons that same day by Sir John Macartney, an officeholder turned anti-unionist. He reminded the House that the clergy had abandoned their claims to tithe on pasturage

1 *Parl. Hist.* xxxv, p. 202.

only because of a hostile resolution by the Irish House of Commons in 1735; and that the effect of this resolution might lapse after the Union, exposing the graziers of Ireland to a burdensome levy.[1] The anti-unionists at once publicized this argument in the pastoral areas, which included many of the unionist strongholds in Connaught. Within a week a meeting of leading privy councillors had framed a Bill stating that tithe of agistment was no longer demandable.[2] This met with the concurrence of the bishops, who had allowed their claims to slumber for sixty years, and excitement subsided. The House of Lords having offered little resistance to the measure, by 28 March the Union resolutions had passed through both houses of the Irish Parliament. It was noticeable that on other issues party alignments in the House of Commons were exceedingly fluid, and showed no conceivable relation to the Union issue. On 29 March J. C. Beresford moved that sympathizers with the 1798 rising should be deprived of the vote. He was supported by the anti-unionist Ogle and the unionist Duigenan, opposed by the Ponsonbys, Castlereagh, and the respected independent unionist Sir Hercules Langrishe, at almost his last parliamentary appearance. The motion was lost by 13 votes to 33. Again, on 6 April, the anti-unionist Lord Mathew's proposal for some recognition of the services against the rebels of the brutal High Sheriff of Tipperary, Fitzgerald, was eventually moved by the Attorney-General, Toler, and passed by 65 votes to 14. The 'liberal' minority included the unionists Arthur Browne, Walter Yelverton, and the Hely-Hutchinsons as as well as the anti-unionists Plunket and Edgeworth.[3]

In the British Parliament the Union Bill met with opposition from two quarters. The Foxite Opposition was reinforced during April 1800 by determined lobbying on the part of the English woollen manufacturers, who feared that low overheads and cheap labour might enable the Irish to compete dangerously with them.[4] They also claimed that it

---

[1] Cornwallis to Portland, 22 Mar. 1800 (H.O. 100/87); Holmes to Castlereagh 22 Mar. '1799' (actually 1800; Holmes was an old man educated before the calendar reform of 1752) (Mt. Stewart MSS.).

[2] Cornwallis to Portland, 26 Mar. 1800 (H.O. 100/87).

[3] H. Grattan, *Life*, v, pp. 148-9.

[4] *An Account of the Proceedings of the Merchants, Manufacturers and others con-*

would be impossible to prevent the re-export of raw wool through Ireland to rivals throughout the world. The centres of this agitation were Yorkshire, where John Foster had first stimulated the alarm during a visit to Harrogate in the autumn of 1799, and the West Country; and a few M.P.s from these areas, of whom the most notable were the members for Yorkshire, William Wilberforce and Henry Lascelles, voted for the reconsideration of the commercial clauses affecting the woollen trade, but were defeated by 133 votes to 58. This was the only spark of excitement in England on the Union. Otherwise the Union resolutions passed both Houses of Parliament with remarkable smoothness, and in the second week of May were referred back to Ireland in the form of a Bill.

By this time the anti-unionists in Ireland were learning to recognize defeat. The lack of spontaneous public feeling on the issue could no longer be disguised. During the spring assizes, the anti-unionists had been rebuffed on several of the grand juries. In Down, a new sheriff refused to accept an anti-unionist petition, and was supported by 16 votes to 7.[1] Londonderry[2] and Galway[3] passed unionist resolutions by big majorities. In Donegal, although no unionist petition could be got up in what had been an opposition stronghold, a respectable grand jury declined to back any further action by the anti-unionists.[4] Only in Tyrone anti-unionist resolutions passed on the casting vote of the sheriff.[5] The outburst of counter-petitioning stimulated in January and February by the anti-unionists had dwindled:[6] and the general apathy

cerned in the wool and woollen trade of Great Britain, Phillips, London, 1800. See my article, 'Some British Reactions to the Irish Act of Union', Economic History Review, 2nd series, xviii, no. 2, Aug. 1965, p. 367.

[1] Castlereagh to Portland, 21 Apr. 1800 (H.O. 100/93).
[2] Beresford to Castlereagh, 14 Apr. 1800 (Castlereagh Correspondence, iii, p. 140).
[3] Martin to Castlereagh, 15 Apr. 1800 (Mt. Stewart MSS.). The majority was 18 to 5.
[4] Galbraith to Littlehales, 14 Apr. 1800 (H.O. 100/93): 'The county of Donegall has not for 20 years seen so full an attendance and the last man on the jury has £1200 a year.'
[5] Same to same, 9 Apr. 1800 (H.O. 100/93).
[6] In the Queen's County on 28 Apr. a meeting of forty anti-unionists under Lord de Vesci unanimously passed a set of resolutions against the measure; but two days later the marquess of Drogheda and thirty-four others presented the Sheriff with a congratulatory address for refusing to convene the county on this matter

was noted not only by relieved officials at Dublin Castle,[1] but even by such staunch anti-unionists as Thomas Goold, who informed the House of Commons:

> He lamented that the public feeling was not sufficiently alive to the question of Union. He lamented that the citizens of Dublin did not exhibit in their countenances the despondency of defeated liberty, and though it was evident that the public sentiment did not keep pace with or sympathise with the opposition within the House, and though that opposition should gradually diminish, he would never acknowledge the triumph of the minister. . . .[2]

Within the House there was now small hope of breaking the solidarity of the Unionist party. Experience had increased Castlereagh's stature as a parliamentarian,[3] and he guided the measure through its last stages with a sure hand. On 13 May he introduced Bills to provide for the method of selecting peers and boroughs to be represented in the United Parliament. Sir John Parnell's motion that leave to introduce the Bill should not be given until the main resolutions came before the House was defeated by 125 votes to 80. On 21 May the main division occurred on Castlereagh's motion for the introduction. At this debate, Cornwallis reported:

> Mr. George Ponsonby, who has been considered as the chief conductor of the Opposition, made only a very short speech, saying that he considered all arguments useless, that he could not hope to change the determination of the majority, but that he would still oppose the measure in every stage till its conclusion. . . . The manner in which the debate was conducted showed that the House was tired with the discussion of the subject, and there was manifest indisposition to enter seriously into fresh debate.[4]

The motion was carried by 160 votes to 100. Including the Speaker, tellers, and several members locked out during the

---

(Coote to Cooke, 30 Apr. 1800 (C.S.O. 516/92/3)). The only other activity which I have discovered at this stage was the collection of a petition, dated 23 Apr. 1800, from 128 unionist inhabitants of Moat, co. Westmeath (Mt. Stewart MSS.).

[1] Cornwallis to Ross, 18 and 21 May 1800 (*Cornwallis Correspondence*, iii. pp. 235 and 237); Cooke to Grenville, 22 May 1800 (*H.M.C. Dropmore MSS.* vi, p. 258).   [2] *Dublin Evening Post*, 17 May 1800.

[3] 'Lord Castlereagh has improved so much as a speaker as to become nearly master of the House of Commons', wrote Cornwallis to Ross on 22 May 1800. This had 'much diminished the unpopularity which his cold and distant manners in private society had produced' (*Cornwallis Correspondence*, iii, p. 235.)

[4] Cornwallis to Portland, 22 May 1800 (H.O. 100/87).

division, the strength of parties was 166 unionists to 104 anti-unionists.

Although interest in the question was flagging, and a number of the country gentlemen were anxious to quit Dublin, attendances diminished little while the Opposition leaders went on dividing the House to the bitter end. At the second reading of the Union Bill on 27 May, Henry Grattan opposed the committal of the Bill; and when this was approved by a 118–73 majority, he moved for its postponement until 1 September, only to be defeated by 124–87. The debate was remarkable for some spirited exchanges between the mover and Castlereagh. All that now remained for the Opposition was to place their views on record by submitting an address to the King requesting him to put an end to the measure. This was attempted less in the hope of inviting Crown intervention, a forlorn hope which would have been embarrassing in its constitutional implications, than in order to publicize their arguments further. The address, compiled by a committee consisting of Foster, Grattan, and Lord Corry was moved by the latter on 6 June, and accordingly entered at full length in the journals of the House. After a debate somewhat less longwinded than usual, it was defeated by 135 votes to 77, and the committee report of the Union Bill was received by a 153–88 majority. An attempt by the fire-eating O'Donel to move that the Bill should be burnt by the common hangman was quashed by the Speaker. Later in the evening the anti-unionists split, about two-thirds of them seceding from the House by way of protest against the passing of the measure. Those who remained dissociated themselves from this gesture, but the Castle was in some fear that the secession foreshadowed the formation of a permanent opposition.[1] However, at the next meeting of the House on 9 June, several prominent anti-unionist country gentlemen declared that, as the Bill had duly passed through Parliament and become the law of the land, they would pledge themselves to acquiesce in it and would endeavour to reconcile their constituents to the new régime.[2]

---

[1] Castlereagh to Portland, 7 June 1800 (H.O. 100/88).
[2] Cornwallis to Portland, 9 June 1800 (H.O. 100/94). Among these M.P.s were Lord Maxwell (M.P. for co. Cavan), Charles Vereker (Limerick city), Richard

Dublin Castle needed especially to detach the moderate anti-unionists from the Opposition, because so many of the small boroughs, from which the ministry had drawn their majority during the Union crisis were to be abolished. Of the 100 members of the House of Commons returned to the United Parliament at the beginning of 1801, fifty had been anti-unionists, forty-eight had supported, while two were county members elected during the recess.[1] Had the anti-unionists remained hostile, they would have represented a formidable addition to the ranks of the Westminster Opposition. But as early as January 1800 Cornwallis had made up his differences with a leading anti-unionist Orangeman, the earl of Enniskillen, who had agreed to support the ministry on all issues save that of Union.[2] The members who promised co-operation on 9 June were all 'right wing' anti-unionists, who had seldom been in opposition on other matters, and had no great desire to run continually in harness with the Ponsonby whigs. Apart from the Ponsonbys and Parsons, the only anti-unionist leaders unreconciled to Dublin Castle in the second half of 1800 were Foster, Parnell, and Downshire. Many of the others played host to Cornwallis during a goodwill tour in August, and the Viceroy found 'no trace of ill-humour with respect to the Union'.[3] Even the capital was tranquil: in August Cornwallis wrote: 'Nothing could be more quiet than Dublin. In our procession . . . the concourse of people was immense, and they all had cheerful countenances, and when I passed they cried out "There he is; that's he", and often added "God bless him". These are not unpleasant circumstances to a man who has governed a country above two years by martial law.'[4] But

Dawson (co. Monaghan), J. C. Beresford (Dublin city), and Edward Lee (Dungarvan).

[1] The anti-unionists included thirty-seven of the sixty-four county members. As the borough members were to be chosen by lot from between the two members elected for each of the surviving constituencies in 1797, it could not be certain how many government supporters would be returned. Early in 1801 some of the backbenchers with seats in the United Parliament were induced to retire, to make way for major officials such as Isaac Corry and Charles Ormsby, who had been unlucky in the draw.

[2] Castlereagh to Portland, 18 Jan. 1800 (H.O. 100/93); Cornwallis to Ross, 22 Feb. 1800 (*Cornwallis Correspondence*, iii, p. 198).

[3] Cornwallis to Ross, 17 Sept. 1800 (ibid., p. 291).

[4] Same to same, 16 Aug. 1800 (ibid., p. 287).

the Lord Lieutenant's troubles were not over. It remained for him to ensure that the British ministry honoured the commitments made to expedite the passing of the Act of Union. The most pressing of these concerned the bestowal of honours on supporters; the most far-reaching question was the future of the Catholics.

Having been empowered to grant any honours requisite to assist the passage of the Act of Union, Cornwallis and Castlereagh had used this authority fairly freely. Their liberality was not without precedent. Fourteen barons and a viscount were created to facilitate the British elections of 1796, and eighteen Irishmen owed their coronets to Lord Harcourt's management of the 1776 elections. The abolition of pocket boroughs deprived many proprietors of the customary means by which they hoped to improve their situations in society; whereas, in previous years, they might have waited for their reward, the Union represented the last opportunity of making a bargain with the Castle. Of the sixteen baronies promised as a result of the Union negotiations, five were granted to borough proprietors,[1] and five to gentlemen who had purchased seats to return Government supporters.[2] Three were granted to county members,[3] and two to veteran government supporters, who had been promised peerages on other occasions.[4] The remaining peerage was bestowed on Sir John Henniker, a Suffolk neighbour of Cornwallis, whose son sat for the purchased borough of Kildare. As Henniker's support was required for the candidacy of the Lord Lieutenant's son, Viscount Brome one of the members for Suffolk, this peerage was a piece of Cornwallis's personal patronage,

---

[1] i.e. the baronies of Castlecoote (to C. H. Coote, proprietor of Maryborough), Clanmorris (John Bingham, Tuam), Dufferin (Sir James Blackwood, Killyleagh), Mount Sandford (Henry Sandford, Roscommon), and Tara (John Preston, Navan).

[2] The baronies of Adare (Sir Richard Quin), Dunalley (Henry Prittie), Ennismore (William Hare), Hartland (Maurice Mahon), and Ventry (Sir Thomas Mullins).

[3] Joseph Blake (co. Galway: Baron Wallscourt), Hon. Clotworthy Rowley (Meath: Baron Langford), and the wife of Sir Thomas Newcomen (co. Longford).

[4] Sir John Blaquiere had been promised a peerage for his services in the raising of militia (p. 101, *supra*). Lodge Morres (Baron Frankfort de Montmorency) had an undertaking from Camden when he left the Ponsonby party in 1795 (Morres to Pelham, 11 July 1797 (Add. MSS 33105)).

totally irrelevant to the Union.[1] In addition, Cornwallis recommended the promotion of nine barons to the rank of viscount, three viscounts to earldoms, and three earls to marquessates as marks of approbation for their support.[2] The duke of Portland protested strongly against all these proposals. His objections were mainly grounded on the need 'to save His Majesty from those sensations which he but too evidently suffers whenever there is occasion to move him to confer honours of this description for mere political purposes.'[3] In particular, the King renewed his old objection to disgusting the English earls by the creation of Irish marquesses; though this did not prevent him or Portland from pressing for a marquessate for the earl of Inchiquin,[4] an absentee Irishman resident in London, who had not so much as contributed a proxy vote to the Union debates.[5] They objected to the selection of the useful Blaquiere as a representative peer, but urged the claims of Sheffield and Grandison, two Englishmen whose Irish titles were minor rewards for public services in Great Britain. Nor would the Home Government grant English peerages to any of the Irish magnates, except the shifty Ely.[6] Cornwallis and Castlereagh, stung by the prospect of having to break their personal pledges to many of the Irish lords, replied in strong terms threatening resignation; and eventually nearly all their recommendations were accepted.[7] This incident is mainly of interest as indicating the levity and ineptitude with which the Home Government was prepared to jeopardize relations

[1] Cornwallis to Portland, 3 June 1800 (H.O. 100/94). Viscount Brome (1774–1823) was M.P. for Suffolk 1796–1805. Sir John Henniker (1724–1803) was M.P. for Sudbury 1761–8, and Dover 1774–84.

[2] Cornwallis recommended the earls of Altamont, Bective, and Ely; Viscounts Caledon, Donoughmore, and Kenmare; and Lords Bantry, Glentworth, Kilconnel, Kilwarden, Longueville, Monck, Somerton, Tullamore, and Yelverton, for promotion. Some of these noblemen had very little, if any, influence in the House of Commons.

[3] Portland to Cornwallis, 25 July 1800 (H.O. 100/88).

[4] Murrough O'Brien (c. 1724–1808), 10th earl of Inchiquin, and 1st marquess of Thomond, resided in London, and was Sir Joshua Reynolds's son-in-law.

[5] Portland to Cornwallis, 13 June 1800 (H.O. 100/94).

[6] Cornwallis to Portland, 17 June 1800 (H.O. 100/94); Castlereagh to Camden, 18 June 1800 (*Castlereagh Correspondence*, iii, pp. 326–9).

[7] Cornwallis to Ross, 25 June 1800; Portland to Cornwallis, 27 June 1800 (*Cornwallis Correspondence*, iii, pp. 269 and 271). Lord Tyrawley was not granted a remainder of his peerage to an illegitimate son.

with the leading Irish. After the decision to admit Cornwallis's recommendations, there was a complete reversal of
policy, and in the remaining months of 1800 Irish peerages
were approved by Westminster almost for the asking. Cornwallis had adopted a practice of forwarding requests for
honours to England, without committing himself to promises
of their fulfilment;[1] but no application was refused by the
Home Government. Of nine baronies created in December
1800, only three went to members of the Irish House of
Commons, of whom one had been an anti-unionist; and there
is little justification for including these peerages among the
'Union creations'.[2] Cornwallis grumbled at this change of
face: 'Everything has been given of late with a most profuse
hand, and the points which I neither asked nor recommended
have been acceded to more readily than those for which the
honour of my Government was engaged, and on which the
success of the Union depended.'[3] Vexed at the ignorance and
neglect of many of the British ministers, Cornwallis contemplated retirement early in the new year. It had not been
decided whether the office of Lord Lieutenant would be continued after he relinquished it.[4]

There remained one delicate aspect of the Union arrangements which had scarcely been touched on. This was the
subject of Catholic concessions. From the outset of negotiations George III had set his face against extending the civil
rights of the Roman Catholics. Even at the moment of
greatest crisis, in January 1799, he had written, '. . . approving the Lord Lieut. of Ireland being directed to use the
greatest efforts to prevent an emancipation of the Roman
Catholics, and declaring that though a strong friend of the
union of the two kingdoms, I should become an enemy to
the measure if I thought a change in the situation of the
Roman Catholics would attend the measure.'[5] Nevertheless

---

[1] Cornwallis to Portland, 9 Nov. 1800 (H.O. 100/94).

[2] Peerages were granted to the unionist M.P.s Frederick Trench and Lord
Charles Fitzgerald, and to the anti-unionist Robert King, brother of the earl of
Kingston. Other creations included a new Chief Justice, a former Chief Secretary
(Douglas), two English admirals, an elderly Irish general, and the marchioness of
Buckingham.

[3] Cornwallis to Castlereagh, 29 Dec. 1800 (*Cornwallis Correspondence*, iii, p. 316).

[4] Cornwallis to Ross, 24 Oct. 1800 (ibid., p. 296).

[5] Memorandum dated 31 Jan. 1799, 8.32 a.m. (Windsor Castle MSS.).

in the autumn of 1799 Castlereagh had asked Pitt's ministry for permission to hold out encouragement to the Irish Catholics. With many of the Protestants hostile, including most of the Orange Lodges, it was essential at that time to ensure that the Catholics did not go over to the anti-unionists. By the unanimous decision of the British Cabinet, Cornwallis and Castlereagh were authorized to state:

that the opinion of the cabinet was favorable to the principle of the measure, that some doubts were entertained as to the possibility of admitting Catholics into some of the *higher offices*, and that ministers anticipated considerable repugnance to the measure in many quarters, and particularly in the *highest*; but that, as far as the sentiments of the cabinet were concerned, His Excellency need not hesitate in calling forth the Catholic support in whatever degree he found it practicable to obtain it.[1]

But at the same time as this decision was communicated to Dublin, an old hand on Irish affairs, Lord Hobart, was warning Pitt: 'As to the Catholics . . . if they are deceived it must proceed from a wrong construction of the opinions you have delivered in public, but unless you think that disappointment will not happen, I am sure you ought privately to apprize Lord Castlereagh of your real sentiments, for I am certain the Irish Govt. is acting under a dangerous error upon that business. . . .'[2] This warning came from an influential source. On Irish affairs the King's ear tended to be dominated by a small group of reactionary 'experts', former Lords Lieutenant and Chief Secretaries such as Westmoreland, Buckingham, Hobart, and Auckland. Soured by their experiences of Irish politics, their narrow outlook commended itself to the rigid conscience of the King; and their influence had already manifested itself during the Fitzwilliam episode.

Given such divergent counsels, Pitt settled for a waiting game, successfully shelving the question until the autumn of 1800. The delay was attributed first to the doubtful outcome of the struggle in the Irish House of Commons, and then to negotiations for an armistice with the French. In fact, Pitt was hesitant in tackling an issue of such delicacy, and

---

[1] Castlereagh to Pitt, 1 Jan. 1801 (P.R.O. 30/8/326). The emphasis is Castlereagh's.
[2] Hobart to Pitt, 2 Nov. 1799 (P.R.O. 30/8/328).

Cornwallis began to fidget. To his old friend Ross, he wrote in October: 'I cannot help entertaining considerable apprehension that our Cabinet will not have the firmness to adopt such measures as will render the Union an efficient advantage to the Empire. . . .'[1] By December both Cornwallis and Castlereagh were urging the ministry to take action on the matter before they were forestalled by the whigs, whose untimely advocacy of the cause might involve 'mischievous consequences'. Opposition was already looming from the Lords Chancellor, Loughborough and Clare. Loughborough, aspiring to a position of royal confidence comparable to that of his predecessor Thurlow, had earlier formulated the doctrine that, while Catholics might exercise all the rights of citizenship appropriate to a subject (including, apparently, the right to vote) they were disqualified from the exercise of any office in which they might figure as representative of the Crown or the legislating authority.[2] But in mid January Cornwallis was growing confident that Pitt might be able to pilot successful relief measures on to the statute book. Lord Spencer had informed Ross that he expected the King would make some concessions: and as for Clare, Cornwallis commented: '*Our* Chancellor will bully and talk big, but he is too unpopular here to venture to quarrel with Administration.'[3]

Apart from Clare, little opposition was apprehended in Ireland. Under-Secretary Cooke, who under Castlereagh's influence had somewhat surprisingly been converted to liberal views on the subject, estimated that sixty-four of the 100 Irish members would support relief measures.[4] The Castle's command of Irish politics seemed adequate. During the recess there had been three county by-elections, all in former anti-unionist strongholds. In Donegal, the veteran radical Alexander Montgomery had been succeeded by the more moderate Lord Sudley. Colonel William Westenra, the candidate favoured by Dublin Castle, had carried Monaghan against the son of the deceased member, Leslie, without any

---

[1] Cornwallis to Ross, 8 Oct. 1800 (*Cornwallis Correspondence*, iii, p. 294).
[2] The doctrine was enunciated at Fitzwilliam's resignation in 1795. Cf. Stanhope, *Pitt*, iii, pp. 263–4; Cornwallis to Castlereagh, 29 Dec. 1800 (Mt. Stewart MSS.).
[3] Cornwallis to Ross, 19 Jan. 1801 (*Cornwallis Correspondence*, iii, pp. 332–3).
[4] Cooke to Castlereagh, 29 Dec. 1800 (Mt. Stewart MSS.).

government assistance.[1] And at an election in January 1801 for the Ponsonby stronghold of Wicklow, Lord Proby, eldest son of the earl of Carysfort, had managed to take the lead from George Ponsonby for a few days, although eventually beaten by the weight of the Fitzwilliam interest.[2] In all these contests the Union seems to have been pretty much of a dead issue. There was certainly no evidence of widespread dissatisfaction with Cornwallis's régime.

But at the end of January 1801 the King intervened; and his feelings moved him so strongly that he conceived the idea of direct interference in Irish politics. The immediate pretext concerned the election of a member for Armagh, one of the surviving close boroughs, whose nominal patron, the archbishop of Armagh, invariably followed the recommendation of the Government of the day. It happened that a new archbishop had been installed at the end of 1800. Contrary to the wish of Cornwallis and Castlereagh, who had advised that a prelate with Irish experience should be chosen, the King had given the post to the bishop of St. David's, William Stuart, a son of the celebrated earl of Bute. In January 1801 it became necessary to find a parliamentary seat for the Irish Chancellor of the Exchequer, Isaac Corry, who had been unlucky in the draw for his old borough of Newry. It was proposed that the archbishop should secure the resignation of the sitting member for Armagh, that rabid Protestant, Dr. Patrick Duigenan, in favour of Corry. Loughborough made it his business to communicate this proposal to the King, who was immediately provoked into violent action against the advocates of Catholic relief. His first intention was 'to apprize the Lord Primate of the ill effect it would produce should he assist any person to a seat in parliament who is supposed to be favorable to the Roman Catholic question, and that at the expence of one supposed a strong friend to the present Church Establishment'.[3] Such direct interference by the King in the return of a member for a House of Commons borough would have been sufficiently

---

[1] Cornwallis to Ross, 16 Aug. 1800 (*Cornwallis Correspondence*, iii, p. 288).

[2] On 26 Jan. the poll stood at Proby, 145; Ponsonby, 118 (Cooke to Castlereagh, 27 Jan. 1801 (Mt. Stewart MSS.)).

[3] George III to Loughborough, 28 Jan. 1801 (Windsor Castle MSS., 9988).

noteworthy in the early years of his reign. Now, after seventeen years of Pitt, the notion was a revelation of the strength of his feelings. Profusely apologizing for venturing to raise the matter, Loughborough at once advised the King 'that no *formal* communication should be made by Your Majesty to the Primate of Ireland on this subject'.[1] The emphasis was Loughborough's; the implication was plain.

It was on the same day that the King made the disagreement public by hectoring Dundas at a levee over the 'Jacobinical' scheme that Castlereagh had brought over from Ireland.[2] The next day (29 January) George III wrote to the Speaker, Addington, requesting him to remonstrate with Pitt against considering so dangerous an idea; and the archbishop of Canterbury and Lord Chief Justice Eldon joined in condemning the scheme.[3] As the archbishop of Canterbury promised to inform Castlereagh of his utmost opposition to the measure and to the election of Corry for Armagh, the King seems to have abandoned the idea of writing to Archbishop Stuart.[4] News of these developments reached Dublin on 2 February. Lord Chancellor Clare was in tantrums, believing that the plan had been adopted before the passage of the Union and sedulously concealed from him throughout.[5] But many of the more moderate Irish peers were strongly in favour of the measure, notably Kilwarden and Shannon who had been foremost in counselling caution to Fitzwilliam six years earlier. Little overt opposition had yet been rallied in Dublin.

Meanwhile events moved swiftly in England. Pitt sent the King a closely reasoned memorandum justifying the removal of Catholic disabilities, minimizing the danger of consequent upheavals, and offering his resignation if after mature consideration the King failed to agree. In conclusion he appealed to the King to refrain from dabbling in politics: '. . . most

---

[1] Loughborough to George III, 28 Jan. 1801, 8 p.m. (Windsor Castle MSS., 9990–1).

[2] W. Wilberforce, *Life*, iii, p. 7.

[3] George III to Addington, 29 Jan. 1801 (Windsor Castle MSS., 9994).

[4] Archbishop Moore to George III, 29 Jan. 1801 (draft of letter from George III to Archbishop Stuart, 29 Jan. 1801) (ibid., 9996–7 and 9998).

[5] Cooke to Castlereagh, 2 Feb. 1801 (Mt. Stewart MSS.). It is an insight into Clare's peculiar judgement of character that he believed his colleagues capable of such a sustained deception.

respectfully but explicitly submitting to you the indispensable necessity of effectually discountenancing in the whole of this interval all attempts to make use of your name or to influence the opinions of any individual or descriptions of men on any part of this subject.'[1] Neutrality was the best Pitt could hope for; but it was too late to expect that the King was either able or willing to throw off the influence of those who, from ambition or conviction, sided against the Prime Minister. George, 'considering the oath that the wisdom of our forefathers have enjoined the kings of this realm to take at their coronation', was adamant against concessions; but he was still hopeful that Pitt's sense of duty would deter him from retiring at all 'to the end of my life'.[2] On 2 February Pitt, nevertheless, submitted his resignation. Two days later the King commissioned Addington to form a ministry. Although the Speaker had been known to favour Catholic concessions when the Union Bill had been in committee, he accepted the commission.

Pitt's action in resigning without attempting to force the issue had been frequently criticized, most weightily by Lecky and Barnes.[3] Such criticism underrates the effect of the crisis on the Irish politics of that time. There seems to have been a determined attempt on the part of the 'inferior cabinet on Irish affairs'—Auckland, Westmoreland, and Hobart—to whip up the Orange members in opposition to any move for Catholic relief. Dr. Duigenan refused to resign his seat at Armagh,[4] and busied himself with trying to secure from the Dublin corporation an address of thanks to the King for his support of the Protestant cause.[5] Anticipating a parliamentary battle, Hobart and Westmoreland summoned Downshire to London, his disgrace forgotten. 'You may be

---

[1] Pitt to George III, 31 Jan. 1801 (Windsor Castle MSS., 10006–13).

[2] George III to Pitt, 1 Feb. 1801; Pitt to George III, 2 Feb. 1801; George III to Pitt, 4 Feb. 1801; Addington to George III, 4 and 5 Feb. 1801 (ibid., 10021–2, 10028–9, 10033–5, 10038, and 10039).

[3] Lecky, *History*, v, p. 442; Barnes, *Pitt*, ch. viii; but cf. Pares, *King George III and the Politicians*, pp. 164–6.

[4] Archbishop of Canterbury to George III, 2 Feb. 1801 (Windsor Castle MSS., 10023). Corry eventually came in for Lord Roden's borough of Dundalk. Roden was an Orangeman, but his son-in-law, the sitting M.P., needed a situation (Cooke to Castlereagh, 22 Feb. 1801 (Mt. Stewart MSS.)).

[5] Cooke to Castlereagh, 24 Feb. 1801 (ibid.').

assured', wrote Hobart, '. . . that your coming to London at this time will be felt as a mark of attachment in the quarter of all others where I know you would most wish to produce such an impression.'[1] Whipping together the remains of his parliamentary following, Downshire prepared to travel to London.[2] In the British House of Lords the earl of Darnley was preparing to table a motion on the state of the nation. After his ambiguous conduct on the Union issue, it was to be expected that the debate would provide an opportunity for the formation of a group of 'King's friends'.

Nor were the Irish whigs solid on the issue. Cooke had found William Ponsonby prepared to support Catholic emancipation at the outset of the crisis.[3] When the extent of Pitt's difficulties became obvious, Cooke reported on the authority of Lord Shannon that 'the Ponsonbys who had been much elated begin to grow serious and grim';[4] especially when William Burton, a veteran member of the cousinhood, declared he would not vote with them for Popery. Few of the 'Protestant' anti-unionists could be expected to follow Cornwallis and Castlereagh on an issue where it was likely they would combine with the ministerialist right wing at Westminster in siding with the King. Even if Pitt had called in the whigs to his aid, he could not have counted on having the numbers. Despite the enlightened sentiments of the whig leaders, there was an unassessed number of back-benchers who might have agreed with William Burton. Party solidarity had not yet reached the stage where a Government leader, deserted by a wing of his own followers, could count on forcing a necessary piece of legislation with Opposition support, as Peel carried the repeal of the Corn Laws in 1846. Had

---

[1] Hobart to Downshire, 6 Feb. 1801 (Downshire MSS.). In an unsigned letter to Downshire about this time Westmoreland wrote: 'I saw his Majesty Tuesday, and in his usual catching and kind mind whilst talking of other people he said "we shall have Downshire now".'

[2] Downshire to Reilly, 15 Feb. 1801 (ibid.): 'Do you know anything of Francis Savage, I have written to him to hasten him to London that he may attend the Catholic Emancipation bill and assist our good King in throwing it out. Will you be so good as to write to the same purpose and hurry him away; I have written to Moore for the same purpose, hurry him off I beseech you, as we do not know how soon this damned question may be agitated.' Savage was M.P. for co. Down, and Moore M.P. for Newry.

[3] Cooke to Castlereagh, 7 Feb. 1801 (Mt. Stewart MSS.).

[4] Same to same, 19 Feb. 1801 (ibid.).

Pitt persevered with Catholic Emancipation, his parliamentary following would have included only his own group of followers—sixty at most—[1]and an unknown number of whigs; and his decision to dodge the issue in the interest of harmony during war-time becomes more readily explicable.

In fact the resignation of Pitt facilitated the absorption of the Irish members into existing party alignments. The Irish whigs naturally gravitated to the Foxite orbit. Former anti-unionists of the 'right wing', such as Foster and Downshire, who might have borne Pitt a grudge, had no objection to assuming an attitude at least of benevolent neutrality towards the Addington Administration. Foster, who had been inclined at first to remain coldly aloof from the United Parliament, was skilfully courted in the early months of 1801 by Liverpool, as one man of business to another. Foster's commercial knowledge was required by the Board of Trade. The hostility of Russia was seriously interfering with the Riga hemp trade, and steps were contemplated to encourage the development of the industry in Ireland, with an assured outlet in the Royal Navy.[2] It was not long before Foster's qualifications led to his appointment to the Board of Trade, upon Liverpool's assurance that it was not the intention of the British Government 'to make Ireland merely a nursery for raw materials for export'.[3] Before long Foster overshadowed Isaac Corry as the ministry's expert on Irish finance, and when he succeeded Corry as Irish Chancellor of the Exchequer in Pitt's second Administration, it was as a convinced opponent of Catholic concessions, on the grounds (among others) that a 'Catholic' régime would demand the repeal of the Union.

During the Union controversy the anti-unionists had frequently called for a general election to test the sentiments of the country. If the 1802 election is any guide, there would have been little significant change in the composition of the House. There was no widespread revulsion against members

---

[1] C. J. Fox to Lauderdale, 12 July 1805 (Lord J. Russell, *Correspondence of C. J. Fox*, iv, p. 98).
[2] Cf. the minutes of the Board of Trade, 1800/1 (B.T. 5/12, P.R.O., London); also Liverpool to Foster, 29 Jan. 1801 (Add. MSS. 38311).
[3] Liverpool to Foster, 3 Mar. 1801 (ibid.).

who had voted for the Union, even in those supposedly open constituencies, the counties. In 1800, twenty-five county members had voted for the Union and thirty-nine against. Of these, sixteen unionists and twenty-five anti-unionists were returned in 1802. Nine other county members elected in 1802 had sat for boroughs in the previous Parliament. Of these, two were unionists, two neutral, and five anti-unionists. The new members included three from unionist families, seven from anti-unionist connexions, and four whose views cannot be indicated. Dividing the neutrals evenly between the two sides, it might have been expected that twenty-four of the county members would have been unionists and forty anti-unionists, a loss of one to the Government. But several of the successful candidates from among the former anti-unionists, such as Hardman and Falkiner the members for Dublin county, enjoyed the patronage of Dublin Castle at the 1802 elections. In Dublin city, the Government favoured the Orange anti-unionists, J. C. Beresford and George Ogle; but the latter was displaced by John Latouche the younger, who had been on the same side as Ogle over Union. W. W. Pole, an anti-unionist, and Eyre Coote, of a zealous unionist family, ran together with government support in Queen's County.[1] Moreover, under Lord Hardwicke (Lord Lieutenant under Addington and Pitt from 1801 to 1805), some of the most outspoken anti-unionists accepted office under the Crown—among them Plunket, Bushe, and Arthur Moore—without any sense of inconsistency with their former denunciations of Pitt's ministry and the Union jobbery.

If further proof was required of the transient nature of the political alignments formed over the Union controversy, it was afforded by the formation of the All the Talents ministry in 1806. As a result of complex and protracted négotiations by William Elliott, now promoted to Chief Secretary under the duke of Bedford as Viceroy, there came into being a system of political alliances which none could have foreseen in 1799. The main factions supporting the Administration were those old rivals, the Ponsonbys and the Beresfords, flanked by Lords Shannon and Donegall. Against them were ranged

---

[1] Marsden to Hardwicke, 17, 21, 22, 24, and 29 July, 2 Aug. 1802; and several undated, around the same time (L.M. Add. MSS. 35723).

Castlereagh, Foster, Longueville, and the marquess of Ely, who for once—his judgement must have been failing with age—had raised his terms too high to come to any accommodation with the ministry in power. Issues of Irish policy no longer divided these factions. Their stands were determined entirely by questions of local patronage and by their relationships to political groups in England.[1] There was no appreciable difference in the attitudes of the former anti-unionists and their opponents, towards the peasantry and the middle-class radicals. Plunket conducted a trenchant prosecution of Robert Emmet after the abortive rising of 1803; while the whig Lord Chancellor George Ponsonby in 1806 sounded very much like the reactionary Lord Chancellor Clare in his reference to possible agrarian disturbances: '. . . If then these measures of conciliation are not to be expected, force must be resorted to, and that if employed in time may produce most useful results. . . .'[2] During the nineteenth century the gradual solidification of Irish party divisions into whig and tory, liberal, and conservative, followed the pattern of events in Great Britain. Despite the significant eruptions of Daniel O'Connell and of the Young Ireland movement in Irish politics, it was not until the elections of 1874 and 1880 that the old families finally lost much of their influence, and a powerful nationalist group, independent of British connexions, came to dominate the electorates of Ireland.

When on 1 January 1801 the Union of Great Britain and Ireland was consummated, the autonomy ceded to the nation-wide Volunteering movement in 1782 was relinquished without any show of popular resistance. It is possible to suggest that Irish nationalism had been cowed by the presence of British troops, reinforced by the relentless corruption of Dublin Castle. I think such an interpretation

---

[1] Irish political negotiations during the duke of Bedford's vice-royalty in 1806–7 are described in great detail in the Grey of Howick MSS. and *H.M.C. Dropmore MSS.*, vol. viii. Two issues much disputed were the disposal to a Beresford adherent of the collectorship of Londonderry, coveted by the Ponsonbys; and the attempts of the Ponsonbys and Lord Longueville to muscle into Cork politics to offset the waning influence of Lord Shannon.

[2] George Ponsonby to Charles Grey, 4 Dec. 1806 (Grey of Howick MSS.).

would be misleading and erroneous. Then as now, politics worked through a subtle and complex interaction of social, economic, and ideological pressures. Only the most old-fashioned nationalists view the Union as the black-and-white melodrama described by McNevin and Jonah Barrington; but it is still usual to attribute too much importance to the role of corruption in passing the Union. This is in part because previous historians of the Union drew much material from the parliamentary speeches made at the time by leading politicians. The anti-unionists had the most eloquent speakers, and their assertions, although of necessity partisan, have frequently been cited; but they were never an entirely satisfactory basis for an objective assessment.

Why was the Union considered necessary? In 1782, as Pitt complained, there had been no satisfactory formal definition of the limits of Irish autonomy; but under existing constitutional practice, the Crown retained supremacy over the appointment of ministers, the armed forces, and foreign policy, and in these important matters continuity of policy between Great Britain and Ireland might have been ensured. But in practice, the affairs of the two islands could not be easily insulated. The commercial mistrust displayed in 1785 might in time have been overcome, as it was in 1800. In 1789, however, the Regency crisis threw together the party politics of the two islands. The Irish whigs lent themselves to Foxite designs, while Pitt found himself committed to the support of a narrow and acquisitive clique of the Protestant Ascendancy.

Even then, had it not been for the increasing menace of revolutionary France, it is possible that Britain might have refrained from interfering overmuch in the domestic affairs of Ireland. There is no evidence to suggest that Pitt's Irish policy was guided by a long-cherished scheme of Union; on the contrary, he and his colleagues gave Ireland as little attention as they could, in the belief that the existing régime in Dublin could keep the country in a state of tranquillity and security. But increasingly the Home Government found itself obliged to direct the actions of the Irish ministers. Westminster provided the initiative for the reforms of 1793; Westminster arbitrated on the Fitzwilliam episode; and finally, Westminster was obliged to find the finance for the Irish Government's recurring deficits in 1797 and 1798— and Pitt, as a vigilant First Lord of the Treasury, was alert to the implications of Ireland's growing financial dependency. Moreover, the Irish Government's handling of the country's internal problems seemed only to result in unrest and insecurity, and by the crisis year of 1798 the bankruptcy of its policy stood revealed. No alternative government could have been found within Ireland, as the whigs were a minority group who refused to act with Pitt. Union, previously a subject for conjecture, was only then adopted by Pitt as the sole adequate solution of the dilemma. It was just possible that a united government might handle Ireland's sectarian, commercial, and political problems more disinterestedly than the existing régime. It could hardly do worse.

Among the anti-unionists who resisted this solution, there were two conflicting views of nationalism. A liberal minority, such as Grattan and Parsons, looked to the growth of an Irish nation in which all should have the opportunity of deserving citizenship, and which would combine its own distinctive ethos with a firm loyalty to the British connexion. This ideal became the inspiration for the more moderate Home Rulers later in the nineteenth century. But it was a minority ideal in 1800; for most of the anti-unionists, the autonomy of Ireland meant the autonomy of the Protestant Ascendancy. Under Westmoreland and Camden, this group had shaped much of the Irish policy to which Britain had been committed. But Pitt was showing disquieting inclinations to liberalism; and if Cornwallis was a harbinger of the new order under the Union, then the Ascendancy would resist. The anti-unionists won the first round of the struggle in Parliament because both wings of the party were agreed on the simple issue of resisting the measure, whereas the Government in its over-confidence had adequately prepared neither its parliamentary management nor the framing of the Union provisions. The anti-unionists then failed to sustain their victory because they were unable to agree on any constructive alternative to Union, owing to the conflicting elements on their side. This failure, and not corruption, ensured the Government's eventual victory.

Few of the anti-unionists seceded from their party. The Government's majority in 1800 was principally secured from interests which had hitherto stood neutral. Many unionist supporters were given places; but neither the unionists nor the whigs thought that there was anything corrupt about rewarding one's followers with office, and it may be doubted whether many members voted against their consciences. To the anti-unionists, the objectionable features about the Union patronage arrangements were that the Cornwallis Administration, in bestowing its favours, was tying up resources of patronage which should have been left available for the needs of future ministries; also that peerages were too liberally handed out to Government supporters at a time when there would be no opportunity for the anti-unionists to redress the balance in some future House of Lords. But no sincere objection could have been made by the anti-unionists to the conventions that a borough was a saleable commodity, or that landlords could assume the right to influence the views of their freeholders. These were commonly accepted practices in eighteenth-century Ireland.

Patronage, however, was but one of the pressures exercised on members of the last Irish Parliament. In addition, not only the county members, but also a number of borough representatives[1] were sensitive to the influence of local opinion in their own town or county. In attempting to determine the sense of articulate public opinion on the Union, it is useless to apply the criteria of nineteenth-century liberalism or twentieth-century democracy. Even among the voters, the forty-shilling freeholders and the smaller shopkeepers were considered unworthy of serious notice,[2] and in each county, public opinion was largely shaped by a comparative handful of the landed class and merchants. Since the decline of the Volunteers, provincial politics in Ireland had tended to relapse into a preoccupation with local and personal issues, in which the landed proprietors exercised influence through the votes of their tenantry; the merchants were of consequence on the city corporations,

---

[1] e.g. Richard Martin in Galway (p. 145); Robert Ward and Sir James Blackwood in Down (p. 195).

[2] See pp. 129 and 151.

and through their commercial interests. They both shaped and reflected the public opinion which Government and Opposition alike needed to court through county meetings, petitions, and resolutions of the grand juries. The strenuous efforts made by both sides to win the counties were no sham fight. In most cases there was a definite correlation between the way a member voted, and the expressions of respectable opinion from his native county. The members for Dublin and its environs, apprehensive of British industrial competition and loss of commerce and importance, voted anti-unionist. The members for Cork and those areas of Connaught hoping to benefit from the provisioning trade and a greater share of overseas commerce voted unionist. The gentry from the ultra-Protestant borderlands of Ulster opposed the measure, whereas Catholic sympathizers tended to support. There is good reason to suppose that voting on the Union issue reflected regional, economic, and religious differences of opinion fairly faithfully. This could not have been expected in an irresponsible legislature, whose members were motivated solely by personal aggrandizement. It is superficial to isolate and exaggerate the importance of corruption. Even at its worst, the Irish Parliament was responsive to what then passed as public opinion; and the Government found it desirable to modify the Union provisions in order to satisfy objections put forward during the passage of the Bill.

It was because of Parliament's sensitivity to outside public opinion that Cornwallis was concerned about the possibility of political interference by the yeomanry. They might have become an instrument of pressure comparable to the Volunteers, and this was an embarrassment which could not be risked during the war with revolutionary France. In disciplining first Enniskillen and then, more severely and spectacularly, Downshire, Cornwallis was acting to check at the outset any attempt by the grandees of the Protestant Ascendancy to gain undue influence with the yeomanry and militia. Lecky minimizes the likelihood of pressure from this source; but contemporaries as varied as Cornwallis, Downshire, and Jonah Barrington thought differently.

The methods by which the Union was passed were not responsible for its subsequent difficulties and ultimate breakdown. Irish separatism survived, not because of cultural and religious peculiarities—similar factors existed in Wales and Scotland—but because these peculiarities were mingled with economic and social grievances which went unredressed. If Pitt had carried his original plans for tithe reform and a measure of emancipation, the Catholic question might have been adequately settled, instead of being left to identify itself with the nationalist cause at the time of O'Connell's agitation. When the reactionary wing of the Protestant Ascendancy joined with George III and the British conservatives to kill Catholic relief in 1801, they were the means of leaving the Union settlement in much the same unfinished state as the old 1782 constitution after the rejection of the commercial propositions. On both occasions, the letter of constitutional changes had been defined, but the accompanying legislation which would have improved the spirit of Anglo-Irish relations was not promulgated. Instead, Ireland was again forgotten at Westminster until it became a trouble-spot, and concessions denied to good behaviour were yielded to potential violence.

Nor had the framers of the Union foreseen that Ireland would never find scope for her capital and labour in an industrial area comparable in importance to Clydeside or Glamorgan. Except in Ulster, a fast-increasing peasantry under a stultifying system of land tenure would press on Ireland's resources of primary production—resources which would be confronted by the famine of 1846 and the agricultural depression of the latter half of the nineteenth century. Possibly Ireland's miseries were little worse than those of the industrial proletariat in parts of Great Britain; but these misfortunes, exacerbated by defects in nineteenth-century administration, stimulated a nationalist resentment against the Union, which tended to colour historical interpretations. The passing of the Act of Union was remembered largely as a by-word for corruption. It is only in recent years that the researches of Namier and those influenced by him have led to a reassessment of the role of patronage in eighteenth-century political thinking. Although the Namierian method of structural analysis may degenerate into a mere essay in head-counting, the technique undoubtedly has useful applications for Irish history.[1] To regard the ruling class who passed the Union as preternaturally corrupt does not help us to understand the actions of its members. Many of them accepted the framework and conventions of politics as they found them, and too often forgot larger issues in the scuffles and manœuvres of party feuding. But when all this is allowed, the story of the Union presents a recognizable narrative of the relations between a colonial ruling minority and the metropolitan power, understandable in terms of commercial, religious, social, and personal relationships. In such a narrative there can be no heroes or villains, but simply the attempt to understand the actions and motives of men confronted with a problem in administering the affairs of their fellows.

[1] Dr. E. M. Johnston, *Great Britain and Ireland, 1760–1800* (Edinburgh, 1963), has made the first important application of this method to Irish politics.

BIBLIOGRAPHY

PRIMARY SOURCES: MANUSCRIPT

(*a*) *British Museum*

Add. MSS. 29475 and 34452–5: correspondence of William Eden, 1st baron Auckland, Chief Secretary of Ireland 1780–2.

Add. MSS. 33100–33116: correspondence of Thomas Pelham, 2nd earl of Chichester, Chief Secretary of Ireland 1795–8.

Add. MSS. 35781–7 and selections from Add. MSS. 35720–67: correspondence of Philip, 3rd earl of Hardwicke, Lord Lieutenant 1801–6.

Add. MSS. 37308 and 38103: correspondence of Richard, 1st marquess Wellesley.

Add. MSS. 38310–11: correspondence of Charles Jenkinson, 1st earl of Liverpool.

Add. MSS. 38716: correspondence of Robert, 2nd earl of Northington, Lord Lieutenant 1783–4.

Add. MSS. 38736: correspondence of Charles, 1st marquess Cornwallis, Lord Lieutenant 1798–1801.

Add. MSS. 40181: correspondence between Charles, 1st marquess Cornwallis, and William, 3rd duke of Portland, 1799.

Add. MSS. 40183: correspondence between Richard, 1st marquess of Buckingham, W. W. Grenville, and others.

(*b*) *Public Record Office, London*

Board of Trade papers, 5/1 to 5/12.

Chatham papers, esp. P.R.O. 30/8/104, 30/8/107, and 30/8/325 to 331.

Home Office papers, 100/1 to 100/112 (1782–1804): Ireland.

(*c*) *Durham County Record Office*

Grey of Howick MSS.: includes some correspondence of the Ponsonby family, 1797–1806.

(*d*) *Hampshire County Record Office, Winchester*

Bolton MSS., Box 1 (papers of Thomas Orde, Chief Secretary of Ireland, 1784–7).

Wickham MSS.: papers of William Wickham, Chief Secretary of Ireland, 1802–3, on loan from Lady E. Bonham Carter, Alton, Hants.

(*e*) *Nottingham University Library*

Correspondence of William, 3rd duke of Portland: little of relevance.

(*f*) *Sheffield City Library*

Wentworth Woodhouse MSS., series F: papers of Wentworth, 4th earl Fitzwilliam, Lord Lieutenant of Ireland, January–March 1795.

(g) West Suffolk Record Office, Bury St. Edmunds

Bunbury MSS., series 18: correspondence of Thomas and Lady Louisa Conolly.

(h) National Library of Ireland, Dublin

Blaquiere MSS.: correspondence of Sir John Blaquiere, Chief Secretary 1772–7, with the 1st earl of Liverpool and others (to 1802).

Buckingham MSS.: patronage correspondence of Richard, 1st marquess of Buckingham, 1782–90.

Fitzgibbon MSS.: estate correspondence and legal papers of the 1st earl of Clare, *c.* 1780–1800: hardly anything on public affairs.

Heron MSS.: letter book, and two patronage lists of members of the House of Commons, of Sir Richard Heron, Chief Secretary 1777–80.

Lord Lieutenant's Union Correspondence (2 vols.). The origins of this collection seem to be unknown to the staff of the National Library. It contains:

(i) Several letters by the 10th earl of Westmoreland, 1793 (evidently once part of the Fane collection, *infra*).

(ii) Several transcripts of official correspondence between Pitt, Portland, Castlereagh, and Cornwallis; the originals are either in the Chatham MSS. or the Home Office files (series 100). The transcripts are on paper watermarked 1835.

(iii) Some original material on paper watermarked 1797 and 1798—mainly about patronage matters, the state of the House of Commons, or specific aspects of the Act of Union. Many of these memoranda are unsigned, and their authorship must be conjectured from handwriting or internal evidence.

The binding of this collection is modern. Presumably the collection was reassembled after dispersal during 'the troubles' of 1920–2, when many documents in the Irish State Paper Office were destroyed.

Roche MSS.: family correspondence of Sir Boyle Roche's wife, 1775–1811.

(i) Public Record Office of Ireland, Dublin

Chief Secretary's Office, correspondence: esp. files C.S.O. 501 to 525.

Fane MSS.: correspondence of John Fane, 10th earl of Westmoreland, Lord Lieutenant 1789–95.

(j) Public Record Office of Northern Ireland, Belfast

Downshire MSS. (D.O.D. 607–9, 1776–98), unclassified beyond June 1798: correspondence of Arthur, 2nd marquess of Downshire.

Macartney MSS. (D.O.D. 572), correspondence of George, earl Macartney, Chief Secretary 1769–72: a few letters about the Union.

Massereene and Ferrard MSS.: includes correspondence of John Foster, Speaker 1785–1800: surprisingly little about the Union.

(k) Private Collections

Mount Stewart MSS.: papers of Robert, viscount Castlereagh, later 2nd marquess of Londonderry: bound in 28 vols.—vols. i–ix cover the period

1793–1801. (By permission of the late marchioness dowager of Londonderry, D.B.E.)

Verner MSS.: papers relating to the earls of Aldborough, 1738–1801. (In possession of Sir James Verner, Bart., Farnham, Surrey).

Wellington MSS.: papers of Arthur Wellesley, later 1st duke of Wellington: election correspondence of borough of Trim, and other Irish political matters, 1790–5. (By permission of the 7th duke of Wellington, K.G.)

Windsor Castle MSS.: correspondence of King George III, 1795–1801. (By gracious permission of H.M. the Queen.)

PRIMARY SOURCES: PRINTED MATERIAL

Auckland correspondence: *The Letters of William Eden, 1st Baron Auckland* (4 vols., London, 1861–2).

Beresford correspondence: *The Letters of the Rt. Hon. John Beresford* (ed. William Beresford, 2 vols., London, 1854).

Castlereagh correspondence: *Memoirs and Correspondence of Viscount Castlereagh* (edited by his brother Charles, 3rd marquess of Londonderry, 12 vols., 1848–54). Vols. i–iv are relevant. All this material has been taken from the Mount Stewart MSS., but where it has been accurately transcribed in the *Castlereagh Correspondence* I give the appropriate reference.

Cornwallis correspondence: *Correspondence of Charles, 1st Marquis Cornwallis* (edited, with notes, by Sir Charles Ross, 3 vols., London, 1859).

Grattan, Henry, jnr. : *Life of Henry Grattan* (5 vols., 1839–46). Contains some useful original correspondence.

Pitt–Rutland correspondence: *Letters Exchanged between William Pitt and Charles, 4th Duke of Rutland, Lord Lieutenant, 1784–7* (ed. by Lord Mahon, 1890).

Stanhope, Viscount: *Life of Pitt* (2 vols., 1879). Includes original correspondence.

Historical Manuscripts Commission
  Beaufort, Donoughmore MSS. (part ii).
  Charlemont MSS. (2 vols.).
  Dropmore MSS. (vols. i–viii).
  Emly MSS.
  Lothian MSS., Blickling.
  Rutland MSS. (vol. iii).
  Stopfortd–Sackville MSS.

Other Original Correspondence will be found in
  BUCKINGHAM, RICHARD, 2nd duke of: *Courts and Cabinets of the Reign of George III* (vol. ii, London, 1848).
  DAY, ELLA, B.: *Mr. Justice Day of Kerry* (Exeter, 1938).

Parliamentary Papers
(*a*) Irish House of Commons Journals (19 vols.; esp. vols, xvii–xix).
(*b*) Reports of Debates
      (i) Parliamentary History (Great Britain) (vols. xxxiv and xxxv, 1798–1800).

(ii)   Parliamentary Register of Ireland (15 vols., 1782–97).

(iii) Parliamentary Register: a report of the debates in the House of Commons in Ireland on Tuesday and Wednesday 22nd and 23rd of January 1799 on the subject of an Union . . . (Moore, Dublin, 1799). Contains reports of all debates until 8 February 1799.

(iv) A report of the important debate in the House of Commons of Ireland on Thursday April 11, 1799 on the Regency Bill, including the admirable speech of the Right Honourable John Foster (Speaker) (Campbell and Shea, 1799).

(v)   A report of the debate in the House of Commons of Ireland on Wednesday and Thursday the 15th and 16th January 1800, on an amendment to the address moved by Sir Laurence Parsons, Bart. on the subject of an union (Moore, Dublin, 1800).

(vi) A report of the debate in the House of Commons of Ireland on Wednesday and Thursday the 5th and 6th February 1800, on delivering a message from His Majesty on an union (Moore, Dublin, 1800).

(vii) Speech of the Rt. Hon. John Foster of the House of Commons of Ireland, delivered in committee on Monday the 17th day of February, 1800 (Moore, Dublin, 1800).

(viii) An accurate report of the speech of William Saurin, Esq. in the Irish House of Commons on Friday the 21st of February on the question of an union with Great Britain (Moore, Dublin, 1800).

(ix) Henry Grattan: *Speeches* (edited by H. Grattan jnr., 1821).

(c) United Kingdom Parliamentary Papers

(i)   Report from the committee appointed to consider the fourth article of the Act of Union between Great Britain and Ireland (Sess. 1801 (63) vol. 3, p. 139).

(ii) Report of the commissioners of Union Compensation, etc. (Sess. 1805 (417), vol. 8, p. 527).

(iii) Proceedings of His Majesty's Government in Ireland respecting the better collection of the revenue (Sess. 1805, vol. v, p. 117).

(iv) Report from the select committee on Irish election laws (Sess. 1817 (281) vol. viii, p. 2).

(v)   Report from the select committee on the expenses of sheriffs at elections, and on the laws for regulating elections in Ireland (Sess. 1820 (226), vol. iii, p. 269).

(vi) Report from the select committee on the Limerick election . . . (Sess. 1820 (229), vol. iii, p. 283).

(vii) Legislative Union: evidence taken before the Irish House of Commons (Sess. 1833 (517), vol. xxxv, p. 541).

(viii) Report of the Commission to enquire into municipal corporations in Ireland (Sess. 1835, vol. xxvii).

Newspapers and Periodicals

The Anti-Union (1799). (British Museum.)
The Belfast Newsletter (1797–1800). (Linen Hall Library, Belfast.)

The Cork Advertiser (1799). (National Library of Ireland, Dublin.)
The Courant (1800). (British Museum Newspaper Annexe, Colindale.)
The Detector (1800). (British Museum Newspaper Annexe, Colindale.)
The Dublin Evening Post (1797–1800). (National Library of Ireland.)
The Olio (1800). (British Museum.)

Pamphlets

(i) *Anonymous*

'An account of the proceedings of the merchants, manufacturers and others concerned in the wool and woollen trade of Great Britain and their application to Parliament that the laws respecting the exportation of wool might not be altered in arranging the Union with Ireland' (Phillips, London, 1800).
'An historical account of the late election of the knights of the shire for the co. of Down . . .' (Dublin, 1784).
'A report of the debate of the Irish bar . . . on the subject of an union . . .' (Moore, Dublin, 1799).
'Cease your funning, or the rebel detected' (Dublin, 1798).
'County of Down Election, 1805 . . .' (Dublin, 1805).
'Reasons against an union . . .', by an Irishman (Dublin, 1798).
'Strictures on the pamphlet entitled *Arguments for and against an Union* . . .' (Dublin, 1798).
'Union or separation', by R. F.   (Dublin, 1799).
'The utility of an Union between Great Britain and Ireland considered', by a friend to both countries (London, 1799).

(ii) *Known Authors*

BALL, CHARLES, 'An Union Neither Necessary or Expedient for Ireland . . .' (Dublin, 1798).
(COOKE, EDWARD), 'Arguments for and against a union between Great Britain and Ireland, considered' (Dublin, 1798).
GOOLD, THOMAS, 'An address to the people of Ireland on the subject of the projected union' (Dublin, 1799).
JEBB, RICHARD, 'A reply to a pamphlet entitled *Arguments for and against an Union*' (Dublin, 1798).
JERVIS, SIR J. W., 'A letter addressed to the gentlemen of England and Ireland on the inexpediency of a federal union' (1798).
JOHNSON, WILLIAM, 'Reasons for adopting a union between Ireland and Great Britain' (Dublin, 1798).
RUDD, PEMBERTON, 'Thoughts on an union . . .' (Dublin, 1799).
SHEFFIELD, JOHN BAKER HOLROYD, 1st baron, 'Observations on the objections made to the export of wool from Great Britain to Ireland' (London, 1800).
SPENCER, JOSHUA, 'Thoughts on an Union' (4th edition, Dublin, 1798).
TAAFFE, THOMAS, 'Reform or Union! . . .' (Dublin, 1799).

Berwick Collection, 144 pamphlets collected by the Revd. Edmund Berwick, relating to the county of Down election for 1790 (National Library of Ireland).

SECONDARY WORKS

(*i*) *1800–50*

BARRINGTON, SIR JONAH, *Historical Anecdotes and Secret Memoirs of the Legislative Union between Great Britain and Ireland* (1st ed. 1809–13; 2nd ed.
1834). The second edition, written when Barrington was aged, embittered,
and in exile is extremely unreliable, but has been frequently cited.
—— *The Rise and Fall of the Irish Nation* (1833, reprinted 1917). Inclined
to melodrama.

COOTE, DR. CHARLES, *History of the Legislative Union between Great Britain
and Ireland* (London, 1802). The most unbiased contemporary account;
draws largely on published speeches.

EDGEWORTH, RICHARD LOVELL, *Memoirs of His Own Life* (2 vols., 1820).
Some reference by an intelligent, moderate anti-unionist.

GAMBLE, JOHN, *View of Society and Manners in Northern Ireland . . . 1812*
(London, 1813). A balanced and interesting survey.

HARDMAN, J., *A History of the Town and Country of Galway* (Dublin, 1820).
Useful, but little directly concerning the Union.

HARDY, FRANCIS, *Memoirs of the Political and Private Life of James Caulfield,
Earl Charlemont, K.P.*, etc. (2 vols., 1812). A whig eulogy, but carefully
revised from original material.

MUSGRAVE, SIR RICHARD, *History of the Rebellions in Ireland . . .* (1st ed.,
Dublin, 1801). A laborious, anti-Catholic collection.

PLOWDEN, FRANCIS, *An Historical Review of the State of Ireland from the
Invasion of that Country under Henry II to the Union with Great Britain on
the 1st of January 1801* (2 vols. *1803*).
—— *A history of Ireland from 1801 to 1810* (3 vols., 1811). Hostile to the
Cornwallis Administration and the Union.

YOUNG, ARTHUR, *A Tour of Ireland* (1776; reproduced in Everyman edition,
last reprinted 1953). Still useful as a description of contemporary agriculture, although one or two of his conclusions have recently been ques-
tioned.

(*ii*) *1850–1964*

BARNES, D. G., *George III and William Pitt* (New York, 1939). Over-
corrects the 'whig interpretation' of relations between King and minister.

BELMORE, SOMERSET LOWRY CORRY, 4th earl of, *Parliamentary Memoirs of
Tyrone and Fermanagh* (1887).

BURKE's *Landed Gentry of Ireland* (1913 ed.). Despite imprecisions, improba-
bilities, and misprints, a mine of information.
—— (1958 ed.). Excludes many families in the earlier volume, but more
carefully compiled and edited.

BURTCHAELL, G. T., *Alumni Dublinensis . . .* (revised ed., 1935).
—— *The Parliamentary Representatives of the County of Kilkenny* (1888).

CLERMONT, THOMAS FORTESCUE, BARON, *A History of the Family of Fortescue,
in all its Branches* (2nd ed., London, 1880). Contains some original
correspondence.

C(okayne), G. E., *Complete Peerage* (1st ed. 1887–98; revised ed., 13 vols., 1910–59).

Connell, K. H., *The Population of Ireland, 1750–1845* (O.U.P., 1950). Some stimulating sidelights on the economic history of the time.

Corkery, M., *The Hidden Ireland* (3rd. ed., London, 1941). The most accessible introduction to the Gaelic culture of the eighteenth century.

Craig, M. J., *The Volunteer Earl* (London, 1948). Life of Charlemont; adds little to Hardy and the material in the H.M.C. volumes.

Curtis, E., *History of Ireland* (London and Dublin, 1936).

Froude, J. A., *The English in Ireland* (3 vols. 1871–4). A tendentious and provocative book, by now largely superseded.

Gill, C., *The Rise of the Irish Linen Industry* (O.U.P., 1925). Still the authority for that branch of Irish commerce.

Gwynn, Stephen, *Henry Grattan* (London, 1936). The most recent biography; a sympathetic account, largely from secondary material.

Harlow, V. T., *The Founding of the Second British Empire* (London, 1952). Vol. i, chapters x and xi. Draws Ireland into the wider context of British colonial policy.

Hore, Walter, *A History of Wexford* (Dublin, 1906).

Hutchinson, K. H., *Tyrone Precinct* (Belfast, 1951).

Hyde, H. Montgomery, *The Rise of Castlereagh* (London, 1933). Draws on the unpublished material in the Mount Stewart MSS. to defend Castlereagh's Irish policy.

Ingram, A., *A History of the Union* . . . (London, 1887). Designed as a corrective to the nationalist interpretation.

Johnston, E. M., *Great Britain and Ireland, 1760–1800* (Edinburgh, 1963). The only important post-Namierian study of Irish politics in this period; breaks considerable new ground.

Lecky, W. E. H., *History of Ireland in the Eighteenth Century* (5 vols., 1892). See esp. vols. iv and v. Still the classic interpretation.

MacDonagh, M., *The Viceroy's Post-bag* (Dublin, 1904). Cases of jobbery from the Hardwicke MSS.; references not given.

McDowell, R. B.: *Irish Public Opinion, 1750–1800*. (Faber, London, 1944). Deals especially with the influence on politics of Dublin and the northern radicals.

MacNeill, J. Swift, *The Irish Act of Union and how it was carried*. (Dublin 1912). The nationalist case at its most virulent.

McNevin, R., *Pieces of Irish history* (Dublin, 1843–8). Formulates the 'conspiracy theory' of the origins of the Act of Union.

Maxwell, Constantia, *Dublin under the Georges* (London and Dublin, 1941). An agreeable and competent social history.

O'Brien, George, *Economic History of Ireland* (London, 1924). Has not been supplanted, but further exploration in this field is required.

O'Hegarty, P., *A History of Ireland under the Union, 1801–1922* (London, 1952). A partisan work, of little value.

O'Sullivan, W., *Economic History of Cork City to the Union* (Cork, 1937). One of the few recent useful regional histories.

Pares, R., *King George III and the Politicians* (Oxford, 1954).

SOMERVILLE, E. Œ. and Ross, M., *An Incorruptible Irishman* (London, 1952). A fanciful life of Charles Kendal Bushe; its main value comes from drawing on some original family material.

STRAUSS, E., *Irish Nationalism and British Democracy* (London, 1951). A promising theme: the colonial nature of Anglo-Irish relations. Treatment marred by cocksure judgements and inadequate research.

Theses

O'SULLIVAN, G., 'Irish Parliamentary Representation, 1800–30.' (B.Litt. thesis, Trinity College, Dublin University.) A rather slight work; useful on the Catholic question.

STEWART, A. T. Q., 'The Transformation of Presbyterian Radicalism in Northern Ireland, 1792–1825.' (M.A., Queen's University, Belfast.) Contends that the Ulster Presbyterians had begun to swing to conservatism before the rising of 1798 and its failure.

INDEX

Note. Individuals are listed under the title which they bore during the Union controversy of 1798–1800, with their subsequent title in brackets afterwards.

PRINTED IN GREAT BRITAIN
AT THE UNIVERSITY PRESS, OXFORD
BY VIVIAN RIDLER
PRINTER TO THE UNIVERSITY